AQUINAS ON EFFICIENT CAUSATION AND CAUSAL POWERS

In this innovative book, Gloria Frost reconstructs and analyzes Aquinas's theories on efficient causation and causal powers, focusing specifically on natural causal powers and efficient causation in nature. Frost presents each element of Aquinas's theories one by one, comparing them with other theories, as well as examining the philosophical and interpretive ambiguities in Aquinas's thought and proposing fresh solutions to conceptual difficulties. Her discussion includes explanations of Aquinas's technical scholastic terminology in jargon-free prose, as well as background on medieval scientific views – including ordinary language explanations of the medieval physical theories which Aquinas assumed in formulating his views on causation and causal powers. The resulting volume is a rich exploration of a central philosophical topic in medieval philosophy and beyond, and will be valuable especially for scholars and advanced students working on Aquinas and on medieval natural philosophy.

GLORIA FROST is Professor of Philosophy at the University of St. Thomas, Minnesota. She has published articles in journals including *Journal of the History of Philosophy*, *British Journal for the History of Philosophy*, *Oxford Studies in Medieval Philosophy* and *Ergo*.

T0371470

AQUINAS ON EFFICIENT CAUSATION AND CAUSAL POWERS

GLORIA FROST

University of St. Thomas, Minnesota

CAMBRIDGE
UNIVERSITY PRESS

Shaftesbury Road, Cambridge CB2 8EA, United Kingdom

One Liberty Plaza, 20th Floor, New York, NY 10006, USA

477 Williamstown Road, Port Melbourne, VIC 3207, Australia

314–321, 3rd Floor, Plot 3, Splendor Forum, Jasola District Centre, New Delhi – 110025, India

103 Penang Road, #05–06/07, Visioncrest Commercial, Singapore 238467

Cambridge University Press is part of Cambridge University Press & Assessment, a department of the University of Cambridge.

We share the University's mission to contribute to society through the pursuit of education, learning and research at the highest international levels of excellence.

www.cambridge.org
Information on this title: www.cambridge.org/9781009225380

DOI: 10.1017/9781009225403

First published 2022
First paperback edition 2024

A catalogue record for this publication is available from the British Library

Library of Congress Cataloging-in-Publication data
NAMES: Frost, Gloria Ruth, author.
TITLE: Aquinas on efficient causation and causal powers / Gloria Frost.
DESCRIPTION: Cambridge, United Kingdom : Cambridge University Press, 2022. | Includes bibliographical references and index.
IDENTIFIERS: LCCN 2022011767 (print) | LCCN 2022011768 (ebook) | ISBN 9781009225427 (hardback) | ISBN 9781009225380 (paperback) | ISBN 9781009225403 (epub)
SUBJECTS: LCSH: Thomas, Aquinas, Saint, 1225-1274. | Causation. | BISAC: PHILOSOPHY / History & Surveys / Medieval
CLASSIFICATION: LCC B765.T54 F76 2022 (print) | LCC B765.T54 (ebook) | DDC 189/.4–dc23/eng/ 20220512
LC record available at https://lccn.loc.gov/2022011767
LC ebook record available at https://lccn.loc.gov/2022011768

ISBN   978-1-009-22542-7   Hardback
ISBN   978-1-009-22538-0   Paperback

To my greatest effects Cecelia, Maria, Thomas and Joseph
and to Jacob my co-cause in all things

Contents

Acknowledgments

There are many colleagues with whom I have discussed this book over the years. While I cannot mention all of them by name, I am nevertheless grateful to all who have shown interest and provided encouragement for this project. I would particularly like to thank those who provided written comments on drafts of chapters and other material that made its way into the book: Jeffrey Brower, Jeffrey Hause, Scott MacDonald, Sydney Penner, Kara Richardson and Can Laurens Löwe. I would also like to thank the anonymous readers for Cambridge University Press for their careful and insightful comments. I am grateful to Hilary Gaskin for her advice and to Nigel Hope for his copyediting. I am especially grateful to Jeffrey Brower for organizing a workshop on this book during the summer of 2020. Jeff Brower, David Cory, Therese Scarpelli Cory, Scott MacDonald and Jake Tuttle generously read and discussed a penultimate draft of the entire manuscript. Their insights and suggestions led to many improvements, and I am grateful to each of them. I gratefully acknowledge the University of St. Thomas Center for Faculty Development for their support in the form of a sabbatical grant and Distinguished Early Career grant that allowed me additional time for research. I am grateful to my family and friends for the many ways in which they have supported me. I would especially like to thank my parents, Marianne and Larry Wasserman, and my husband, Jake Frost. Finally, as in all things, *Deo gratias*.

Abbreviations for Aquinas's Works

Compend. Theo.	*Compendium theologiae*
De malo	*Quaestiones disputatae de malo*
De mixt. element.	*De mixtione elementorum*
De operat. occult.	*De operationibus occultis naturae ad quendam militem ultramontanum*
De pot.	*Quaestiones disputatae de potentia*
De prin. nat.	*De principiis naturae*
De spirit. creat.	*Quaestio disputata de spiritualibus creaturis*
De ver.	*Quaestiones disputatae de veritate*
De virt.	*Quaestiones disputatae de virtutibus*
In De anima	*Sentencia libri De anima*
In De caelo	*In libros De caelo et mundo expositio*
In De causis	*In librum De causis expositio*
In De sensu	*Sentencia libri De sensu et sensato*
In Div. nom.	*Super librum Dionysii De divinis nominibus*
In Gen. et Cor.	*In librum primum De generatione et corruptione expositio*
In Meta.	*In duodecim libros Metaphysicorum expositio*
In Peri Herm.	*Expositio libri Peryermeneias*
In Phys.	*In octo libros Physicorum expositio*
In Post Anal.	*Expositio libri Posteriorum Analyticorum*
In Sent.	*In quatuor libros Sententiarum*
Q.D. de anima	*Quaestiones disputatae de anima*
Quodl.	*Quaestiones quodlibetales*
ScG	*Summa contra gentiles*
ST	*Summa theologiae*
Super Io.	*Super Evangelium S. Ioannis lectura*

I cite divisions within texts according to the following abbreviations: d. = distinction, q. = question, a. = article, ob. = objection, lec. = lectio,

c. = chapter. Citations refer to the corpus of the text unless otherwise indicated. Roman numerals are used to indicate book numbers of works with multiple books, e.g. *In I Sent.* = first book of the Sentences.

Whenever possible I cite the Leonine edition of Aquinas's texts. The abbreviation used for this edition is "Leon." Editions used for works not contained in the Leonine edition are listed in the Bibliography.

Introduction

Our everyday experience of the world reveals that the things around us are constantly changing. Clouds move across the sky, the grass outside grows taller, eggs hatch and chicks mature, fires consume forests and each day the sun rises and sets. It is apparent that the material world does not stay the same. Rather, material things differ as times goes on. Philosophers of every era have sought to answer the question of how and why things change. Why is it that new things come to be and old things pass out of existence? Why do persistent things differ over time? Theories of causation pose answers to these questions. They explain why the world in structured in such a way that one thing happens and another follows. Many, if not all, of our explanations of phenomena are causal. Typically, when we want to explain why something happened, we appeal to a causal history. We think that we have explained something once we have arrived at what caused it. Once we know that a certain type of thing causes another, we can predict future effects based on the presence of an adequate cause. We can even manipulate future effects by bringing about their causes. Natural scientists work to identify the specific causes of specific effects. It is the job of philosophers to explain what causation itself is.

Philosophical theories of causation are supposed to tell us what sorts of entities causes are. For example, when a fire consumes a forest, should the cause of the trees' perishing be identified as the fire or the event of burning? Philosophical theories are also supposed to tell us how causes relate to their effects and what conditions something must meet to be identified as the cause of an effect. For example, do causes merely make their effects probable or do causes necessitate their effects? Causation is a notoriously difficult concept to understand. Modern and contemporary philosophical work on causation has for the most part aimed to reduce causation to more familiar concepts. On most contemporary theories of causation, causation is analyzed as a certain logical relationship which obtains between events. For example, one prominent theory claims that

I

what it is for an event A to cause an event B is for A and B to exemplify a regularity such that when event A happens event B follows. Another theory claims that causation can be understood in terms of counterfactual dependence such that event A is the cause of event B if it is true that had A not happened then B would not have happened either.

The goal of this study is to reconstruct Thomas Aquinas's thinking about causation. Aquinas exemplifies an older, premodern way of thinking about causation which views causation as a *sui generis* phenomenon which cannot be reduced to any other more familiar concepts. According to Thomas Aquinas, causation is a relationship of ontological dependence. Causes are responsible for the being of their effects; and effects depend on their causes for their existence. Efficient causes are the type of causes which are responsible for bringing about changes in the material world. On the pre-modern view that Aquinas exemplifies, efficient causation essentially involves exercises of causal power. Aquinas thinks that substances are the entities which function as efficient causes; and they cause other things to change by exercising active powers. For example, fire causes other substances in the material world to undergo the change of burning by exercising its active power to burn. Substances undergo change on account of possessing a feature known as a passive power. For example, when a log is burned by fire it undergoes burning in virtue of its passive power to be burned. Iron, by contrast, cannot be burned because it lacks the relevant passive power. On Aquinas's view, efficient causation is a real interaction which occurs between substances in virtue of inherently causal features that each possesses. Thus, the causing of an effect cannot be reduced to a logical regularity or counterfactual about the cause and its effect. Rather, substances and their causal powers are what explain why certain regularities and counterfactuals are true. The goal of this study is to reconstruct the intriguing details of Aquinas's theories about efficient causation and causal powers.

The study focuses on Aquinas's views about instances of efficient causation that occur between non-rational, terrestrial material substances. These instances of efficient causation fall under the type of efficient causation that is called natural efficient causation. Natural efficient causation explains the changes we observe with regularity in the material world, such as grass growing and the sun rising. Other examples of natural efficient causation include a fire's burning of a log and a frog's begetting of another frog. Distinctively human actions that are done through the powers of intellect and will are excluded from the scope of natural efficient causation. Actions done by immaterial agents, such as God and angels, are likewise excluded from the scope of natural efficient causation. Like his Aristotelian counterparts, Aquinas recognizes other types of causation beyond efficient causation, such as formal and final causation. This study treats of other types of causation only insofar as they are relevant for understanding efficient causation. The study reconstructs and analyzes Aquinas's views on three main topics regarding natural efficient causation: (1) the nature of the relationship that obtains between a natural efficient cause and its effect, (2) the various ontological elements that are involved in paradigm cases of natural efficient causation, and (3) how to understand more complicated cases of natural efficient causation, such as cases in which multiple efficient causes cooperate and cases in which efficient causes produce effects for which they have no active power.

Rationale and Methodology

Aquinas's views on the workings of natural efficient causes and powers are important since Aquinas is a central figure in the history of philosophy and causation is a central philosophical topic. Yet, Aquinas's views have additional significance given their placement in the trajectory of historical thinking about causation. In the early modern period, philosophers turned away from the ancient and medieval view that substances are endowed with inherently causal features by which they bring about changes in one another. Many of the assumptions at work in contemporary philosophical debates emerged in this period. Recent studies on causation in early modern philosophy have emphasized that modern discussions and theories of causation cannot be fully appreciated without understanding their medieval background.[1] For example, in their *Stanford Encyclopedia of Philosophy* entry on Hume and Causation, William Morris and Charlotte R. Brown write: "The medieval synthesis Thomas Aquinas (1224–74) forged between Christian theology and Aristotle's science and metaphysics set the terms for the early modern causation debate."[2] It should be noted that in many cases, early modern figures forged their views in opposition to later medieval Aristotelians, such as Suárez. However, the framework of

[1] Walter R. Ott, *Causation and Laws of Nature in Early Modern Philosophy* (Oxford: Oxford University Press, 2009) and Tad M. Schmaltz, *Descartes on Causation* (New York: Oxford University Press, 2008).
[2] See section 5 of William Edward Morris and Charlotte R. Brown, "David Hume," in Edward N. Zalta (ed.), *The Stanford Encyclopedia of Philosophy* (Spring 2021 Edition), https://plato.stanford.edu/entries/hume/, accessed May 31, 2021.

Aquinas's thinking (e.g. his concepts, terminology and questions) exerted great influence on these later Aristotelians.

Though Aquinas is perhaps the most studied medieval figure, there is surprisingly little scholarship that focuses explicitly on his views on natural efficient causation and natural powers.[3] Most of the scholarship on Aquinas's views on efficient causation and causal powers focuses exclusively on the case of human beings and God. In recent decades there have been important studies focusing on the human powers of intellect and will, as well as the perceptual powers that humans share with other animals.[4] Recent studies have also examined the distinctive features of human action.[5] With respect to divine causation, there have been recent studies both on how the sacraments and grace are causes and on how God causes effects in the ordinary course of nature.[6] By recovering Aquinas's views on natural efficient causation and causal powers, the present study will complement the existing literature on human and divine exercises of efficient causation. Aquinas thought that through our observation of and reflection upon natural causes and their operations we can acquire insight into efficient causes with higher powers. When explaining the workings of the human intellect and will or even God's activity, Aquinas often makes references and analogies to natural causes.[7] Thus, by uncovering Aquinas's

---

[3] Three of the most extensive discussions of Aquinas's views on causality and action are these mid-twentieth century books: Cornelio Fabro, *Participation et causalité selon St. Thomas D'aquin* (Louvain: Publications Universitaires de Louvain, 1961); Joseph Finance, *Être et agir dans la philosophie de Saint Thomas* (Paris: Beauchesne, 1945); Francis X. Meehan, *Efficient Causality in Aristotle and St. Thomas* (Washington, DC: Catholic University of America Press, 1940). There are no more recent book length studies devoted principally to Aquinas's views on power, causation and action as such. There is a recent book chapter which summarizes some of Aquinas's views on causation: Michael Rota, "Causation," in *The Oxford Handbook of Aquinas*, ed. Brian Davies and Eleonore Stump (Oxford: Oxford University Press, 2012), 104–14.

[4] See for instance Anthony Kenny, *Aquinas on Mind* (London and New York: Routledge, 1993) and Robert Pasnau, *Thomas Aquinas on Human Nature: A Philosophical Study of Summa Theologiae 1a, 75–89* (Cambridge: Cambridge University Press, 2002). For a recent study of Aquinas's views on the operation of intellect, see Therese Scarpelli Cory, *Aquinas on Human Self-Knowledge* (Cambridge: Cambridge University Press, 2014). On perceptual powers, see Anthony J. Lisska, *Aquinas's Theory of Perception* (Oxford: Oxford University Press, 2016).

[5] Stephen Brock, *Action and Conduct: Thomas Aquinas and the Theory of Action* (Edinburgh: T&T Clark, 2000) and Can Laurens Löwe, *Thomas Aquinas on the Metaphysics of the Human Act* (Cambridge: Cambridge University Press, 2021).

[6] For recent studies on the sacraments, see Reginald Lynch, *The Cleansing of the Heart: The Sacraments as Instrumental Causes in the Thomistic Tradition* (Washington, DC: Catholic University Press, 2017) and Marilynn McCord Adams, *Some Later Medieval Theories of the Eucharist* (Oxford: Oxford University Press, 2012). On divine causation in the natural world, see Michael J. Dodds, *Unlocking Divine Action: Contemporary Science and Thomas Aquinas* (Washington, DC: Catholic University of America Press, 2012).

[7] See for example *ST* I q. 25, a. 2 and *ST* I q. 84, a. 3.

understanding of natural efficient causation, this study will deliver insights applicable to these other areas of his thought in which scholars of Aquinas have shown great interest.

Perhaps the reason Aquinas's views on natural efficient causation and causal powers have not been studied in great depth, despite their importance, is because Aquinas himself wrote no separate treatise on these topics. To reconstruct his views, a reader must look to discussions scattered throughout his corpus. Since the topics of efficient causation and causal powers are relevant to understanding many issues in philosophy and theology, we find Aquinas discussing these topics in both expected and unexpected contexts. There are passages in nearly every one of Aquinas's works which illuminate his views on efficient causation and causal powers. I have combed through Aquinas's corpus to find the most important passages about efficient causation and causal powers and using them as a basis, I reconstruct his views in a systematic way.

Whenever one aims to reconstruct a historical thinker's views using multiple texts written across the span of many years, one faces the question of whether the figure's thinking developed over time. Aquinas's views on causation and causal powers appear to have remained remarkably stable over his career. While there certainly are issues about which Aquinas changed his mind over time, these topics do not seem to be among them. To illustrate the consistency of his thought over time, the notes often include references to the same thesis in multiple works from different points in his career.[8] In the few cases in which there appear to be conflicts between the views that Aquinas asserts in different works, I explicitly discuss whether his claims can be reconciled or whether they must be interpreted as a change of position.

Organization of the Study

The book is organized thematically around the central elements of Aquinas's theories. The first chapter aims to introduce the reader to the big picture of Aquinas's thinking about efficient causation and causal powers. This chapter is a good place for all readers to begin, even those who wish to read the later chapters in isolation or out of order. In addition to discussing in more depth some of the key theses which were introduced above, the first chapter introduces some further ontological elements

---

[8] On the dating of Aquinas's works see Jean-Pierre Torrell, *Saint Thomas Aquinas: The Person and His Work* (Washington, DC: Catholic University Press of America, 1996).

which Aquinas thinks are involved in paradigm (i.e. *per se*) instances of efficient causation. The significance of Aquinas's views is highlighted by contrasting them with competing historical theories. The chapter also provides important information about Aquinas's sources and terminology.

The second chapter considers in more depth Aquinas's views on the relationship between an efficient cause and its effect in paradigm instances of efficient causation. It recovers Aquinas's thinking about the modal and temporal relationship between a *per se* natural cause and its effect. The chapter also discusses Aquinas's rejection of self-motion and action at a distance.

The next four chapters of the study explore Aquinas's views on the elements that are involved in paradigm instances of natural efficient causation. Chapter 3 recovers Aquinas's views on active power and examines in greater detail his thinking about the connection between form and active power and the diffusiveness of goodness. Chapter 4 examines Aquinas's views on another aspect of the agent that is crucial to explaining why it acts. Aquinas thought that in addition to active powers, natural agents had a natural inclination or impetus toward exercising those powers, and to the fullest extent possible. Powers explain why substances are able to act and natural inclination explains why they do in fact exercise their powers whenever they are in appropriate circumstances. This chapter also examines Aquinas's views on how ends or goals function as final causes of natural agents' actions. Aquinas's views on this topic are closely related to his understanding of natural inclination.

In addition to the agent's active power and natural inclination, Aquinas thought that the features of the substance upon which an agent acted, namely the patient, were also crucial to understanding efficient causation. Chapter 5 recovers Aquinas's thinking on passive potentiality, which is the feature of the patient through which it undergoes action.

The next chapter, Chapter 6, reconstructs Aquinas's thinking about what an agent's action is ontologically and how it relates to the passion that the patient undergoes and the motion or change that the agent causes. For instance, when fire burns a log, what is the fire's action of burning? Is it something distinct from the burning that the fire causes and the log undergoes? Or are all of these realities one and the same? Chapter 6 examines Aquinas's answers to these questions.

While the first six chapters of the book unpack Aquinas's views about the conditions and elements involved in the most proper and basic instances of efficient causation in the natural world, the final two chapters focus on more complicated cases of efficient causation. Chapter 7 examines various ways in which an effect can be attributed to an agent as an efficient cause even when the agent acts at a prior time and is not active in the immediate production of the effect. The final chapter recovers Aquinas's thinking on various ways in which efficient causes can act through the power of other causes. It discusses how efficient causes can be used as instruments by other causes to produce effects, as well as how certain efficient causes essentially depend on the powers of higher efficient causes to act.

PART I

The Elements of Paradigm Instances of Efficient Causation

CHAPTER I

Background and Overview of Aquinas's Theories

It is helpful for the reader to encounter a general overview of Aquinas's theories before delving into its particular details and complications in subsequent chapters. This chapter provides an introduction to Aquinas's views on efficient causation and causal powers, as well as some background and context necessary for appreciating his views. The chapter first introduces Aquinas's views on the nature of the relationship between an efficient cause and its effect and the various elements involved in paradigm cases of efficient causation. After presenting an overview of Aquinas's theories, the chapter next contrasts Aquinas's views with competing historical theories of causation. Comparison with these other theories helps to highlight what is philosophically significant in Aquinas's theories. The chapter also discusses Aquinas's sources and situates his views relative to medieval debates about causation. This background provides some context for appreciating what is original or controversial in Aquinas's theories. Finally, the chapter includes an introduction to the technical terminology in which Aquinas expresses his views on efficient causation and causal powers. Aquinas uses a variety of Latin terms to refer to the various conceptual elements in efficient causal situations. To aid the reader, these terms are introduced here at the beginning of the study.

1.1 Overview of Aquinas's Views on Efficient Causation and Causal Powers

As noted in the introduction, Aquinas understands the concept of causation in a much broader way than modern and contemporary philosophers. Since the early modern period, philosophers, for the most part, have conceived of causes as those things that are responsible for bringing about changes. Aquinas, by contrast, thinks of the causes which bring about changes, namely efficient causes, as only one type of cause alongside other species of causes. We can best understand Aquinas's views on efficient causation by first examining the nature of causation in general and then what is proper to the class of efficient causes.

Causation in General and Defining Features of Efficient Causation

Aquinas conceives of the notion of a "cause" as a species of a wider category called "principle." A principle is a beginning or that from which anything else follows. For example, one thing can follow from another according to number, as six follows from seven, or according to time, as one thing happens after another. The lower number and the earlier times are considered principles since there is an order of numbers or times in which they precede another term which follows them. Causes are a specific type of principle and what is proper to causes is that existence follows from them.[1] In Aquinas's view, the relationship between causes and their effects is one of existential dependence. He writes regarding causes in general: "[T]he name cause implies a certain influence on the being of the thing caused."[2] Elsewhere he writes: "Indeed it is necessary for an effect to depend on its cause. For this is part of the notion of effect and cause."[3] In Aquinas's view, causation is a two-way ontological relationship: Effects depend on their causes for their existence; and causes give rise to the existence of their effects. Causes need not bring their effects into being *simpliciter*. A cause may be responsible for something which already exists coming to exist in a new way. For example, the sun might cause an already existing apple to exist as ripened or reddened. While all causes influence being, some causes only influence how something exists.

Aquinas's conception of the cause–effect relationship is noteworthy because alternative theories of causation, as will be explained below, deny that the causal relationship is an ontological one and instead see it as a logical relationship, such as counterfactual dependence or logical entailment. From Aquinas's perspective, it is the real dependence of an effect

---

[1] *De prin. nat.* c. 3 (ed. Leon., vol. 43, 42–43): "Sed tamen causa videtur addere supra principium communiter dictum, quia id quod est primum, sive consequatur esse posterius sive non, potest dici principium … Sed causa solum dicitur de illo primo ex quo consequitur esse posterioris: unde dicitur quod causa est ex cuius esse sequitur aliud." Meehan claims that unlike Aquinas, Aristotle did not distinguish between "principles" and "causes." See Meehan, *Efficient Causality in Aristotle and St. Thomas*, 170–71.

[2] *In V Meta.* lec. 1 (ed. Marietti, 208, n. 751): " nomen causa, importat influxum quemdam ad esse causati." All translations from Latin to English are my own unless otherwise noted.

[3] *De pot.* q. 5, a. 1 (ed. Pession, 35): "Effectum enim a sua causa dependere oportet. Hoc enim est de ratione effectus et causae …"

upon its cause, rather than a logical or conceptual relationship, that unifies the multitude of different instances of causation as instances of causation.

Following Aristotle, Aquinas acknowledged four different species of causation: formal, material, efficient and final.[4] The different species of causes are distinguished from one another according to the different way each cause influences the being of its effect. As is well known, Aquinas followed Aristotle in conceiving of material objects as composed of matter and form.[5] The matter of a substance causes the being of the substance by composing it, as clay composes a statue. The form causes the being of the substance by actualizing matter in a specific way. The form of a cat, for example, actualizes matter in such a way that the form and matter together compose a cat, rather than a dog or some other type of substance. Material substances depend on both their matter and their form to exist, but they depend on each in a different way. Matter causes the being of a substance by composing it, while form causes the being of a substance by actualizing the matter out of which it is composed. Thus, the material and formal cause are two distinct species of cause since they influence the being of that which they cause differently.

The efficient cause is the cause that is responsible for uniting form with matter. Aquinas writes: "For the efficient cause is the cause of a thing insofar as it induces form or disposes matter."[6] Aquinas recognized that matter cannot actualize itself, and so, another cause must be responsible for actualizing a form in matter. This is the role of the efficient cause.[7] For example, the sculptor who induces the shape of the statue in clay is the efficient cause of the statue. The male parent of the cat is its efficient cause since, according to Aristotelian biology, it induces the form of the cat in the female parent's menstrual blood. By uniting form with matter, efficient causes are responsible for changes in the material world.

The last of the four causes, the final cause, is the end or goal that explains why an efficient cause acts. The final cause causes an effect by being desired or sought after. If, for example, a person walks for the sake of maintaining her health, then health is the final cause which explains why

---

[4] *ST* II-II q. 27, a. 3 (ed. Leon., vol. 8, 226): "Est autem quadruplex genus causae: scilicet finalis, formalis, efficiens et materialis ..."

[5] On Aquinas's hylomorphism see Jeffrey E. Brower, *Aquinas's Ontology of the Material World: Change, Hylomorphism, and Material Objects* (Oxford: Oxford University Press, 2014).

[6] *De pot.* q. 5, a. 1 (ed. Pession, 35): "Nam efficiens est causa rei secundum quod formam inducit, vel materiam disponit."

[7] *De prin. nat.* c. 3 (ed. Leon., vol. 43, 42): "Oportet ergo praeter materiam et formam esse aliquod principium quod agat, et hoc dicitur esse efficiens, vel movens, vel agens ..."

she is walking. Health causes her walking to exist because her seeking of health is what caused her to begin to walk. Aquinas thought that final causality was operative in natural efficient causation as well. Though natural causes cannot cognize the goals for which they act, they have inclinations toward certain goals built within them. These end-directed inclinations are causes of the actions of natural efficient causes. This will be discussed in greater detail in Chapter 4. With this general background in place, we can look now at the distinctive way in which efficient causes cause their effects.

Regarding efficient causes, Aquinas writes: "For that which causes something through its operation causes it as an efficient cause."[8] Elsewhere he states: "An efficient cause is a cause insofar as it acts."[9] Action, also called operation, is the unique way in which efficient causes influence the being of their effects. While all causes influence the being of their effects, efficient causes are the only causes that produce their effects *by acting*. In Aquinas's view, actions are exercises of active power. He writes: "Action is properly the actuality of a power ..."[10] Elsewhere he states: "[N]othing is able to act except through an active potentiality existing in it ..."[11] Accordingly, efficient causes are set apart from the other types of causes insofar as they cause by exercising powers. Above, I described efficient causes as those causes which are responsible for uniting form with matter. It should be noted that though Aquinas thinks that natural causes exercise efficient causation by inducing a form in a preexisting subject which functions as matter, he denies that efficient causation as such essentially involves inducing a form in matter or causing a change in some preexisting subject. Aquinas views God's creation of the universe from nothing, as well as his conservation of created substances, as types of efficient causation.[12] Yet, creation and conservation do not involve causing

---

[8] *De ver.* q. 28, a. 8 (ed. Leon., vol. 23, 3/1, 843): "Nam quod causat aliquid per operationem, causat per modum causae efficientis ..."

[9] *In V Meta.* lec. 2 (ed. Marietti, 213, n. 775): "Nam efficiens est causa inquantum agit." See also *De ver.* q. 22, a. 2.

[10] *ST* I q. 54, a. 1 (ed. Leon., vol. 5, 39): "Actio enim est proprie actualitas virtutis ..."

[11] *ScG* II c. 60 (ed. Marietti, 191, n. 1375): "[N]ihil est potens agere nisi per potentiam activam in ipso existentem ..."

[12] There has been some debate in the literature about whether Aquinas thinks creation and conservation are types of efficient causation. For an overview of the debate and defense of the view that he regards these divine acts as types of efficient causation, see Julie Swanstrom, "Creation as Efficient Causation in Aquinas," *American Catholic Philosophical Quarterly* 93:1 (2019): 1–27. Meehan also defends this view in *Efficient Causality in Aristotle and St. Thomas*, 184–85. For a passage in which Aquinas lists creation, conservation and natural change as types of efficient

a change in something preexisting. What these types of efficient causation have in common with the efficient causation that is exercised by created natural substances is that all involve causing an effect through action, namely through an exercise of active power. Action is what is essential to efficient causation as such. With this general background in place, we can now turn to the specific elements involved in paradigm instances of natural efficient causation.

Per se *Efficient Causation: The Paradigm Instance of Efficient Causation in the Natural World and Its Elements*

Aquinas thinks that certain instances of efficient causation which occur between material substances are the most fundamental and proper instances of causation in the material world. Other instances of natural efficient causation happen in virtue of these cases. The most proper and fundamental cases of natural efficient causation are called *per se* instances of efficient causation, and they involve several key elements which the subsequent chapters examine in greater detail. Aquinas thinks that instances of *per se* efficient causation include each of the following: (1) an *efficient cause*, which also called *an agent*, (2) an *action* which the agent performs by its (3) *active power* due to (4) a *natural inclination* for an end or goal. In addition to the four features just listed, all of which pertain to the agent, instances of efficient causation also include: (5) something upon which the agent acts, namely a *patient*, with an appropriate (6) *passive power* and (7) a *motion* or change which the agent causes and the patient undergoes as its (8) *passion*. In what follows, Aquinas's views about each element will be briefly explained. The subsequent chapters will expand on these explanations and provide the textual support for the views which I attribute to Aquinas here.

Agents, Patients and Motions

Let us begin by understanding the most obvious elements which are involved in efficient causation. According to Aquinas, efficient causation always involves an efficient cause, namely an agent. Aquinas clarifies that

---

causation see his *In Div. nom.* c. 4, lec. 5 (ed. Marietti, 115, n. 352): "[H]aec enim tria videntur ad rationem causae efficientis pertinere: ut det esse, moveat et conservet."

the entity that acts as an agent or efficient cause is always a complete substance, rather than one of its metaphysical or integral parts.[13] For example, the entire fire that is on a stove is the efficient cause which heats water. The agent of heating is not the fire's form of heat, nor a particular material part of it. Aquinas acknowledges that certain metaphysical features, namely active powers, explain why substances can act, but he emphasizes that the entire substance is the agent that acts in virtue of these features.

Aquinas thinks that natural efficient causes cause their effects in a particular way, namely by initiating a motion in another substance, called a patient. Motion is the process by which a persisting material substance gains one specific form, while losing a contrary form.[14] It is important for the reader to understand that Aquinas's conception of motion is much broader than our contemporary understanding. Today we tend to equate motion with locomotion, namely movement from one place to another. For Aquinas, however, in addition to locomotion, there are also quantitative and qualitative motions. For example, when a pot of water goes from being cold to being hot, it undergoes the motion of heating. The motion of heating is the process by which the water acquires the form of heat and loses the form of coldness. Because Aquinas understands motion to encompass more than locomotion, I will at times refer to motions as "changes." In Aquinas's view, motions occur gradually and they take time.[15] They terminate in a new form which is acquired by the patient substance. For example, heating water takes time and during it

---

[13] *ST* II-II q. 58, a. 2 (ed. Leon., vol. 9, 10): "Actiones autem sunt suppositorum et totorum, non autem, proprie loquendo, partium et formarum, seu potentiarum: non enim proprie dicitur quod manus percutiat, sed homo per manum; neque proprie dicitur quod calor calefaciat, sed ignis per calorem." See also *ST* I q. 75, a. 2 ad 2; *ST* I q. 77, a. 1 ad 3 and *Q.D. de anima* 12. On the definition of a substance or supposit see *ST* I q. 29, a. 2. On the principle "actions are of supposits" see Alain de Libera, "Les actions appartiennent aux sujets: petite archéologie d'un principe leibnizien," in *Ad ingenii acuitionem: Studies in Honor of Alfonso Maierù*, ed. Stefano Caroti et al. (Louvain-La-Neuve, BE: Fédération Internationale des Instituts d'Etudes Médiévales, 2007), 199–219, and Richard Cross, "Accidents, Substantial Forms, and Causal Powers in the Late Thirteenth Century: Some Reflections on the Axiom 'actiones sunt suppositorum,'" in *Compléments de substance: études sur les propriétés accidentelles offertes à Alain de Libera*, ed. Christophe Erismann and Alexandrine Schniewind (Paris: Vrin, 2008), 133–46. For a recent discussion of the principle in relation to Aquinas's theory of the human person and its acts of cognition see Brian Carl, "Action, Supposit, Subject: Interpreting *Actiones Sunt Suppositorum*," *Nova et Vetera* 17:2 (2019): 545–65.

[14] *In V Phys.* lec. 3 (ed. Leon., vol. 2, 238): "Omnis enim motus est mutatio ab una specie determinata in aliam speciem determinatam."

[15] See for instance *ScG* II c. 19.

the water gradually becomes hotter. Through the motion of heating, the water acquires the form of heat which it previously lacked.[16] In some passages, Aquinas describes efficient causes as the causes which "induce form."[17] Yet, in other passages, he describes efficient causes as "principles of motion."[18] Since natural efficient causes induce forms in their patients by way of motion, the effect of a natural efficient cause can be considered in a twofold manner. The effect of a natural efficient cause is both the motion which it initiates in its patient and the form which is the terminus of that motion.[19] Since natural efficient causes cause forms to be in their patients by way of motion, Aquinas also refers to them as "movers."[20]

Motion is not the only type of change for Aquinas. Generation and corruption are changes in which substances come into and go out of being.[21] Unlike changes which are motions, they do not involve a persisting subject which loses one accidental form and acquires a new one. Aquinas recognizes that natural efficient causes can cause generation and corruption. For example, dogs can generate other dogs and fires can cause trees to go out of existence by burning them. However, natural efficient causes only cause generation and corruption by causing prior qualitative motions in a patient.[22] For example, the fire causes the tree to be corrupted into ash in virtue of heating and blackening it.

---

[16] While motions in general involve gaining and losing forms, there are exceptions. According to Aquinas's views on intension and remission, changes of qualitative increase and decrease do not result in a substance acquiring a new form, but rather acquiring a new degree of participation in a form. For example, when already hot water becomes hotter, it does not gain a new form, but rather participates more perfectly in the form of heat which it already possesses. I discuss Aquinas's views on this topic in my paper "Aquinas on the Intension and Remission of Accidental Forms," *Oxford Studies in Medieval Philosophy* 7 (2019): 116–46.

[17] See fn. 6.

[18] *In I Meta.* lec. 4 (ed. Marietti, 23, n. 70): "causa est efficiens, quae est unde principium motus."

[19] For a passage in which Aquinas claims the form is the effect of the agent, see *De malo*, q. 5 a. 5 ad 16.

[20] See, for example, the text in fn. 7.

[21] *In I Phys.* lec. 13 (ed. Leon., vol. 2, 46):

> tres sunt species mutationis, scilicet generatio et corruptio et motus. Quorum haec est differentia, quia motus est de uno affirmato in aliud affirmatum, sicut de albo in nigrum; generatio autem est de negato in affirmatum, sicut de non albo in album, vel de non homine in hominem; corruptio autem est de affirmato in negatum, sicut de albo in non album, vel de homine in non hominem.

[22] *In I Gen. et Cor.* c. 10, lec. 24 (ed. Leon., vol. 3, 20): "Praeterea quaelibet forma substantialis propriam dispositionem requirit in materia, sine qua esse non potest: unde altera est via ad alterationem et altera ad corruptionem."

Aquinas's Physics

To fully appreciate Aquinas's views about the motions that natural efficient causes cause in their patients, as well as the examples he uses in discussing efficient causation, it is necessary to understand something of his views about the makeup of the physical universe. Aquinas's conception of the physical world was far different from the perspective of our contemporary science. Unlike many contemporary scientists, Aquinas sees qualitative forms as irreducible to quantitative features of substances. For instance, while today's scientists would reduce heat to the motion of molecules, Aquinas saw heat as an irreducible quality of substances. Aquinas, following Aristotle, held that there were four types of elemental substance: fire, air, water and earth. Every other terrestrial substance was generated by mixing these four elements together in various proportions. Each element was distinguished from the others in virtue of having a distinct combination of four basic qualities: hot, cold, wet and dry. Fire, for example, is hot and dry, while water is cold and wet. Other sensible qualities, such as textures and colors, were seen as "secondary" qualities which arose in virtue of the primary qualities.[23] Though substances possessed secondary qualities in virtue of possessing certain degrees and combinations of primary qualities, Aquinas thinks that secondary qualities are irreducible to primary ones. For example, redness and sweetness and real accidental forms that inhere in sweet and red substances over and above the primary qualities which give rise to them. The primary qualities were regarded as that through which material substances acted to cause changes in one another's primary qualities.[24] Changes in secondary qualities followed upon the more basic changes to primary qualities. For example, changes of texture or health or sickness were seen as caused in virtue of causing changes to a

---

[23] On medieval theories of primary and secondary qualities see Anneliese Maier, "The Theory of the Elements and the Problem of Their Presence in Compounds," in *On the Threshold of Exact Science*, trans. Steven Sargent (Philadelphia: University of Pennsylvania Press, 1982), 124–42; and Robert Pasnau, "Scholastic Qualities, Primary and Secondary," in *Primary and Secondary Qualities: The Historical and Ongoing Debate*, ed. Lawrence Nolan (New York: Oxford University Press, 2011), 41–61.

[24] *In II De anima* lec. 24, n. 11 (ed. Leon., vol. 45/1, 171): "[T]angibilia sunt qualitates activae et passivae elementorum, secundum quas accidit universaliter alteratio in corporibus." See also *ST* I q. 78, a. 3 (ed. Leon., vol. 5, 254): "non omnia accidentia habent vim immutativam secundum se; sed solae qualitates tertiae speciei, secundum quas contingit alteratio." See also *Sentencia Super Meteora* I, c. 2. Note that "tangible qualities" and "qualities of the third species" are other ways of referring to the "primary qualities."

substance's wetness and dryness or heat and coldness.[25] Within this physical theory, paradigm instances of natural efficient causation involve an agent causing its patient to acquire a form of one of the primary qualities. Such an example, which I will refer to often in the book, is the case of fire which causes heat in water. On Aquinas's view, this example involves the agent fire and the patient water and a motion of heating which terminates in the form of heat. The motion of heating and the form of heat are irreducible to any quantitative features of the water.

So far we have seen Aquinas's view that paradigm instances of natural efficient causation involve an agent, a patient and a motion or change that the agent causes in the patient. Aquinas thinks that we must posit some further elements within the agent and the patient to explain how it is that each is able to respectively cause and undergo the specific type of motion in question. Since not all substances can heat other things or be heated, there must be something within fire that explains how it is able to cause heating and something within water which explains how it is able to undergo heating.

Active Power, Passive Power and Natural Inclination

Active power is that which explains how an agent is able to cause a specific type of change. Aquinas identifies the active powers of material substances with their inherent forms. More specifically, Aquinas maintains that a material substance is able to induce a certain form in another substance by virtue of having that same form in itself. For example, fire is able to induce the form of heat in water through its own form of heat. In *per se* instances of efficient causation, the agent actualizes a new form of the same species as its own in its patient. According to Aquinas, forms are by their nature communicable. They enable their bearers to actualize forms of the same species in other substances which are suitable recipients for the form. However, not every type of form is an active power for affecting material change. Aquinas thinks that the elemental qualities of hot, cold, wet and dry are the only forms that can immediately affect material change. For example, through its form of heat, a fire can make other things hot, but it cannot make other material objects red through its form of redness. Forms that are not active powers for causing material change, nevertheless, are active powers for causing changes in the perceptual and intellectual faculties of cognitive beings. For instance, though redness is not a form through which an apple can make another substance turn red, it is nevertheless a form through which an apple acts on an animal's power of sight, thereby enabling an act of seeing red.[26]

Passive power is the aspect of the patient that allows it to undergo a specific type of change. A passive power is a capability to receive a certain type of form. For example, the passive power for undergoing heating is a capacity to take on the form of heat. Material substances have receptivity for form in virtue of both their matter and the other forms that actualize them. Matter as such is a principle of receptivity. However, to receive any specific type of form, it must be actualized by other forms that prepare it to receive the further form in question. Not just any substance can be burned. The substance must have an oily or fatty quality to be combustible. This illustrates that to be burned, material substances must have certain qualitative forms that make them susceptible to receiving the further forms involved in a change of burning.

To explain why an agent acts on its patient, Aquinas thinks that a further feature of the agent must be invoked beyond its active power. Something else must be posited to explain why the agent does in fact exercise its power, as well as why the agent exercises its power to the fullest extent possible. This is the role of natural inclination. A natural inclination is an impetus within a natural agent that drives it to exercise its proper powers whenever an appropriate circumstance obtains. For example, when fire comes into contact with water it is not indeterminate whether fire will heat the water or not. Fire always exercises its power to heat, unless something impedes it. Aquinas thinks that fire's natural inclination toward heating is what explains why it exercises its power whenever it is able. Furthermore, fire does not stop heating until it makes the water as hot as it possibly can. Natural inclination is what drives natural agents to exercise their powers as much as possible. Natural inclinations are always inclinations for some determinate type of action or effect. Natural inclination impels a natural agent toward an action or effect in a way analogous to how a human agent's will inclines it toward reaching a certain goal. The action or effect which a natural agent's inclination regards is known as the agent's end or final cause. Ends or final causes cause natural agents to act insofar as natural agents have natural inclinations for them. For instance, heat causes fire to heat insofar as fire acts on account of its natural inclination toward heating.

---

[26] On Aquinas's account of perception, see Lisska, *Aquinas's Theory of Perception*.

Action and Passion

There are two elements which are left to discuss, namely action and passion. Action is the realization or manifestation of the agent's active power and passion is the realization or manifestation of the patient's passive potentiality. The action of heating for example is the realization of the fire's active power to heat and the passion of being heated is the realization of the patient's passive potentiality to undergo heating. But what are actions and passions ontologically? Aquinas thinks that the motion which the agent causes and the patient undergoes constitutes both the agent's action and the patient's passion. For example, the motion of heating which water undergoes constitutes the agent's action of heating and patient's passion of being heated. Yet, correlative actions, passions and motions are not simply identical with each other. An action is a motion taken together with its ontological dependence on an agent. Motions ontologically depend on an agent insofar as they arise from them as their origin. Likewise, a passion is a motion taken together with its ontological dependence on a patient. Motions depend on a patient insofar as they exist in them as their subject. For example, when fire heats water, the fire's action of heating is not merely the change occurring in the water, but rather it is that change considered precisely insofar as it is arising from the fire's active power. Similarly, the water's passion of being heated is not merely the change of heating, but that change considered precisely insofar as it is happening to the water as its subject.

Relational Conditions for Efficient Causation

In addition to the ontological elements involved in *per se* efficient causation, Aquinas thinks that there are some relational conditions which must be met between the agent and the patient. First, the agent and the patient must be distinct from each other. The agent and the patient must be other since an agent causes a form through possessing the same type of form in actuality and a patient receives a form through having that form potentially. Since the same subject cannot have the same form actually and potentially, the agent and the patient must be other. They need not be distinct substances, however. One part of a substance can be that through which the substance acts on another part. This is because one part of a substance can have a form in actuality, while another has it in potentiality. For example, if one of my hands is hot, I can touch my other hand and make it hot. The second relational condition which must be met between the agent and the patient is that the agent must be in contact with the patient. Aquinas thinks that an agent can only act where its power is present. A fire in my backyard cannot burn a tree across the street since the power of the fire is not located where the tree is. Aquinas does think that an agent's power can be put into contact with a patient in a different location through a medium. For example, the fire can warm my hands even when I am not touching it since the fire's power to heat can extend to my hands through the medium of the air. This is to say that the fire heats my hands in virtue of heating the air which is in contact with both the fire and my hands.

There are many questions which arise about each element involved in *per se* efficient causation. The next five chapters take up each of the elements described above, explaining each in detail and examining the conceptual questions which arise. It is likely that many readers are already thinking of counterexamples to Aquinas's basic model of *per se* efficient causation. It is not hard to come up with examples of cases of efficient causation which involve an agent producing an effect for which it has no corresponding active power or inclination toward that effect. Aquinas himself recognizes that there are examples of efficient causation in nature which do not involve the elements involved in the paradigm case of *per se* efficient causation. For example, he acknowledges efficient causes which "accidentally" produce effects for which they have no corresponding power or inclination. He writes about the case of a fire which cools a substance in virtue of opening its pores.[27] Fire has no active power to cool and no inclination toward this effect, yet Aquinas thinks that fire is a genuine efficient cause of the change of cooling in this case. The study will also examine the details of Aquinas's thinking on these non-paradigm cases, as well as more complicated cases involving many cooperating agents. For now, however, I focus only on Aquinas's analysis of the most proper or paradigm instances of efficient causation since this is the core of his theory. Within the core of Aquinas's theory there are already several ideas which are quite striking, especially when they are situated relative to other theories of causation.

1.2   Competing Models of Causation: Humeanism and Nomicism

The conceptual significance of Aquinas's views on efficient causation and causal powers can be brought out by considering two competing

---

[27] *In IX Meta.* lec. 2, n. 1789.

understandings of causation from the history of philosophy, Humeanism and Nomicism. These alternative theories continue to shape the assumptions operating in contemporary discussions of causation. Accordingly, it may benefit the contemporary reader to see Aquinas's views contrasted with them.

The British empiricist David Hume (1711–76) is perhaps the historical philosopher who has most influenced the manner in which contemporary philosophers think about causation. As is the case for any historical figure, the proper interpretations of Hume's views on causation are subject to debate.[28] My goal here is not to defend a particular interpretation of Hume, but rather to introduce some key theses about causation which are often attributed to him. I will refer to those theses as comprising the "Humean" model of causation, even though some scholars might deny that Hume himself truly defended all of them. The key theses of the Humean model of causation are these: First, there is no real power or production in the natural world. We cannot see, feel, or intuit one object producing another. All we experience through our senses is one event happening in conjunction with another. Empiricists claim that it follows from our lack of experience of powers and production that we have no license to posit them as real features of the world. Likewise, there is no justification for maintaining that causes are necessarily connected to their effects. Hume argues that all we experience is a cause's conjunction with its effect. We assume that the same causes will be conjoined with the same effects in the future because they were in the past. However, just as we have no sense impression of power and production, we likewise have no sense impression of a necessary connection between cause and effect. Rather, this necessary link is a projection of our minds. This is significant because what gives causation its predictive value is the assumption that causes necessitate their effects. If causes necessitate their effects, then when a cause is present, we can infer that its effect will follow. However, if causes do not necessitate their effects there is no justification for assuming that an effect will follow when its cause is posited.

The second thesis of the Humean model has to do with how we should understand claims about causation given that there is no real power or production in the world. According to the Humean model, causation is a logical relationship between events which regularly happen in conjunction

---

[28] For a summary of the various aspects of Hume's views on causation, as well as a very useful annotated bibliography of secondary literature, see C. M. Lorkowski, "Hume, David: Causation," in *The Internet Encyclopedia of Philosophy*, www.iep.utm.edu/, accessed April 1, 2021.

with one another. There is no real, metaphysical connection between causes and effects. We refer to one event as the cause of another event if the second event regularly follows the first. However, on the metaphysical level the world is a collection of loose and separate events unfolding in temporal succession.

The contrast between Aquinas's model of causation and the Humean model should be apparent. On Aquinas's view, efficient causation is a real, irreducible metaphysical phenomenon. Efficient causes produce their effects and their effects really depend on their causes for their being. In the next chapter, we will see that Aquinas himself recognized that we have no sense experience of production or power, and yet, by intellectual reasoning we can know that there must be real efficient causation in nature and that powers are necessary to explain how this efficient causation happens. Furthermore, also in contrast with Humean assumptions, Aquinas maintains that the fact that efficient causes do not logically necessitate their effects does not undercut the metaphysical reality of causation. Since efficient causes can always be impeded in their production of their effects, it is possible for a natural cause to exist without its effect. Though causes, taken only in themselves, do not necessitate their effects, they nevertheless are productive of the being of their effects in the situations in which they do cause them.

Much contemporary work on causation has assumed that Hume was correct in his rejection of causation as involving exercises of power and genuine production. Many contemporary philosophers believe that claims about causal dependence are reducible to claims about other non-causal relationships between events. Much contemporary literature on causation focuses on developing the right non-causal relationship between events to which causal statements can be reduced. For instance, according to David Lewis's counterfactual analysis of causation, one event e causally depends on another event c if and only if, if c were not to occur e would not occur.[29] Though the Humean approach to causation continues to be predominant, in recent decades a number of contemporary philosophers have argued against it. In its place, they have advocated for a return to the pre-modern view that objects have real causal powers.[30] Many of the philosophers pursuing this growing research agenda have explicitly described their project as a revival of the Aristotelian perspective.

[29] David Lewis, "Causation," *Journal of Philosophy* 70:17 (1973): 556–67.
[30] For an overview of contemporary work on causal powers, see Jonathan Jacobs (ed.), *Causal Powers* (Oxford: Oxford University Press, 2017).

A second model of causation that has also been prominent in both the history of philosophy and contemporary philosophy is the "nomic" model. According to nomicism, laws of nature are central to understanding causation in the natural world. On the Humean model, statements about what universally happens in the world, e.g. "Salt dissolves in water," are nothing more than statements about what regularly happens. There is no explanation for why these regularities are true and no necessary connection exists between the events which the statements are about. The nomic model, by contrast, claims that statements about what universally happens in the world express necessary laws that govern the universe. On this model, laws about necessary relationships between events are part of the very fabric of reality, and these laws are instantiated in particular instances of causation. For example, there is a certain necessary relationship between salt's being dropped in water and its dissolving. This law is what determines that a particular grain of salt dissolves when dropped into a particular cup of water. Laws of nature, on the nomic model, do not merely report the regularities that happen in the world. Rather, they necessitate or produce the regularities. A law of nature is what accounts for why two particulars are related to each other as cause and effect. In the early modern period, laws of nature were expressly associated with theism and were thought to have been established by God.[31] In contemporary philosophy, laws of nature are seen as brute features of the universe and they are not traced to any divine lawgiver.[32]

Aquinas's model of causation also differs in crucial ways from the nomic model. As we will see, this difference has not always been adequately recognized.[33] Aquinas denies that terrestrial natural causes, considered in themselves, necessitate their effects. This is because such causes are always able to be impeded. Nevertheless, Aquinas thinks that we can formulate universal, generalizations about what effects will follow from causes on the assumption that the causes are not impeded. Aquinas agrees with the nomic model that there is a deeper metaphysical explanation for the regularities in nature. Yet, he disagrees about what that explanation is. On the nomic model, laws of nature are extrinsically imposed on objects and these extrinsic laws determine that entities of the same universal types

---

[31] For an overview of Descartes's view of laws of nature as established by the divine will, see Ott, *Causation and Laws of Nature in Early Modern Philosophy*, 51–60.
[32] For an important contemporary account of laws of nature, see D. M. Armstrong, *What Is a Law of Nature?* (Cambridge: Cambridge University Press, 1983).
[33] See Section 2.3.

behave according to certain regularities. On Aquinas's model, by contrast, the regular patterns of behavior of material substances have an intrinsic rather than an extrinsic source. Natural substances of the same kind have the same types of intrinsic causal powers and this is why they behave in similar ways. It is the regular behavior of natural entities, which stems from their causal powers, that makes certain laws true. This is the reverse of the nomic model, which prioritizes the laws and appeals to them to explain regularities in the behavior of natural entities. For example, on the nomic model, the law of nature that water dissolves salt is what determines that a particular instance of water dissolves a particular grain of salt. On Aquinas's model, things are reversed. The generalization that water dissolves salt is true because the instances of water that exist in the world have a power to pull sodium chloride ions apart and regularly do so. The nomic model assumes that laws exercise "top down" control over natural events. Aquinas, by contrast, believes that the powers of natural entities determine "from the bottom up" which generalizations obtain.

1.3   Aquinas's Sources

Aristotle

Like much of his natural philosophy, Aquinas's theory of efficient causation draws heavily on Aristotle as a source.[34] Aquinas's hylomorphic conception of the material world and the fourfold division of causes are, as is well known, taken from Aristotle. Aquinas's demarcation of the realities involved in efficient causation (e.g. agents, patients, powers, actions and passions) and his understanding of the conditions that must be met for material substances to act upon one another are likewise drawn from Aristotle. The *Physics* and *Metaphysics* are the two Aristotelian works in which causation is discussed most extensively and Aquinas's commentaries on these works, especially the *Physics*, contain many of his most lengthy and detailed discussions of causation. Though some scholars disagree, I think it is reasonable to view Aquinas's Aristotelian commentaries as sources for his own views, rather than mere expositions of Aristotle. However, care must be exercised in interpreting

---

[34] For a brief account of Aquinas's use of Aristotle as a source, see James Doig, "Aquinas and Aristotle," *The Oxford Handbook of Aquinas*, ed. Brian Davies and Eleonore Stump (Oxford: Oxford University Press, 2012), 33–41.

these texts since they also include summaries of positions which are not Aquinas's own.[35]

While Aristotle is perhaps the source who had the most influence on Aquinas's views on efficient causation and causal powers, Aquinas's theories nevertheless cannot be reduced to Aristotle's.[36] At times Aquinas departs from Aristotelian views to accommodate theological doctrines unknown to Aristotle. For example, in defining efficient causation Aquinas, unlike Aristotle, had to make room for creation and conservation as types of efficient causation. Thus, while Aristotle defines efficient causation as a source of motion or change, Aquinas defines it as causation that produces being.[37] At other times, Aquinas does not explicitly contradict Aristotle's views, but he goes beyond them. The debates of his period required Aquinas to give accounts of matters that Aristotle did not address in great detail. Examples that will be discussed below include debates about the relationship between the soul and its powers and the nature of the sameness and difference between action, passion and motion.

Averroes (Ibn Rushd) and Avicenna (Ibn Sina)

Aquinas, and his medieval Christian contemporaries, did not read Aristotle in a vacuum. The commentaries of Averroes and Avicenna shaped their understanding of Aristotle's views and highlighted where the interpretive difficulties lie.[38] At times the Islamic commentators point out apparent inconsistencies within Aristotle's texts, and they disagree with each other on how to interpret Aristotle's positions. The Islamic commentators shaped Aquinas's views on many topics and his views on efficient causation are no exception.

Aquinas's views about how efficient causes act for the sake of an end is one example of how his understanding of Aristotelian concepts was heavily shaped by these Islamic sources. One of the main arguments Aquinas puts forth to establish that efficient causes act for the sake of an end rests on the counterfactual claim that if agents did not act for a goal, then they would

---

[35] For an overview of the scholarly positions on the significance of Aquinas's Aristotelian commentaries and citations to relevant literature, see John Wippel, *The Metaphysical Thought of Thomas Aquinas* (Washington, DC: The Catholic University of America Press, 2005), xix–xx.

[36] For a summary of differences between Aristotle's and Aquinas's views on efficient causation, see Meehan, *Efficient Causality in Aristotle and St. Thomas*, 399–405.

[37] See Meehan, *Efficient Causality in Aristotle and St. Thomas*, 185–88.

[38] For a brief overview of Aquinas's interaction with these sources, see David Burrell, "Aquinas and Jewish and Islamic authors," in *The Oxford Handbook of Aquinas*, ed. Brian Davies and Eleonore Stump (Oxford: Oxford University Press, 2012), 65–72.

not act at all. He explicitly attributes this argument to Averroes.[39] Aquinas also draws on Avicenna's thought to explain how it can be that the end causes an agent's action if the end does not exist until after the action has been completed. Aquinas follows Avicenna's claim, *contra* Averroes, that the end is a final cause insofar as it is in the intention of the agent.[40] This move to make the end in the intention that which exercises final causality enables these authors to show how the end can be prior to the action which it causes.[41] Aquinas likewise draws on Avicenna when he explains how it can be that natural causes act for the sake of ends even though they lack the ability to deliberate about ends. Aquinas cites Avicenna's example of a harpist who plays chords without deliberating about the notes. This is supposed to show that it is possible for an agent to act for an end without deliberation.[42]

In addition to shedding light on various interpretive possibilities for Aristotelian texts and positions, the Islamic commentators also passed on to Aquinas concepts and ideas which were their own and not found in Aristotle. For example, in two of Aquinas's most extensive discussions of causation in his commentaries on Aristotle's *Physics* and *Metaphysics*, he explicitly cites and endorses a fourfold division of types of efficient causes, which he attributes to Avicenna.[43] As we will see in Chapter 7, Aquinas uses Avicenna's division between perfecting, preparing, assisting and advising causes to identify various ways in which one efficient cause can be involved in the causation of another efficient cause's action and effects.[44] These more fine-grained notions of different types of causes, which are not found in Aristotle, gave Aquinas the conceptual resources needed to discuss particularly complicated and non-standard cases of efficient causation.

---

[39] See Section 4.1 for discussion of this argument and fn. 6 for the text in which Aquinas attributes this argument to Averroes.

[40] On the debate between Avicenna and Averroes on final causality and its influence on scholastic figures see Robert Pasnau, "Intentionality and Final Causes," in *Ancient and Medieval Theories of Intentionality*, ed. Dominik Perler (Leiden: Brill, 2001), 301–23 and "Teleology in the Later Middle Ages," in *Teleology: A History*, ed. Jeffrey McDonough (Oxford: Oxford University Press, 2020), 90–115.

[41] See Section 4.2, especially fn. 30.   [42] See Section 4.2, especially fn. 16.

[43] *In V Meta.* lec. 2 and *In II Phys.* lec. 5. The explicit mention of Avicenna occurs only in the *Metaphysics* text. On Avicenna's views on efficient causation see Kara Richardson, "Avicenna's Conception of the Efficient Cause," *British Journal for the History of Philosophy*, 21 (2013): 220–39; and her entry, "Causation in Arabic and Islamic Thought," in Edward N. Zalta (ed.), *The Stanford Encyclopedia of Philosophy* (Winter 2015 Edition), https://plato.stanford.edu/archives/win2015/entries/arabic-islamic-causation/, accessed May 31, 2021, especially Section 2.2.2.

[44] See especially Section 7.1.

In addition to offering interpretations of Aristotle and new non-Aristotelian concepts, Aquinas's Islamic sources also gave him resources for reconciling the Aristotelian philosophical framework with his theistic worldview. One such example relevant to efficient causation regards how efficient causes are defined. Above when discussing Aristotle as a source for Aquinas, it was noted that Aristotle defined efficient causes as those causes which are sources of motion or change. Aquinas, however, defines efficient causes as causes that produce being in order to make room for God's acts of creation and conservation to be conceived of as exercises of efficient causation.[45] It was from Avicenna's texts that Aquinas encountered the idea that divine activity, though it does not involve motion or change, should nevertheless be conceived of as a type of efficient causation alongside the efficient causation exercised by creatures, rather than something *sui generis.*[46]

Neo-Platonic Sources

In addition to Aristotle and his Islamic commentators, Aquinas's philosophical thought was greatly influenced by neo-Platonic sources.[47] The neo-Platonic source that was most influential on Aquinas's thinking about causation is the *Liber de Causis*. The *Liber de Causis* is a ninth-century text by an unknown author which was translated into Latin in the twelfth century.[48] It draws heavily on the Greek neo-Platonist Proclus to present an array of theses about hierarchical ordered causes. Many scholastic figures, including Aquinas, wrote commentaries on this work and it is cited frequently in their other works.[49] Its theses about primary and secondary causes greatly influenced medieval discussions of ordered causes and particularly the causal relationship between God and creatures. Perhaps most influential was the very first proposition of the work, which

---

[45] See also Section 1.1.

[46] See for example *In II Sent.* d. 1, q. 1, a. 2 ad 1 (ed. Mandonnet-Moos, vol. 2, 18–19): "Ad primum ergo dicendum, quod, secundum Avicennam, I Suff., cap. x, et VI Metaph., cap. I, duplex est agens: quoddam naturale, quod est agens per motum, et quoddam divinum, quod est dans esse, ut dictum est."

[47] On Aquinas and neo-Platonism, see Wayne Hankey, "Aquinas, Plato, and Neo-Platonism," in *The Oxford Handbook of Aquinas*, ed. Brian Davies and Eleonore Stump (Oxford: Oxford University Press, 2012), 55–64.

[48] The modern edition of this work is Adriaan Pattin (ed.), '*Le Liber de causis*: Édition établie à l'aide de 90 manuscrits avec introduction et notes par A. Pattin O.M.L.', *Tijdschrift voor Filosofie* 28 (1966): 90–203.

[49] For a list of some of the scholastic commentaries on this work see Pattin, 122–30.

stated that the first cause is *more* of a cause of the effect than the second.[50] The work advocated for the primacy of causes with higher natures when such causes jointly cause effects with causes of a lower nature.

1.4   Situating Aquinas among His Medieval Contemporaries

It is natural to wonder how Aquinas's views compare with others in the medieval period. Was he somehow original or unique? Or was he merely a representative of a standard view? Medieval views about causation have yet to be extensively researched and there are still many gaps to be filled in about our knowledge of the views of particular thinkers. Yet, some observations can be made about the different approaches to efficient causation that were represented in the period and their predominance. We know from Aquinas's own writings, as well as other research, that there were medieval thinkers who opposed the general model of efficient causation that he defends. As we saw above, Aquinas maintained that natural efficient causes influence the being of their effects and such effects depend on their causes for their being. While this general conception of efficient causation was widespread among scholastic thinkers, there were some medieval figures, primarily in the Islamic tradition, who rejected it and instead defended a view known as occasionalism.[51] According to occasionalism, God is the only active efficient cause and thus particular substances in the material world do not actively produce any effects. Created substances function merely as passive occasions for God to act. For example, when fire comes into contact with cotton, the fire does not truly burn the cotton. Rather, fire's contact with cotton is merely an occasion for God to produce burning in the cotton. Occasionalism is similar to Humeanism insofar as it denies that creatures have active powers and maintains that those entities that we consider to be causes and effects (e.g. as when we claim that fire causes burning) merely exist in conjunction with each other. Aquinas knew of the occasionalist position and argued against it in several places in his works.[52]

---

[50] *Le Liber de causis* (ed. Pattin, 134): "Omnis causa primaria plus est influens super causatum suum quam causa universalis secunda."
[51] On Islamic occasionalism see Dominik Perler and Ulrich Rudolph, *Occasionalismus: Theorien der Kausalität im arabisch-islamischen und im europäischen Denken* (Göttingen: Vandenhoeck & Ruprecht, 2000).
[52] On Aquinas's critique of occasionalism see M. Fakhry, *Islamic Occasionalism and Its Critique by Averroës and Aquinas* (London: Routledge, 1958).

Occasionalism was not the only competing approach to efficient causation on offer in the medieval period. There were medieval figures who conceptualized efficient causation in a manner which bears some similarity with the nomic view discussed above.[53] Many believe that the notion of a law of nature is a post-medieval concept invented by Descartes.[54] Research has shown, however, that there were medieval figures such as Robert Grosseteste and Roger Bacon who discussed general laws that governed natural causation and prioritized these laws of nature over the immanent features of material substances (e.g. active forms) in causal explanations of natural events.[55] Aquinas, however, does not engage with these views in his works and currently there is no evidence of major medieval debates about the role of laws of nature in efficient causation.

While there is evidence of some alternative views in the medieval period, the majority of medieval scholastic figures accepted the key features found in Aquinas's conception of efficient causation. More specifically, there was a general consensus among medieval scholastic thinkers that (1) natural efficient causes influence the being of their effects, and (2) efficient causes act through active powers. These central features of Aquinas's model of causation are broadly Aristotelian and, as is well known, Aristotle heavily influenced scholastic figures. Thus, many other Christian medieval thinkers of Aquinas's period view efficient causal situations as involving the same entities included in Aquinas's account. While there was broad consensus among medieval Aristotelians that efficient causal situations involve an agent, a patient, a motion or change, active and passive powers, an action and a passion, there were disagreements about the precise nature of these realities.

It lies outside of the scope of this project to examine the many debates in which scholastic figures engaged about the ontological realities involved in efficient causation. As will become clear, there are many nuances in Aquinas's views on this topic and many interpretive issues to consider. It is simply not possible to examine other figures' positions with the same level of detail and care in a book of this length. What follows is a brief overview of some of the central scholastic debates about causation. This overview is intended to give the reader some perspective about which positions defended by Aquinas were subject to disagreement.

---

[53] See Section 1.2.   [54] Ott, "Causation and Laws of Nature in Early Modern Philosophy," 51.
[55] See for example Yael Kedar, "Laying the Foundation for the Nomological Image of Nature: From Corporeity in Robert Grosseteste (c. 1168–1253) to Species in Roger Bacon (1220–1292)," in *Robert Grosseteste and the Pursuit of Religious and Scientific Learning in the Middle-Ages*, ed. J. P. Cunningham (New York: Springer, 2016), 165–85.

Active Causal Powers: What Are Powers? How Are They Individuated?

While scholastic figures agreed that agents acted through active causal powers, there were many debates about what exactly these powers are and how many of them are required to account for the various actions substances perform. Many scholastic writings on these questions about active powers focused specifically on the active powers of living organisms, particularly humans. Yet, some positions and arguments defended in these debates had a wider application to all created active powers.

Regarding the question of what active powers are in themselves, we saw above that Aquinas maintains that active powers are forms. For instance, the power by which fire heats water is the form of heat in the fire by which it is hot. Other figures denied that powers could be identified with forms. Henry of Ghent, for example, claimed that powers by their nature are related to actions. The power to heat, for example, by its nature is related to heating. Thus, Henry reasoned that powers cannot merely be absolute, namely non-relational items, such as forms. Rather, in his view, powers are relationships to actions, which are founded on absolute items. So, fire's power to burn, is not itself the fire's heat, but rather a relatedness that fire has to heating in virtue of its heat.[56]

Another major disagreement among scholastic thinkers focused on the relationship between a substance's active powers and its substantial form. More specifically, the debate centered upon whether the human substantial form was the active power through which human beings engaged in their characteristic activities of knowing, willing and sensing, or whether these human powers were accidental forms distinct from the human substantial form. While this debate focused specifically on the human being and its powers, some of the arguments proceeded from general claims that had implications for how all substantial forms relate to the powers by which substances operate.[57] As we will see, Aquinas argues that

[56] On Henry's position See Cross, "Accidents, Substantial Forms, and Causal Powers," 137; J. T. Paasch, *Divine Production in Late Medieval Trinitarian Theology: Henry of Ghent, Duns Scotus, and William Ockham* (Oxford: Oxford University Press, 2012), 117–21; Simona Vucu, "Henry of Ghent and John Duns Scotus on Self-agency and Self-motion: An Inquiry into the Medieval Metaphysics of Causal Powers," PhD diss., University of Toronto, 2018, ProQuest Dissertations Publishing, 10641101, 141–49.
[57] For discussion of one such argument in Aquinas see Section 3.8. For a discussion of thirteenth century positions on the soul and its powers, see P. Künzle, *Das Verhältnis der Seele zu ihren Potenzen: Problemgeschichtliche Untersuchungen von Augustin bis und mit Thomas Von Aquin* (Freiburg: Universitätsverlag, 1956). For a briefer overview of the debate and discussion of the critique of Aquinas's position, see Adam Wood, "The Faculties of the Soul and Some Medieval

no substance acts immediately through its substantial form. The powers by which substances immediately act are accidental forms distinct from their substantial form. Against this position, other scholastic figures, such as Henry of Ghent and John Buridan, held that powers such as the human intellect and will were identical with the human substantial form, namely the soul.

Another related debate concerned how active powers are individuated. As we will see, Aquinas maintains that powers are individuated by the acts that immediately arise from them. In his view, each action that immediately arises from a substance entails a distinct active power through which the action is performed. For example, the acts of heating and illuminating entail two separate active powers in fire, namely a power to heat and a power to illuminate. Aquinas allows that two different types of action can arise from the same active power if and only if one act happens in virtue of the other, for example, as melting happens in virtue of heating.[58] John Buridan critiqued the position that powers are individuated by actions. In his view, it is not necessary to posit a distinct power to account for each type of action that a substance can perform. He thought that there are "multi-track" powers which enable various types of actions. He was among those who held that the human soul was identical to its powers. Thus, he saw the soul as an example of a single power from which many different types of actions immediately arose.[59]

Action, Passion and Motion: How Do They Relate to One Another?

As we saw above, Aquinas maintains that natural efficient causation always involves motion. The agent causes motion and the patient undergoes it. For example, in the case of fire heating water, fire causes heating and water undergoes it. But how does the fire's action of heating and the water's passion of undergoing heating relate to the motion of heating itself? Medieval scholastic thinkers debated about how to analyze the ontological relationship between action, passion and motion. Aristotle claimed that one and the same motion was both the agent's action and the patient's passion.[60] His scholastic followers, however, developed different accounts

---

Mind-Body Problems," *The Thomist* 75(2011): 585–636. For a detailed discussion of Aquinas's position and arguments, see Wippel, *Metaphysical Thought of Thomas Aquinas*, 275–94.

[58] See Section 3.2.

[59] On Buridan's views see Can Laurens Löwe, "Aristotle and John Buridan on the Individuation of Causal Powers," *Oxford Studies in Medieval Philosophy* 6 (2018): 189–222.

[60] See his *Physics*, Bk. III, lec. 3.

of the nature of the sameness and the difference that obtains between these realities. On one end of the spectrum, thinkers such as Ockham argued that action and passion differ only conceptually from the motion involved in efficient causation. Action and passion are merely two different concepts of the same reality.[61] On the other end of the spectrum, thinkers such as Peter Auriol argued that an agent's action must be an entity that exists prior to and is separable from the motion that is caused through it.[62] Aquinas's own position, which has been subject to interpretive debate, lies somewhere between these two extremes. I will show in Chapter 5 that while he maintains that action and passion are irreducible to motion, correlative actions and passions are nevertheless inseparable from the motion which they involve.

The Conditions for Efficient Causal Interactions: Must the Agent and the Patient be Distinct? Can Some Substances Act at a Distance?

In addition to debates about the precise nature of the entities involved in efficient causal interactions, there were disagreements among medieval scholastics about the conditions which needed to be met for efficient causation to occur. As already mentioned, Aquinas held that the agent and the patient must be other in order for the agent to communicate a form to the patient in action. By contrast, other medieval figures believed that self-motion was possible. It is well known that many medieval thinkers thought that the human will could move itself to act. Yet, there were also medieval figures, such as John Duns Scotus, who believed that even natural agents, namely those lacking intellect and will, could engage in self-motion. Scotus thinks that growth is an example of self-motion in which a substance acts through one of its qualitative forms, e.g. heat, to induce a new quantitative form in itself.[63]

---

[61] On Ockham's view see Susan Brower-Toland, "Causation and Mental Content: Against the Externalist Reading of Ockham," in *The Language of Thought in Late Medieval Philosophy: Essays in Honour of Claude Panaccio*, ed. J. Pelletier and M. Roques (Cham: Springer, 2017), 59–80, particularly section 3.

[62] On Auriol's critique of Aquinas's views on action, see Gloria Frost, "What is an Action? Peter Auriol vs. Thomas Aquinas on the Metaphysics of Causality," *Ergo* 6:43 (2020): 1259–85. See also Can Laurens Löwe, "Peter Auriol on the Metaphysics of Efficient Causation," *Vivarium* 55:4 (2017): 239–72. On Scotus's views in comparison with Aquinas's see Can Laurens Löwe, "John Duns Scotus versus Thomas Aquinas on Action–Passion Identity," *British Journal for the History of Philosophy* 26:6 (2018): 1027–44.

[63] On Scotus's views on self-motion, see Peter King, "Duns Scotus on the Reality of Self-Change," in *Self-Motion from Aristotle to Newton*, ed. Mary Louise Gill and James Lennox (Princeton: Princeton University Press, 1994), 227–90 and Yul Kim, "Why Does the Wood Not Ignite Itself? Duns

Another condition for efficient causal interactions that was debated was the "contact" condition. Aquinas held fast to the Aristotelian view that the agent must be in physical contact with the patient in order to act upon it. Contact with the patient could be immediate, as in cases where the agent and the patient were touching one another, or contact could be mediated by an intermediary, known as a "medium," which touches both the agent and the patient. Aquinas supported the contact condition with a claim that an agent can only act where its power is physically present. Thus, an agent must be in physical contact with something in order to act upon it. However, other scholastic figures rejected the contact condition and maintained that action at a distance does occur in the physical world.[64] Thinkers such as William of Ockham supported this view by educing cases in which an agent appears to act at distance, such as magnetism and the action of a sensible object on the power of vision.[65]

Debates about Natural Inclination and Final Causality: Are Natural Inclinations Necessary? Are There Final Causes in Nature?

In Aquinas's view, part of the explanation for why natural causes exercise their powers in action is that they have a natural inclination toward their proper activities. Natural inclinations are tendencies within natural causes which impel them toward certain goals, which can be either an action or a product. Aquinas views natural inclinations as explaining why natural causes exercise their active powers whenever they are in contact with appropriate patients. This position was challenged by later figures. Ockham, for example, claims that the explanation for why fire goes from not acting to acting is the removal of an impediment or its coming into contact with a suitable patient.[66] He sees natural inclinations as unnecessary to explain why natural causes act when in appropriate circumstances. Ockham likewise attacked the view that natural causes act for the sake of ends or goals that function as final causes of natural actions. Ockham

---

Scotus's Defense of the Will's Self-Motion," *American Catholic Philosophical Quarterly* 95:1 (2021): 49–68.

[64] Francis J. Kovach provides an overview of the medieval positions on the possibility of action at distance in his "Aquinas's Theory of Action at a Distance: A Critical Analysis," in *Scholastic Challenges to Mediaeval and Modern Ideas* (Stillwater, OK: Western Publications, 1987), 147–78, at 149–51.

[65] On Ockham's arguments for action at a distance see André Goddu, "William of Ockham's Arguments for Action at a Distance," *Franciscan Studies* 44 (1984): 227–44.

[66] See Henrik Lagerlund, "The Unity of Efficient and Final Causality: The Mind/Body Problem Reconsidered," *British Journal for the History of Philosophy* 19:4 (2011): 587–603, at 593.

relegates final causality to the realm of voluntary activity since only voluntary agents can know and choose to act for the sake of goals. He sees natural agents as determined to act in the same way by their natures, and thus, finds no need for ends or goals to explain why natural agents perform the same determinate actions.[67] Ockham was not alone in banishing final causes from the natural realm. Others such as, John Buridan, likewise saw final causes as playing no role in natural efficient causation.[68]

In light of the many debates that occurred about efficient causation and causal powers in the medieval period, Aquinas's views are best portrayed as a particular way of developing a general approach to causation that was widespread among scholastic thinkers. What the general approach agrees on is that efficient causes produce the existence of their effects and they do so by exercising powers. Yet, among those who shared these two commitments, there were disagreements about the nature of powers and actions and the conditions which must be met for an exercise of active power.

1.5   Aquinas's Terminology

Aquinas relies on several technical concepts and terms to express his views on efficient causation and causal powers. The purpose of this section is to offer the reader a brief introduction to those concepts and terms and to note the English terms I have chosen to translate Aquinas's Latin.

Terminology for Causes: causa, causa efficiens, causa agens

As mentioned above, for Aquinas, *causa*, namely cause, is a broad term which encompasses all four Aristotelian causes. Aquinas uses the term *causa efficiens*, namely efficient cause, to refer to the type of cause which causes its effect by action. Given that efficient causes cause by acting, Aquinas also refers to the efficient cause as the *causa agens*, namely agent cause. *Agens* can be literally translated as "acting one"; however, I will follow the standard practice of translating *agens* as "agent." It is clear that

---

[67] For an overview of Ockham's views which situate them relative to Aquinas and other earlier thinkers, see Jordan Watts, "Natural Final Causality at the University of Paris from 1250–1360," PhD diss., The Catholic University of America, 2015, ProQuest Dissertations Publishing, 3705758.

[68] For discussion of Buridan's views see Lagerlund, "The Unity of Efficient and Final Causality" and Watts, "Natural Final Causality at the University of Paris from 1250–1360," 279–322. On another medieval critique of final causality, see Kamil Majcherek, "Walter Chatton's Rejection of Final Causality," *Oxford Studies in Medieval Philosophy* 7 (2019): 212–42.

Aquinas thought that the terms "efficient cause" and "agent cause" were interchangeable because sometimes when he lists the four causes, he replaces the "efficient cause" with "agent cause."[69] At points in this study, when the context makes clear that it is the efficient or agent cause that is being discussed, I may drop the qualifier of "efficient" or "agent" and simply refer to this cause as "cause" and this form of causation simply as "causation."

As already noted above, Aquinas at times refers to natural efficient causes as "movers" since they act on their patients through motion.[70] The term "mover," however, is not interchangeable with "agent" and "efficient" cause since there are other efficient causes and agents, such as God, which cause effects without motion.

Terminology for Powers and Action: potentia ad esse *vs.*
potentia ad agere, potentia activa, potentia passiva, immanent *vs.*
transeunt, actio *and* passio

Aquinas uses the term *potentia* to refer to powers in general and he uses the term *actio* to refer to the activity which arises from a power.[71] As we will see below, he does use some other terms to refer to specific types of powers and actions, yet *potentia* and *actio* are the terms he uses to refer to these realities taken generally. This terminology is significant insofar as it reveals that Aquinas conceptualizes powers and actions through the lens of the Aristotelian distinction between potentiality and actuality. Potentiality and actuality are basic notions which cannot be defined in terms of prior concepts. Aquinas thinks that we can best understand potentiality and actuality in terms of how they relate to each other. Potentiality relates to actuality as what is imperfect, incomplete or unfulfilled relates to its perfection, completion, fulfillment or manifestation. This relationship is further grasped by considering analogies. An actuality relates to its corresponding potentiality just as one who is awake relates to one who is sleeping or just as one who is seeing relates to one with his eyes closed.[72]

Aquinas maintains that there are two types of potentialities: potentialities for being (*potentia ad esse*) and active potentialities

---

[69] *ScG* III c. 10 (ed. Marietti, 12, n. 1938): "Omnis causa vel est materia, vel forma, vel agens, vel finis."
[70] See text in fn. 7.
[71] *ST* I q. 25, a. 1 (ed. Leon., vol. 4, 290): "potentia activa est principium agendi in aliud"; see also *De operat. occult.* (ed. Leon., 43, 184): "dicimus potentiam principium intrinsecum quo agens agit, vel patiens patitur." *ST* I q. 54, a. 1.
[72] *In IX Meta.* lec. 5.

(*potentia ad agere*).[73] Form is the actuality which fulfills or completes a potentiality for being and action is that which fulfills, manifests or completes a potentiality for acting.[74] For example, Socrates's potential to be tan is fulfilled by the form of tan-ness, and his potential to run is fulfilled by the action of running. Aquinas claims that there are two types of active potentialities: one whose action passes outside of itself into another, just as the act of building terminates in a house, and another whose action remains in the agent, as the act of seeing.[75] The former are often referred to as "transeunt" and the latter as "immanent."

Aquinas uses the term *potentia passiva*, namely passive potentiality, to refer to that through which substances undergo actions.[76] For example, Socrates is able to be tanned by the sun through a passive potentiality in him to be tanned. Though not all commentators agree, I will argue that "potentiality for being" and "passive potentiality" refer to one and the same type of potentiality, which is contrasted with active potentiality.[77]

Just as Aquinas uses the term *actio* to signify the actuality of an active potentiality, he likewise uses *passio*, namely passion, to signify the act of a passive potentiality.[78] In addition to signifying the acts of potentialities, *actio* and *passio* are numbered among the ten Aristotelian categories.[79] The categories delineate the types of beings that are found in the created world. In Chapter 6, I will discuss the differences between action as an accident in the category of action and action as the completion of a potentiality.[80]

I will translate Aquinas's term *potentia* as "potentiality" in order to preserve his conceptualization of substances' causal features through the lens of the potentiality vs. actuality distinction. Yet, often when I am writing about Aquinas's views, I will refer to active potentialities as "active powers" or "causal powers" since this is how the active features of

---

[73] *ST* I-II q. 55, a. 2 (ed. Leon., vol. 6, 351): "Unde, cum duplex sit potentia, scilicet potentia ad esse et potentia ad agere ..." See also *De pot.* q. 1, a. 1 (ed. Pession, 9): "Unde et similiter duplex est potentia"; *De Malo* q. 1, a. 5; *ST* I q. 48, a. 5; and *ST* I, q. 105, a. 5.

[74] *ST* I q. 48, a. 5 (ed. Leon., vol. 4, 496): "Actus autem est duplex: primus, et secundus. Actus quidem primus est forma et integritas rei: actus autem secundus est operatio."

[75] *De ver.* q. 14, a. 3 (ed. Leon., vol. 22 2/2, 446): "Activa autem potentia duplex est: quaedam quidem cuius actio terminatur ad aliquid actum extra, sicut aedificativae actio terminatur ad aedificatum; quaedam vero est cuius actio non terminatur ad extra, sed consistit in ipso agente ut visio in vidente ..."

[76] *ST* I q. 25, a. 1 (ed. Leon., vol. 4, 290): "potentia activa est principium agendi in aliud: potentia vero passiva est principium patiendi ab alio ..."

[77] See Section 5.4.

[78] *In III Phys.* lec. 5 (ed. Leon., vol. 2, 112): "Et actus quidem activi vocatur actio; actus vero passivi vocatur passio."

[79] See Section 6.4.   [80] See Section 6.4.

substances are often referred to today both in the secondary literature on medieval philosophy and in contemporary philosophical discussions. I will similarly use "passive power" to refer to passive potentialities.

Other Power Terms: virtus, vis, virtualiter

In addition to *potentia*, Aquinas uses two other Latin terms which can be translated into English as "power." They are *vis* and *virtus*. *Potentia* is the most general of these terms insofar as Aquinas uses it to refer to every kind of potentiality or power. *Vis* and *virtus* are narrower terms used to refer to particular classes of powers. The term *virtus* is associated with perfection or excellence. Aquinas says that the term *virtus* refers to a perfected potentiality.[81] To understand what Aquinas means by this it is necessary to grasp a distinction between two types of powers. There are some powers which can be exercised without the agent acquiring any further perfection, while other powers require the acquisition of a further form in order to be exercised. An example of the second sort of power is a human being's power to play music. Human beings as such are capable of playing music. However, in order for a human being to actually play music, it is necessary to first learn how to play an instrument. A human being's potential to play music must be perfected by some musical habit, e.g. habitual knowledge of how to play the violin, before it can be exercised in actually playing music. The term *virtus*, which I will translate as "power," refers to those potentialities which have been perfected in such a way that they can be exercised in a determinate act. The term *habitus*, namely "habit," refers to the form that perfects a potentiality by ordering it to a determinate act.[82] Aquinas thinks that active natural powers, such as fire's power to heat, are of themselves *virtutes* (plural of *virtus*) since they do not require a further perfection to be exercised. Fire, for example, does not need to acquire a habit to exercise its power of heating. Natural active powers are of themselves ordered to a determinate act.[83] Since this study focuses

---

[81] *ST* I-II, q. 55, a. 2 (ed. Leon., vol. 6, 351): "Unde, cum duplex sit potentia, scilicet potentia ad esse et potentia ad agere, utriusque potentiae perfectio virtus vocatur."

[82] *ST* I-II q. 54, a. 1 (ed. Leon., vol. 6, 341): "Habitus autem sunt quaedam qualitates aut formae inhaerentes potentiae, quibus inclinatur potentia ad determinatos actus secundum speciem."

[83] *ST* I-II q. 55, a. 1 (ed. Leon., vol. 6, 349): "potentia dicitur esse perfecta, secundum quod determinatur ad suum actum. Sunt autem quaedam potentiae quae secundum seipsas sunt determinatae ad suos actus; sicut potentiae naturales activae. Et ideo huiusmodi potentiae naturales secundum seipsas dicuntur virtutes."

primarily on natural powers, it omits discussion of habits and unperfected powers (i.e. those which are not *virtutes*).

The term *vis*, which I will also translate as "power," refers to a certain type of perfected power (*virtus*).[84] Aquinas uses the term *vis* to refer to the higher powers of living beings by which they are able to change themselves.[85] Examples of such operations include nutrition and growth. The living being is both the agent of these operations and that which is transformed by the operation. These operations are contrasted with operations, such as heating, in which the agent acts upon something outside of itself, as when fire heats water. Aquinas sees the operation which arises from a *vis* as a more perfect form of action because the thing which is changed by the action is itself the agent of the action. It is not subordinated to another which operates upon it. A specific *vis* is typically named by Aquinas by the operation which it enables. For example, Aquinas refers to the power by which plants and animals nourish themselves as the *vis nutritiva*.[86]

One other technical term of Aquinas's which merits some explanation is the adverb *virtualiter*, namely virtually, which is derived from *virtus*. Aquinas almost exclusively uses this adverb to modify the verb "to exist." A reader can be easily misled when Aquinas writes of things "existing virtually."[87] In English the term "virtual" means "almost" or "nearly." Thus, it may seem that something which exists virtually would be something that has a strange, shadowy state between non-existence and existence. For Aquinas, however, the linguistic connection between *virtualiter* and *virtus* is very important. To say that something exists virtually is to say that a power exists which can produce it. Aquinas speaks of effects as preexisting virtually in their causes.[88] This is not to say that the effect exists in some shadowy way in the cause, but rather to say that the power to produce the effect exists in its cause. The effect is the fulfillment or

---

[84] On the meaning of *vis*, see for instance *In III Sent.* d. 23, q. 1, a. 3, p. 1 ad 3 (ed. Mandonnet-Moos, vol. 3, 707): "vis accipitur pro omni eo quod est principium operationis perfectae, quod importat nomen virtutis . . ."

[85] *De virt.* q. 1, a. 1 (ed. Odetto, 708): "vis dicitur, secundum quod res aliqua per potestatem completam quam habet, potest sequi suum impetum vel motum." On how the various grades of living beings engage in self-motion see David Cory, "Thomas Aquinas on How the Soul Moves the Body," *Oxford Studies in Medieval Philosophy*, 8 (2020): 146–87.

[86] See, for instance, *ST* I q. 78, a. 2.

[87] *De pot.* q. 3, a. 11 ad 12 (ed. Pession, 75): "effectus in causa activa virtualiter praeexistit."

[88] *In Div. nom.* c. 9, lec. 4 (ed. Marietti, 318, n. 846): "[O]mnes enim effectus praeexistunt virtualiter in sua causa, *secundum* eius *virtutem.*"

completion of the cause's power, so the effect can be said to exist virtually when the active potentiality for it exists.

Other Terms for Efficient Causal Activity: actio vs. operatio, agere vs. facere, influere

In describing what efficient causes do, Aquinas often uses the verb *agere*, namely to act, which is the verb form of *actio*. He explains that "to act is to exercise some action."[89] Elsewhere though he explains the verb *agere* in terms of the agent communicating that by which it is actual (i.e. its form), he writes: "To act indeed is nothing other than to communicate that by which the agent is actual, insofar as it is possible."[90] As explained above, Aquinas thinks that material substances act through that by which they are actual, namely their forms, to cause actualities of the same kind in their patients. Thus, the meaning of "action" can be described in terms of communicating actuality.

Aquinas uses the verb *agere* in both a general way to refer to any efficient causal activity that arises from a power and in a narrow way to refer to only the causal activity that remains in an agent, e.g. knowing and willing.[91] When he uses *agere* in the more narrow way to refer to immanent causal activity, he uses the term *facere* and *factio* to refer to another sort of efficient causal activity, namely transeunt causality, which passes over into another outside of the agent.[92] I will translate *facere* as "to do" or "to make" depending on the context and *factio* as "a doing" or "a making."

Operare and its noun form *operatio* are another pair of terms that Aquinas uses to describe efficient causal activity. These terms are synonyms for *agere* and *actio*. Like *agere* and *actio*, *operare* and *operatio* are used at times in a general way to refer to all efficient causal activity, namely both

---

[89] *De ver.* q. 5, a. 9, ad 4 (ed. Leon., vol. 22 1/2, 165): "agere est aliquam actionem exercere." There is a discussion of Aquinas's use of action related terminology in Marianne T. Miller, "The Problem of Action in the Commentary of St. Thomas Aquinas on the *Physics* of Aristotle," *Modern Schoolman* 23:3–4 (1946): 135–67; 200–26.

[90] *De pot.* q. 2, a. 1 (ed. Pession, 24): "Agere vero nihil aliud est quam communicare illud per quod agens est actu, secundum quod est possibile."

[91] *ST* I-II q. 57, a. 4 (ed. Leon., vol. 6, 367): "Differt autem facere et agere quia, ut dicitur in IX Metaphys. factio est actus transiens in exteriorem materiam, sicut aedificare, secare, et huiusmodi; agere autem est actus permanens in ipso agente, sicut videre, velle, et huiusmodi."

[92] Ibid.

immanent and transeunt, and also at times in a narrow way to refer only to immanent causality.[93]

In addition to the terms Aquinas uses to refer exclusively to efficient causality, there are some verbs which Aquinas uses to refer to the causation exercised by all four species of cause (e.g. final, material, formal, efficient). These terms are *diffundere*, namely "to diffuse," and *influere*, "to influence." Aquinas writes "it belongs to a cause to influence the effect, and not the reverse."[94] "To diffuse" and "to influence" signify the causality exercised by every species of cause on its effect. Each type of cause influences its effect and diffuses being to its effect. As we have seen, each does so in a different way. Aquinas notes that in addition to being used in a broad sense that applies to each of the four causes, *diffundere* and *influere* are also used in a narrow way to apply specifically to efficient causal activity.[95]

Terminology Associated with Natural Inclination: inclinatio naturalis, appetitus naturalis, tendere, finis

As we saw above, Aquinas thinks that natural substances have an *inclinatio naturalis*, namely "natural inclination," which determines them toward exercising their powers to produce determinate types of effects. Aquinas also refers to natural inclination as *naturalis appetitus*, namely "natural appetite," and as an *impetus*.[96] Natural inclinations are always directed at some action or effect, which is called an "end" (*finis*). For example, Aquinas writes, "[W]e call the end that toward which the impetus of the agent tends."[97] Elsewhere he writes: "The end is that in which the appetite

---

[93] For an example of the general usage, see *ScG* II, c. 1 (ed. Marietti, 114, n. 853): "Est autem duplex rei operatio, ut philosophus tradit, in IX *metaphysicae*: una quidem quae in ipso operante manet et est ipsius operantis perfectio, ut sentire, intelligere et velle; alia vero quae in exteriorem rem transit, quae est perfectio facti quod per ipsam constituitur, ut calefacere, secare et aedificare." For an example of the narrow usage, see *In I Sent.* d. 40, q. 1, a. 1 ad 1 (ed. Mandonnet-Moos, vol. 1, 942): "et tales actiones, quae proprie operationes dicuntur, in ipsis operantibus tantum sunt."

[94] *In III Sent.* d. 29, q. 1, a. 7 ad 1 (ed. Mandonnet-Moos, vol. 3, 942): "causae autem est influere in causatum, et non e converso." For a text in which *influere* is used to describe the cause–effect relationship across different species of causes, see *De ver.* q. 22, a. 2 (ed. Leon., vol. 22 3/1, 616): "Sicut autem influere causae efficientis est agere, ita influere causae finalis est appeti et desiderari."

[95] *De ver.* q. 21, a. 1 ad 4 (ed. Leon., vol. 22 3/1, 594): "Ad quartum dicendum, quod diffundere, licet secundum proprietatem vocabuli videatur importare operationem causae efficientis, tamen largo modo potest importare habitudinem cuiuscumque causae sicut influere et facere, et alia huiusmodi."

[96] *In V Meta.* lec. 6 (ed. Marietti, 226, n. 829): "In naturalibus quidem est impetus, sive inclinatio ad aliquem finem, cui respondet voluntas in natura rationali; unde et ipsa naturalis inclinatio appetitus dicitur."

[97] *ScG* III c. 2 (ed. Marietti, 3, n. 1869): "hoc dicimus esse finem in quod tendit impetus agentis …"

of the agent or mover rests . . ."[98] Aquinas uses the verb *tendere*, namely to
tend, to describe the efficient cause's movement toward its end.[99] Aquinas
also uses the noun *intentio*, namely intention, which is derived from
tendere, to describe a natural agent's intrinsic directedness toward an
end. For example, he writes: "In natural things, the intention of the end
belongs to an agent according to its form through which the end is fitting
to it . . ."[100] Through its form, a natural substance has a natural inclination
toward a certain end. This inclination which the agent has toward an end
is described by Aquinas as an intention in the agent. In English the term
"intention" is typically reserved only for cognitive activity. Thus, it may
seem that when Aquinas writes of the "intention of the end" in natural
things, he is suggesting that they somehow cognize the ends to which they
tend. However, Aquinas writes that "'intention,' just as its name sounds,
signifies 'to tend toward something.'"[101] For him, to say that a natural
cause has an "intention of the end" merely signifies that it has an inclination toward that end.[102] For instance, to attribute to fire an intention of
heating is merely to say that it has a natural inclination toward heating.

Relational Terms: ordo *vs.* relatio, dispositio

The realities in Aquinas's material world, especially those involved in
efficient causation, are in many ways interconnected. Aquinas uses the
technical term *ordo*, namely "order," to discuss the interconnectedness
between various realities. Aquinas describes order as a "proportion."[103]
More specifically, he explains that order refers to the proportion between a
principle and that which follows from it.[104] Above we saw that a principle
is a beginning from which anything else follows.[105] As we saw, causes are a
certain type of principle from which existence follows. Thus, the term
"order" is used to capture the connection between causes and effects. In
addition to causes and effects, there are many other realities involved in

[98] *ScG* III c. 3 (ed. Marietti, 5, n. 1880): "Finis est in quo quiescit appetitus agentis vel moventis . . ."
[99] See, for example, the text in fn. 88.
[100] *ScG* II c. 20 (ed. Marietti, 144, n. 1079): "In rebus enim naturalibus, intentio finis competit agenti
secundum suam formam, per quam finis est sibi conveniens. . ."
[101] *ST* I-II q. 12, a. 1 (ed. Leon., vol. 6, 94): "intentio, sicut ipsum nomen sonat, significat in aliquid
tendere."
[102] *De prin. nat.* c. 3 (ed. Leon., vol. 43, 42): "et hoc intendere nichil aliud erat quam habere
naturalem inclinationem ad aliquid."
[103] *In VIII Phys.* lec. 3 (ed. Leon., vol. 2, 374): "omnis autem ordo proportio quaedam est."
[104] *ST* I q. 42, a. 3 (ed. Leon., vol. 4, 439): "[O]rdo semper dicitur per comparationem ad aliquod
principium."
[105] See Section 1.1.

efficient causation which are said to be "ordered" to each other. Aquinas describes potentiality as "ordered" to actuality.[106] Thus, powers, as potentialities, are ordered to the actions that are their corresponding actualities. At times, Aquinas also uses the term "order" to refer to the interconnection between multiple causes which cooperate toward a joint effect.[107]

It is important to note that the term *ordo* is not interchangeable with the term *relatio*, namely relation. Order is a broader category than relation. Relations, for Aquinas, are one specific type of order, namely an order which obtains between two substances.[108] A relation obtains between two entities in virtue of an accident each has.[109] For example, two white substances, in virtue of their accidental forms of whiteness, also bear a relation to one another. Since only substances can be the bearers of accidents, relations only obtain between substances. Non-substances can be ordered to one another. But they cannot be related to one other because they do not have accidents upon which a relation can be founded. For example, while Aquinas thinks that it is true to say that powers are ordered to actions, he does think that they bear a relation to one another, when "relation" is understood in its technical sense because powers and actions do not have any accidents by which they can be related.

Another relational term which Aquinas frequently uses when discussing aspects of efficient causality is *dispositio*, namely "disposition." In English, the term "disposition" is often used to signify a person's qualities of mind or character, so it may not be apparent that this is a relational term. However, in Aquinas's terminology, the meaning of "disposition" is closely connected to the notion of "order." He writes: "[D]isposition implies a certain order, as was said. Therefore, someone is not said to be disposed through a quality except with reference to something else."[110] For Aquinas, a disposition is a qualitative form in a substance by which it is referred to something else. He maintains that both agents and patients have dispositions that order them toward specific actions and passions. Regarding patients, Aquinas writes: "It is necessary that that which is able

---

[106] *ST* I q. 77, a. 3 (ed. Leon., vol. 5, 251): "potentia, secundum illud quod est potentia, ordinatur ad actum. Unde oportet rationem potentiae accipi ex actu ad quem ordinatur..."
[107] *ST* I q. 116, a. 2 ad 1 (ed. Leon., vol. 5, 554): "Essentialiter vero fatum est ipsa dispositio seu series, idest ordo, causarum secundarum."
[108] *De pot.* q. 7, a. 9 ad 7 (ed. Pession, 208): "relatio ... nihil est aliud, quam ordo unius creaturae ad aliam ..."
[109] *In III Phys.* lec. 1 (ed. Leon., vol. 2, 102): "cum relatio habeat debilissimum esse, quia consistit tantum in hoc quod est ad aliud se habere, oportet quod super aliquod aliud accidens fundetur ..."
[110] *ST* I-II q. 49, a. 2, ad 1 (ed. Leon., vol. 6, 311): "dispositio ordinem quendam importat, ut dictum est. Unde non dicitur aliquis disponi per qualitatem, nisi in ordine ad aliquid."

to undergo something have within itself some disposition which is the cause and principle of such an undergoing and this principle is called passive potentiality."[111] Dispositions in a patient are qualities of it which make it susceptible to receiving the form which the agent causes in it by its action.[112] For instance, dryness disposes a substance toward undergoing burning. As the passage just quoted suggests, Aquinas equates the dispositions of a patient, which order it toward undergoing specific actions, with its passive potentialities. In the case of the agent, dispositions are qualities which order the agent toward actions. However, dispositions of the agent cannot be merely equated with the active potentialities by which they perform actions. Dispositions of an agent are qualities which impact how the agent performs actions through its active potentialities. Dispositions of an agent account for whether the agent acts well or poorly or with difficulty or ease.[113] Quickness, for example, is a disposition which enables an agent to run well.[114] Quickness cannot be equated with the power to run. Rather, it is a further quality that impacts how the agent acts through its power to run.

Many technical terms were introduced in this section. This terminology was introduced at the beginning of the study so that the reader would be familiar with technical terms as they arise and so that it would not be necessary to interrupt discussions of concepts throughout the study to introduce terminology. However, individual readers may wish to refer back to this section as they progress through the study.

1.6   Conclusion

This chapter introduced the key theses of Aquinas's theory of efficient causation and causal powers. We have seen that for Aquinas, efficient causation is a distinctive type of ontological dependence. All causes influence the being of their effects and all effects depend on their causes. The distinctive way in which the efficient cause influences the being of its effect

---

[111] *In V Meta.* lec. 14 (ed. Marietti, 257, n. 963): "Oportet autem illud, quod est possibile ad aliquid patiendum, habere in se quamdam dispositionem, quae sit causa et principium talis passionis; et illud principium vocatur potentia passiva."

[112] *In IV Sent.* d. 4, q. 2, a. 3, qc. 2 (ed. Mandonnet-Moos, vol. 4, 178): "Ad secundam quaestionem dicendum, quod actus activorum recipiuntur in passivis secundum suam dispositionem ..."

[113] *ST* I-II, q. 49, a. 2

[114] *De virt.* q. 1, a. 1 ad 9 (ed. Odetto, 710): "dispositio dicitur tribus modis ... *Alio modo* per quam aliquod agens disponitur ad agendum, sicut velocitas est dispositio ad cursum." The quality of the patient that disposes it to receive a form is one of the other types of disposition discussed in this passage.

is through action. Actions, as we have seen, are exercises of active powers. Aquinas maintained that the most proper exercises of natural efficient causation, namely *per se* efficient causation, involved a number of elements which were introduced in this chapter. The goal of this chapter was to introduce the "big picture" of Aquinas's views and to provide some pertinent conceptual and historical context for his views. It is likely that the reader has many questions about the material in this chapter. The goal of the subsequent chapters is to examine each of the individual elements of Aquinas's views in more depth.

CHAPTER 2

Efficient Causation
The Paradigm Case and Its Features and Conditions

Aquinas thinks that causation is a relationship of ontological dependence. Causes influence the being of their effects and effects depend on their causes for their existence. The unique way in which the efficient cause influences being is by action. The goal of this chapter is to examine in further detail Aquinas's thinking about the nature of the relationship that obtains between an efficient cause and its effect, as well as some conditions that must be met for an instance of natural efficient causation to occur. The chapter analyzes Aquinas's views on the following questions: First, do efficient causes and their actions exist temporally prior to their effects? For example, when fire heats water, does fire cause the heating before the water undergoes it? Second, do natural efficient causes act and produce their effects with necessity? For example, must fire heat water whenever they exist together or is it possible for fire and water to exist together and yet the fire fails to heat the water? Third, can an agent act upon itself or must its patient be distinct from itself? For example, can a fire heat itself? Lastly, must an agent be in contact with its patient to act upon it? For example, can a fire heat an object which it is not physically touching?

As we have already seen, Aquinas thinks that not all instances of efficient causation are equivalent. There are certain instances of efficient causation, namely *per se* cases, which are more fundamental and proper. Other types of efficient causation happen in virtue of these cases. The chapter focuses on how Aquinas would answer the questions above for *per se* cases. Accordingly, the chapter begins by reconstructing Aquinas's views about what defines *per se* instances of efficient causation in the natural world. The chapter next examines Aquinas's views on the temporal and modal relationship that obtains between *per se* natural efficient causes and their effects. The chapter shows that Aquinas thought that such causes are simultaneous with their effects. The chapter considers the implications of this view, as well as how Aquinas reacts to instances of efficient causation in which it is obvious that a later effect depends on a temporally prior efficient cause.

Regarding the modality of natural efficient causation, contemporary scholars debate about whether Aquinas thought that natural efficient causes necessitate their effects. The chapter aims to bring greater clarity to Aquinas's thinking about the modality by which natural causes operate by examining distinctions he draws between different types of natural efficient causes and different types of necessity. Finally, the chapter examines Aquinas's views on important conditions that must be met for efficient causation to occur. We will see that Aquinas thinks that the agent and the patient must be other and they must be in contact with each other. The chapter analyzes the arguments by which Aquinas rejects self-motion and action at a distance.

2.1   Paradigm Instances of Efficient Causation in the Natural World: *Per se* vs. *per accidens* Causation

In Chapter 1, we saw that *per se* instances of efficient causation involve certain elements, particularly an agent with an active power and a natural inclination toward the effect which it produces.[1] For example, fire is a *per se* cause of heating insofar as it heats through an active power to heat and has an inclination toward heating. In this section, we will look more closely at the defining features of *per se* instances of efficient causation and how other instances of efficient causation can deviate from these features. Then we will move on in the subsequent sections to examine the temporal and modal features of *per se* instances of natural efficient causation.

The term *per se* means "through itself" in Latin. Aquinas's description of such a cause illustrates the fittingness of this terminology. Aquinas writes that a *per se* cause "produces its effect through the power of its nature or form, thus it follows that the effect is in itself intended by the cause."[2] According to this description, there are two conditions which a *per se* cause meets. The first condition has to do with the power through which the cause acts. A *per se* cause produces its effect through a form which belongs to it by its nature. When fire heats, for example, it heats through a form in it, namely heat, which it has in virtue of being a fire. Being hot is a form which fire has by its nature and thus, it causes heating through itself, that is, through being what it is. By contrast, there are some causes which cause effects not in virtue of a power which belongs to them by their nature, but

---

[1] See Section 1.1.
[2] *ST* I-II q. 85, a. 5 (ed. Leon., vol. 7, 115): "secundum virtutem suae naturae vel formae producit effectum: unde sequitur quod effectus sit per se intentus a causa."

rather because of a power which is accidentally conjoined to them. Aquinas's example of such a cause is a white thing which efficiently causes a house.[3] White things do not by their nature have a power to build houses. Yet, it may happen that a white thing causes a house because the white thing also happens to be a builder. The house is not built by a white thing through a power it has in virtue of being a white thing, but rather the house is built through a power to build which is accidentally conjoined to a white thing. *Per se* causes cause effects through powers that belong to them in virtue of what they are. Since *per se* causes cause their effects through themselves we can expect that similar causes will cause similar effects. For example, since fires cause heat through a power which belongs to them by their nature, we can expect that all fires will cause heat. We cannot similarly expect that all white things can build houses since the white things that do build houses do so by a power that lies outside of the nature of whiteness.

The second condition which is met in *per se* instances of efficient causation is that the effect is intended by the cause. We saw in Section 1.5 that for Aquinas what it is for a natural cause to intend an effect is for it to have a natural inclination toward the effect.[4] In cases of *per se* efficient causation, the efficient cause has an impetus or directedness toward the effect that it causes. Whenever a cause produces an effect by a power that belongs to it by its nature, it will likewise have a natural inclination toward the effect in question. This is because, as we will see in Chapter 4, the same form that is an agent's active power for an effect is likewise that in virtue of which the agent has a natural inclination toward that effect.[5] For example, the same form of heat which is that by which fire heats is also that in virtue of which fire has an impetus toward heating.

Aquinas contrasts *per se* causes with *per accidens* causes. In *per accidens* instances of efficient causation, the efficient cause still operates toward the effect and the effect still depends on the efficient cause for its being.[6] Yet, the

---

[3] *In V Meta.* lec. 2, n. 789.

[4] *De prin. nat.* c. 3 (ed. Leon., vol. 43, 42): "et hoc intendere nichil aliud erat quam habere naturalem inclinationem ad aliquid."

[5] See Section 4.1.

[6] It has recently been argued in the secondary literatures that Aristotle was an eliminativist about accidental causes, viewing them as non-productive of effects. See Tyler Huisman, "Aristotle on Accidental Causation," *Journal of the American Philosophical Association* 2 (2016): 561–75. There is clear evidence that Aquinas did not hold this view about accidental causes as such. In his *De potentia*, he explicitly claims there are two types of accidental causes. In addition to the non-productive accidental causes that are called causes in virtue of their conjunction with *per se* causes (e.g. the white thing which builds a house), Aquinas says there is an accidental cause "which does something toward the effect." *De pot.* q. 3, a. 6, ad 6 (ed. Pession, 19): "Una quae aliquid operatur ad effectum; sed

efficient cause does not intend the effect. According to Aquinas, a cause is "called a *per accidens* cause of an effect because that effect which follows is outside of the intention of such a cause. . ."[7] In the case of a natural efficient cause, what it means for an effect to be "outside of the efficient cause's intention" is that the efficient cause lacks a natural inclination toward the effect which it produces. Aquinas recognized that efficient causes always operate in an environment which includes other efficient causes and a patient which is characterized by a variety of different forms. Sometimes efficient causes produce effects for which they have no inclination due to how the patient receives their causality. For instance, fire can sometimes cool a substance if through heating, the substance's pores are opened and an inner heat is lost.[8] In this example, the fire does indeed cause cooling through its action; however, cooling is not an effect toward which fire is inclined. There is no intrinsic impetus in fire toward the end of cooling. Furthermore, the fire has no active power for cooling. For Aquinas, it is not the case that all effects are produced through a unique power for producing the specific type of effect in question. Some effects are efficiently caused in virtue of an exercise of a power for producing a different type of effect.

Though Aquinas thinks that *per accidens* efficient causation is a genuine way in which an efficient cause may produce an effect, he nevertheless thinks that *per se* causation is more fundamental than, and explanatory of, *per accidens* causation. He writes: "*Per se* causes are prior to *per accidens* causes."[9] Elsewhere he similarly states: "Every *per accidens* cause is reduced to a *per se* cause."[10] In his view, an agent efficiently causes an effect for which it has no active power and natural inclination in virtue of causing a prior effect according to *per se* causation. For example, the fire which cools a substance by opening its pores, causes the cooling in virtue of causing heating. The heating is caused by the fire according to *per se* causation since it is both caused through a power for heating and intended. In Aquinas's view, *per accidens* causation derives its efficacy from *per se* causation. This is to say that agents efficiently cause effects for which they have no active power, and therefore do not intend, in virtue of causing the

---

dicitur causa eius per accidens, quia praeter intentionem ille effectus a tali causa . . ." See also *In I Sent.* d. 46, q. 1, a. 2 ad 3.

[7] *De pot.* q. 3, a. 6 ad 6 (ed. Pession, 19): "dicitur causa eius per accidens, quia praeter intentionem ille effectus a tali causa sequitur. . ." See also *In I Sent.* d. 46, q. 1, a. 2 ad 3.

[8] *In IX Meta.* lec. 2, n. 1789.

[9] *ScG* II c. 39 (ed. Marietti, 155, n. 1155): "Causa per se prior est ea quae est per accidens."

[10] *ScG* III c. 10 (ed. Marietti, 12, 1937): "Omnis autem causa per accidens reducitur ad causam per se." See also *ST* I-II q. 75, a. 1.

specific effects toward which their powers incline them. For every *per accidens* effect there is some causally prior *per se* effect; and every *per se* effect is causally explained by the exercise of a specific power in the agent which corresponds to that effect.

In addition to *per accidens* efficient causes, we will see in Chapter 7 that Aquinas also acknowledged some other types of efficient causes which do not meet the criteria of a *per se* efficient cause. Aquinas acknowledges, for example, that the efficient cause which induces the disposition *d* in a patient *p* that is necessary for *p* to receive a further form *f* can be considered an efficient cause of *f* even if *f* is induced in *p* by a different efficient cause. Such a cause is called a "preparing" efficient cause. It prepares for a final form *f* insofar as it efficiently causes the disposition *d*, which is a passive potentiality for receiving *f*. For example, an efficient cause which dries a wet log can be considered a preparing cause of its burning since it is necessary for the log to be dry to undergo burning. The cause which prepares for burning by drying the log might not itself be the efficient cause which induces burning in the log. Furthermore, it might lack an inclination toward burning things. For these reasons, a preparing efficient cause would not meet the criteria of a *per se* efficient cause.

It is clear that Aquinas thinks that *per se* efficient causes are not the only types of efficient causes. Yet, it is important to begin by understanding this paradigm type of efficient cause because, as we will come to see in Chapter 7, other instances of efficient causation happen in virtue of *per se* instances of efficient causation. For instance, the preparing efficient cause causes the disposition for a final effect through *per se* efficient causation. Either the disposition will itself by a *per se* effect of the efficient cause or a *per accidens* effect ultimately caused through *per se* efficient causation. It is important to note that the features discussed in the subsequent sections which hold true of *per se* efficient causation may not apply to other types of efficient causation. It is clear, for example, that preparing efficient causes operate prior in time to the final effect which is attributed to them by way of their preparation. For example, the substance that dries the log acts prior to the burning, which is induced by another cause. Similarly, the modal relationship that obtains between a natural efficient cause and its *per se* effects will differ from the modal relationship, which applies to other types of natural efficient causes and their effects.

Before moving on to examine the various features and conditions of *per se* efficient causation, it is worth mentioning again that Aquinas's specific examples of *per se* causation in the material world were shaped by Aristotelian physical theories, which differ greatly from contemporary scientific theories. As we saw, Aquinas thought that there were four primary, elemental qualities of material substances, namely hot, cold, wet and dry, and all other qualities, such as textures and colors, were possessed in virtue of possessing varying degrees of the primary qualities. On this theory, all qualitative changes are caused in virtue of causing changes to a substance's primary elemental qualities. Aquinas writes: "just as through some alteration of hot and cold a man is changed from health to sickness and vice versa, so also is a body made to have a shape through alteration of hardness and softness."[11] Since all qualitative change is caused through causing changes to primary, elemental qualities, the most basic instances of efficient causation in the material world will be those which involve changing such a quality. These changes, as well as the changes in secondary qualities which follow from them, are brought about through the primary qualities. Aquinas writes: "The tangible qualities are the active and passive qualities of the elements, according to which all change happens to bodies."[12] The four forms of hot, cold, wet and dry are the powers through which all bodily change happens. Non-living substances have no further powers for changing material substances beyond these four.[13] Thus, in Aquinas's view the most basic and uncomplicated examples of *per se* efficient causation in the material world will be cases in which one substance causes a primary quality in another substance, such as a hot thing heating another substance or a cold thing cooling another. With this background in place, we can now move on to see Aquinas's views on the temporal and modal relationships that obtain between a *per se* cause and its effect.

2.2 Efficient Causation and Time: Efficient Causes Need Not Be Temporally Prior to Their Effects

A standard contemporary view tracing back to David Hume is that causes must be temporally prior to their effects. On the Humean model, causes

[11] *In I Gen. et Cor.* c. 4, lec. 10 (ed. Leon., vol. 3, 299): "sicut per aliquam alterationem calidi et frigidi mutatur homo de sanitate in aegritudinem aut e converso, et per alterationem mollis et duri perducitur corpus ad aliquam figuram." Differences of hard and soft are themselves dependent upon differences in primary elemental qualities.
[12] *In II De anima*, lec. 24, n. 11 (ed. Leon., vol. 45/1, 171): "[T]angibilia sunt qualitates activae et passivae elementorum, secundum quas accidit universaliter alteratio in corporibus." See also *ST* I q. 78, a. 3 (ed. Leon., vol. 5, 254): "non omnia accidentia habent vim immutativam secundum se; sed solae qualitates tertiae speciei, secundum quas contingit alteratio."
[13] *In I Meteor.* lec. 2 (ed. Leon., vol. 3, 328–29): "Alia vero principia corporum inferiorum sunt quatuor, propter primas tangibiles qualitates, quae sunt principia agendi et patiendi, scilicet calidum, frigidum, humidum et siccum . . ."

and effects are conceived of as events and the cause is, by definition, the event which obtains at a prior time.[14] For instance, the event of a white billiard ball's striking a blue one precedes the event of the blue billiard ball's moving and sinking into the corner pocket. Thus, the former event is defined as the cause of the latter. Aquinas, by contrast, denies that causes that are actually operating are temporally prior to their effects. A cause which is functioning as a cause in actuality, as opposed to merely a potential cause, exists at the same time as its effect. Aquinas writes in his *Physics* commentary: "[T]he difference between causes in actuality and causes in potentiality is that causes operating in actuality exist and do not exist simultaneously with those things of which they are the causes in actuality."[15] A cause is a cause in actuality as long as it is actually causing something. Thus, causes in actuality exist simultaneously with the effects that arise through their power. For example, consider the case of fire heating water on a stove. Fire is a cause in actuality just as long as the water is undergoing the motion of heating. When the motion ceases, fire ceases to be a cause in actuality since there is no longer an effect arising from its active power. What it is for a fire to be an efficient cause in actuality, rather than a potential efficient cause, is for it to be actually heating something.

Aquinas's view that causes in actuality are simultaneous with the effects arising through their power is connected with his position, which we will see in Chapter 6, that action and passion are the same motion.[16] According to him, that which the agent causes and that which the patient undergoes are one and the same motion. For example, the one process of heating is both that which fire causes and that which water undergoes. Aquinas denies that agents first perform an action which then gives rise to a

[14] On Hume's views about causation and time and neo-Humean theories, see Daniel Hausman, *Causal Asymmetries*, Cambridge Studies in Probability, Induction and Decision Theory (Cambridge: Cambridge University Press, 1998), 36–54.

[15] *In II Phys.* lec. 6 (ed. Leon., vol. 2, 74): "inter causas in actu et causas in potentia est ista differentia, quod causae operantes in actu simul sunt et non sunt cum eis quorum causae sunt in actu . . ." See also *In V Meta.* lec. 3 (ed. Marietti, 217, n. 794): "Nam causae in actu particulares sunt simul et tolluntur cum suis effectibus, sicut hic medicans cum hoc convalescente, et hic aedificans cum hoc aedificato: non enim potest aliquid actu aedificari, nisi sit actu aedificans. Sed causae secundum potentiam non semper removentur cum effectibus; sicut domus et aedificator non simul corrumpuntur."

[16] See especially 6.2. The relationship between the thesis that action and passion are the same motion and the view that causes in act are simultaneous with their effects is discussed in *In II Post Anal.* lec. 10, c. 12 (ed. Leon., vol. 1, 365): "Quamvis autem motus in suis partibus successionem habeat, tamen simul est cum causa movente. Simul enim dum movens movet, mobile movetur, eo quod motus nihil est aliud quam actus mobilis a movente, secundum quem movens dicitur movere et mobile moveri."

subsequent motion which is the patient's passion. For example, fire's action is not some prior event which initiates the heating in water. The heating in the water just is the action of fire insofar as it arises immediately from the fire's power. The heating is also the water's passion insofar as it undergoes it. Since the agent's action and the patient's passion are the same temporally extended process, the agent is acting as long as the patient is being affected, and vice versa. The action by which the agent is a cause in actuality lasts just as long as something is being affected by the agent.

It must be noted that, as we saw in Chapter 1, there is a twofold way of considering the effect of a natural efficient cause.[17] As we saw, natural efficient causes cause their effects by initiating motion, and thus, the effect of an efficient cause can be considered as both the motion itself, which arises through the cause's power, and the end point of that motion. The motion is the process by which the cause causes the endpoint, yet the motion is itself an effect of the cause since it depends on the cause for its being.[18] For example, the motion of building is the process by which a builder causes its effect, which is a house. Yet, the motion of building is also an effect of the builder insofar as building depends on the builder to exist. Likewise, the effect of fire which boils water is both the motion of heating and the final temperature of 212 degrees Fahrenheit. While efficient causes in actuality are simultaneous with the motions effected through their power, they are indeed prior to the final result or end product of those motions. This is because it takes time for that final effect to be produced through the motion which the agent efficiently causes. Aquinas writes:

> To understand this, it must be considered that an efficient cause which acts through motion necessarily precedes its effect in time because the effect does not exist until the end of the action; however, every agent must be the beginning of its action.[19]

---

[17] See Section 1.1.

[18] Aquinas thinks that the motion by which the efficient cause causes the final effect can also be considered a cause of the final effect. See *In II Post Anal.* lec. 12, c. 10 (ed. Leon., vol. 1, 365): "Unde sicut motus est causa quietis consequentis, ita prima pars motus est causa subsequentis, et sic deinceps." However, it should be emphasized that motion itself is not an efficient cause since efficient causes are substances which exercise powers. Motion is said to be a cause of its term insofar as it is that by which an efficient cause produces its effect.

[19] *ST* I q. 46, a. 2 ad 1 (ed. Leon., vol. 4, 482): "Et ad hoc intelligendum, considerandum est quod causa efficiens quae agit per motum, de necessitate praecedit tempore suum effectum, quia effectus non est nisi in termino actionis, agens autem omne oportet esse principium actionis." Aquinas adds immediately after this: "Sed si actio sit instantanea, et non successiva, non est necessarium faciens esse prius facto duratione; sicut patet in illuminatione." See also *De aeternitate mundi* (ed. Leon., vol. 43, 86): "Sed terminus actionis simul est cum ipso facto; ergo non repugnat intellectui, si

Aquinas's point can be illustrated with the case of the builder. Though a builder in actuality exists simultaneous with the building of the house, he nevertheless exists prior to the house, which is the end-point of the act of building.[20] The act of building takes time and the house only exists at the end of the temporal process. The builder in actuality is the origin of the temporally extended act of building through which the house is actualized. Thus, he must exist at the beginning of the process, prior to the existence of the house. Furthermore, although Aquinas holds that efficient causes in actuality are simultaneous with the motions that arise through their power, he nevertheless would acknowledge the obvious fact that the end-points of those motions can persist after the efficient cause stops acting and even after the efficient cause ceases to exist. For example, a building can persist after the builder stops acting and even after he dies.

Though natural causes generally initiate motion, Aquinas acknowledges some rare cases in which natural agents cause effects instantaneously, that is, without the process of motion, and these agents need not exist temporally prior to their effects. One example he gives is the sun with its effect of light.[21] Since Aquinas understood the sun to produce light instantaneously, he thought it possible for the sun and its effect of light to come into being together at the same moment. In such a case, there would no respect in which the cause is temporally prior to its effect. For Aquinas, the essence of efficient causation is the exercise of an active power and in some cases, even in the natural world, this happens without motion. In such cases, cause and effect are simultaneous, but nevertheless the effect depends on the cause for its being and thus, the cause retains an ontological priority over the effect.

It is important to note that although Aquinas denies that causes in actuality are temporally prior to their effects, he nevertheless acknowledges

---

ponatur causa producens effectum suum subito non precedere duratione causatum suum. Repugnat autem in causis producentibus per motum effectus suos, quia oportet quod principium motus precedat finem eius."

[20] Aquinas also claims that potency must be temporally prior to the actions of natural causes. *ST* I q. 66, a. 1 ad 2 (ed. Leon., vol. 5, 154–55): "Ad secundum dicendum quod natura producit effectum in actu de ente in potentia: et ideo oportet ut in eius operatione potentia tempore praecedat actum, et informitas formationem." See also *In II Sent.* d. 1, q. 1, a. 2 ad 1.

[21] *De pot.* q. 3, a. 13 ad 5 (ed. Pession, 79): "Nec oportet omnem causam effectum duratione praecedere, sed natura tantum sicut patet in sole et splendore." *In III Sent.* d. 18, q. 1, a. 3 ad 3 (ed. Mandonnet-Moos, vol. 3, 563): "Non enim semper necessarium est ut causa causatum praecedat tempore, sed quandoque sufficit quod praecedat natura."

that all causes are naturally prior to their effects. He writes: "Every cause, insofar as it is a cause, is naturally prior to its effect."[22] Thus, causes in actuality that act by motion are naturally prior to the motions which they cause and causes that act without motion are likewise naturally prior to the effects which they cause. To claim that a cause is naturally prior to its effect is to state that the effect depends on the cause for its being and not vice versa. The effect derives its existence from the cause, but the cause does not exist in virtue of the effect.[23] For example, although the sun and its light might exist simultaneously, there is nevertheless an ontological difference in how they relate to each other. The light depends on the sun for its existence, but the sun does not similarly exist through the light's action.

Aquinas's view that causes in actuality are simultaneous with their effects leads to the question of how Aquinas makes sense of obvious cases in which there seems to be a great temporal delay between the action of a cause and an effect that we attribute to it. Our experience tells us that earlier events do often cause much later ones. For example, taking a medicine prescribed by a doctor usually does not cause an immediate relief of symptoms. Rather, the effects of the medicine typically manifest several minutes or even hours later. If causes in actuality are simultaneous with their effects, how can Aquinas's account make sense of situations in which an earlier exercise of efficient causation leads to a later effect? For instance, how can Aquinas maintain that the doctor's giving of a medicine at time *t1* is the cause of a cure which happens later at time *t2*?

Regarding this issue, it is important to remember that Aquinas thinks that there are other types of efficient causation besides *per se* efficient causation. As we will see in Chapter 7, Aquinas thinks that another type of efficient cause is a preparing efficient cause.[24] A preparing efficient cause effects a change in a patient through which the patient acquires a disposition required for undergoing a subsequent change. For example, an agent that heats a metal which is later molded into a new shape is a preparing cause for the change in shape. The agent that heats the metal is not a *per se* cause of the change in shape, that is, it does not bring about the shape change through an active power that intends this effect. Yet, nevertheless the change in shape depends on the action of the preparing cause since without first being heated, the metal's shape cannot be changed. Preparing

---

[22] *De prin. nat.*, cap. 4 (ed. Leon., vol. 43, 44): "[O]mnis causa, inquantum est causa, naturaliter prior est causato ..." See also *ST* III q. 78, a. 5 ad 3.
[23] *De ver.* q. 2, a. 8 (ed. Leon., vol. 22 1/2, 69): "Remoto autem priori removetur posterius, sed non e converso."
[24] See Section 7.1.

causes necessarily act prior in time to the final effect for which they prepare. Furthermore, it is possible for there to be a great delay between the action of the preparing cause and the subsequent change for which it prepares.

The notion of a preparing cause can help us analyze examples in which a series of changes occur leading up to a final effect. The medicine case is such an example. When the patient ingests medicine, it is put into contact with saliva and eventually stomach acid, which prepares it to be absorbed into the body. A series of changes then occur at the molecular level, which eventually terminate in alleviation of symptoms. The immediate *per se* agent of each change in the process can be considered a preparing cause of temporally subsequent changes. For instance, the stomach acid, through dissolving the medicine, disposes the medicine to undergo the change of absorption and so can be considered a preparing cause of this later change. At every point in the process, there will be a simultaneously acting *per se* efficient cause, such as saliva or stomach acid, which brings about the immediate change. However, the changes immediately brought about by each simultaneously acting *per se* cause can also be attributed to causes which acted earlier to prepare for the change. For example, the act of ingesting the medicine can be considered a preparing cause of the final change which terminates in health since it brought the medicine into contact with the agent that acted upon it to transform it into the state needed to effect the final change. While Aquinas thinks that *per se* causes in actuality act simultaneously with the changes they cause, he also acknowledges that we can attribute temporally later effects to earlier agents according to this other type of non-*per se* efficient causality.

Furthermore, Aquinas also thinks that when there are series of agents and patients such that the first moves the second and the second moves the third and so on, the first agent's action upon the second agent can be seen as a cause of the second's action upon the third, and so on. If the second would not have moved the third unless the first moved it (i.e. the second), Aquinas thinks there is the dependence present which is required for considering the second's action on the third an effect of the first agent's efficient causality.[25]

---

[25] *In II Post Anal.* lec. 12, c. 10 (ed. Leon., vol. 1, 365):

> Et hoc indifferenter sive hoc consideretur in uno mobili, quod movetur continue a principio usque ad finem; sive in diversis mobilibus, quorum primum movet secundum, et secundum tertium. Et licet simul dum primum movens movet, primum motum moveatur, tamen primum motum remanet movens postquam desiit moveri, quo movente simul movetur secundum mobile. Et ita successive moventur mobilia, quorum unum est causa motus

2.3   The Modality of Natural Efficient Causation

This section concerns Aquinas's views on the modality by which natural
efficient causes operate. For example, do fires necessarily burn combustible
objects or is it possible for fire to be in contact with something combustible and yet fail to burn it? If natural causes do necessarily produce their
effects, what is the nature of the necessity at stake? Is it absolute or logical
necessity or a weaker sense of causal necessity? Aquinas's views about the
modality by which efficient causes produce their effects has been subject to
much scholarly disagreement. In this section, I will first present an interpretation of Aquinas's views on this topic and then I will situate this
interpretation in terms of scholarly disagreements.

   Aquinas's most extended discussion of the modality of efficient causation occurs in his *Summa contra Gentiles* where he enumerates the ways in
which there can be absolute necessity in created things. Absolute necessity
is the modality which attaches to things that cannot fail to be. Strictly
speaking, Aquinas thinks that everything that exists could have possibly
not existed if God had chosen not to create it. Yet, he thinks that on the
assumption that God chooses to create certain types of creatures, it follows
that there will be certain absolute necessities in the created world. For
example, Aquinas thinks that if there are human beings, then they must
necessarily be rational and animals. This follows from the human form.
Likewise, if there are material beings composed of contrary elements, they
will necessarily be corruptible.[26] Aquinas considers in the *Summa contra
Gentiles* whether it is similarly the case that if certain natural efficient
causes exist then their actions and effects must necessarily follow. In
addressing this topic, Aquinas claims that natural efficient causes must of
necessity have their proper powers. However, their actions and effects do
not follow from their powers of necessity since they are able to be impeded.
Aquinas writes: "It is necessary for fire to have the power of heating;
however, it is not necessary for it to heat since it is able to be impeded
by something extrinsic."[27] It is part of the very nature of fire to have the

alterius, sicut de his quae proiiciuntur manifestat Philosophus in VIII Physic. Per hunc ergo
modum contingit quod causa non est simul cum eo cuius est causa, in quantum scilicet
prima pars motus est causa secundae, vel primum motum movet secundum.

[26] *ScG* II c. 30 and *In II Phys.* l. 15.
[27] *ScG* II c. 30 (ed. Marietti, 144, n. 1076): "[N]ecessarium est ipsum habere virtutem calefaciendi,
    tamen non necesse est ipsum calefacere; eo quod ab extrinseco impediri potest." *In V Meta.* lec. 5
    (ed. Marietti, 224, n. 826): "Forma enim non semper facit motum in actu, sed quandoque in
    potentia tantum: sicut quando impeditur motus naturalis ab aliquo exteriori prohibente, vel etiam
    quando impeditur actio naturalis ex materiae defectu."

power to heat, yet the action of heating may not follow from fire if extrinsic conditions prevent it.

Further on in the text, Aquinas explains in greater detail how a natural cause might be prevented from acting and producing its effect. Aquinas notes that both a natural efficient cause and its patient must be properly disposed in order for the efficient cause to act and cause its effect. What it is for the patient to be properly disposed is just for it to have the relevant passive potentiality necessary for undergoing the agent's action. In addition to having an active power, the agent must also have the right sort of disposition to act through its active power. Even an efficient cause with a power to cause a certain effect may not actually be able to cause that effect if some other form in the cause weakens its power. This is what it means for an agent to lack the disposition necessary for action. For example, Aquinas claims that the size of an agent makes its power stronger or weaker.[28] Thus, a very small fire, even though it has the power to heat, might be unable actually to heat certain patients because of the weakness in its power to heat. Given that the appropriate disposition is required for an agent to act through its power and for the patient to undergo the agent's action, Aquinas thinks that the modal character of the respective dispositions is relevant for determining whether an agent's action follows from it of necessity.[29] He writes:

> If therefore the dispositions according to which the effect follows of necessity is absolutely necessary in both the agent and the patient, there will be absolute necessity in the agent cause, just as there is in those which act from necessity and always. If, however, the disposition is not absolutely necessary, but able to be removed, there will not be absolute necessity from the agent cause unless on the supposition of the disposition of both [i.e. the agent and the patient] required for acting, just as in those things which are sometimes impeded in their operation either by a defect of power or by the violence of something contrary. Hence, these do not act always and from necessity, but rather for the most part.[30]

---

[28] See *ScG* III c. 69 which is discussed Section in 3.7. Aquinas thinks that there are also other factors that impact the strength or weakness of an agent's power. Most importantly is the degree to which the agent participates in the form which is the active power. See *De virt.* q. 1, a. 11; *ST* I q. 25, a. 1 and *ScG* II c. 8.

[29] Though Aquinas does not mention this in *ScG* II c. 30, he thinks that even when the agent and the patient have the proper dispositions, action only follows if God concurs with the created agent's action. On Aquinas's views about God's causation of creaturely actions, see *De pot.* q. 3, a. 7; *ScG* III, c. 67; and *ST* I, q. 105, a. 5. I discuss his views in my "Three Competing Views of God's Causation of Creaturely Actions: Aquinas, Scotus and Olivi," in *Divine Causation*, ed. Gregory Ganssle (New York: Routledge, 2021), 66-81.

[30] *ScG* II c. 30 (ed. Marietti, 144, n. 1078):

> Si igitur talis dispositio secundum quam de necessitate sequitur effectus, fuerit necessaria absolute et in agente et in patiente, erit necessitas absoluta in causa agente: sicut in his quae

Aquinas thinks that there are some agents which are such that it is necessary that they are suitably disposed to act through their power. Put otherwise, they cannot lose the disposition required for action. Aquinas explains earlier in the text that for some of these agents, the disposition of the patient does not matter. This is to say that regardless of what changes of quality the patient undergoes, the agent can always act upon it. If both the agent and the patient necessarily possess the requisite dispositions for action, then the action of the agent is absolutely necessary. If the agent exists together with the patient, then the agent's action must occur. In Aquinas's view, the only natural agents that act with absolute necessity are the heavenly bodies. He writes elsewhere that terrestrial bodies are necessarily altered by the sun.[31] The sun's actions on terrestrial bodies occur with absolute necessity since the sun cannot lose the disposition it needs to act and regardless of their various dispositions, all terrestrial bodies of every species and quality are subject to alteration by the sun.

In the same *Summa contra Gentiles* text quoted above, Aquinas explains that if the relevant dispositions of the agent and patient are not absolutely necessary, then the agent will not act and produce its effect with absolute necessity. Since the agent and patient can exist without the necessary dispositions, it can happen that both the agent and the patient exist and yet the agent does not act. Aquinas writes in his *De malo*: "It is false that with the cause posited, even if it is of itself sufficient, that the effect is necessarily posited, since the cause is able to be impeded, as for example, when fire is impeded from burning wood by throwing water on it."[32] Causes which are able to be impeded are able to exist without their actions. Aquinas considers the agent's or the patient's loss of the disposition required for action as a type of impediment.

---

    agunt ex necessitate et semper. Si autem non fuerit absolute necessaria sed possibilis removeri, non erit necessitas ex causa agente nisi ex suppositione dispositionis utriusque debitae ad agendum: sicut in his quae impediuntur interdum in sua operatione vel propter defectum virtutis, vel propter violentiam alicuius contrarii; unde non agunt semper et ex necessitate, sed ut in pluribus.

[31] *ScG* II c. 28 (ed. Marietti, 142, n. 1061): "In rerum autem propagatione, ubi iam creatura efficiens invenitur, potest esse necessitas absoluta a causa efficiente creata: sicut ex motu solis inferiora corpora necessario immutantur." See also *In II Phys.* lec. 15 (ed. Leon., vol. 2, 98): "Et similiter quod habet necessitatem ex causa efficiente, est necessarium absolute; sicut necessarium est esse alternationem noctis et diei propter motum solis."

[32] *De malo* q. 16, a. 7 ad 14 (ed. Leon., vol. 23, 317): "Falsum enim est quod causa posita, etiamsi de se sit sufficiens, necesse sit effectum poni: quia potest impediri, puta ignis a combustione lignorum per iniectionem aquae."

In a different section of the *Summa contra Gentiles*, Aquinas enumerates three types of impediments that can prevent a natural cause from producing its effect. First, the cause's own power might be too weak to cause its effect. Moderately hot water, for example, might have too weak a power to cook food. Second, the cause might be impeded by an exterior agent. For example, a flame-resistant suit might impede a fire from burning a firefighter's body. Lastly, indisposition of the patient upon which the agent attempts to act can also impede the agent from acting. A cold piece of metal, for example, cannot be reshaped by human hands because it is indisposed to receive this action.[33] Aquinas thinks that impediments of natural causes are rare. Thus, for the most part, the effects of natural causes follow from them.[34] This will be discussed in more detail below.

For now, it is worth noting that Aquinas claims that if it is supposed that the required dispositions are present in the agent and the patient, that is, there are no impediments, then the agent's action follows with necessity. Aquinas thinks that in addition to absolute necessity, there is another type of necessity known as conditional necessity or necessity of supposition.[35] Effects that are absolutely necessary cannot not exist given the existence of their causes. By contrast, effects that are conditionally necessary or necessary from supposition can fail to exist even given the existence of their causes; however, they are necessary given the existence of their causes together with certain extrinsic conditions. Conditional or suppositional necessity characterizes the actions and effects of terrestrial natural efficient causes. The actions and effects of terrestrial substances do not simply follow from the existence of such substances, but these actions and effects do follow from the existence of their efficient causes when it is assumed that such causes are not impeded. Put otherwise, on the condition that no impediments are present, the actions of natural efficient causes follow with necessity. Aquinas writes in his commentary on the *Metaphysics*: "with regard to irrational potentialities, it is necessary when

---

[33] *ScG* III, c. 73 (ed. Marietti, 105, n. 2488):

> In rebus autem inanimatis causarum contingentia ex imperfectione et defectu est: secundum enim suam naturam sunt determinata ad unum effectum, quem semper consequuntur nisi sit impedimentum vel ex debilitate virtutis, vel ex aliquo exteriori agente, vel ex materiae indispositione; et propter hoc causae naturales agentes non sunt ad utrumque, sed ut frequentius eodem modo suum effectum producunt, deficiunt autem raro.

[34] Ibid. See also, for example, *In II Sent.* d. 39, q. 2, a. 1 ad 3.

[35] *De prin. nat.* c. 4 (ed. Leon., vol. 43, 44): "Et notandum quod duplex est necessitas, scilicet necessitas absoluta et necessitas conditionalis." *In IV Sent.* d. 17, q. 1, a. 2, qc. 3 (ed. Mandonnet-Moos, vol. 4, 836): "quod duplex est necessitas; scilicet necessitas absoluta, et necessitas ex suppositione."

an active approaches a passive in that disposition through which the
passive is able to undergo and the active is able to act, it is necessary that
one undergoes and the other acts; as when fire is applied to something
combustible."[36] When it is assumed that all of the extrinsic conditions are
met for a natural efficient cause to act, it is simply not possible for it to be
in contact with its patient and fail to act.

As mentioned above, Aquinas thinks that impediments to natural causes
are rare. He writes: "the effects of natural causes follow from them for the
most part, and they fail in the minority of cases. . ."[37] It usually happens
that when a natural cause and its patient exist, so too does the natural cause
act and produce its effect. For the most part, agents and patients remain in
the right disposition for action to occur. Aquinas thinks that since impediments to natural causes are rare, it is possible to make "conjectural"
predictions from natural cause to effect. For example, one can predict that
taking a medicine will most likely cause health.[38] It is possible that the
medicine will be impeded from producing its effects, but since it is rare
that natural causes are impeded, it is likely that the medicine's effect will
follow it. The question can be raised of why it is rare that natural causes are
impeded. What is the basis for thinking that natural causes will be
unimpeded for the most part?

To answer this question, it is important to first note that natural causes
are of themselves determined toward performing their proper actions. As
we saw in Chapter 1 and will see in more detail in Chapter 4, natural
causes have a natural inclination or impetus toward action.[39] When the
natural cause is considered in itself, it is not a toss-up whether it will act. It
has an intrinsic drive toward operation. Impediments come about through
the interactions which natural causes have with one another. If an agent or
a patient loses a disposition needed for acting or being acted upon, it is
through the action of another cause upon it. Thus, the most proximate
explanation for why natural causes are rarely impeded is due to the
arrangement of natural causes in the actual world. This is to say that the
individual natural causes in the material world do not often interact in
such a way that they cause each other to lose the dispositions necessary for
action. If the arrangement of natural causes were different, it could have

[36] In IX Meta. lec. 4 (ed. Marietti, 435, n. 1818): "in potentiis irrationabilibus necesse est, quando
passivum appropinquat activo, in illa dispositione qua passivum potest pati et activum potest agere,
necesse est quod unum patiatur et alterum agat; ut patet quando combustibile applicatur igni."
[37] In I Sent. d. 39, q. 2, a. 2 ad 4 (ed. Mandonnet-Moos, vol. 1, 934): "causae naturales consequuntur
effectus suos in majori parte, et deficiunt in minori . . ." See also ScG III c. 73 and ST I q. 115, a. 6.
[38] In I Sent. d. 38, q. 1, a. 5.   [39] See Section 4.1.

been the case that natural causes frequently impeded one another. For example, suppose the weather patterns were such that it was perpetually raining every day on earth. Under these conditions, it would be frequent that fire is impeded from burning things since combustible substances would often be wet. It would be rare that fire does burn other substances. Aquinas thinks that it is not simply a matter of chance that natural causes are arranged in our world in such a way that they are for the most part unimpeded. Rather, he thinks that this is due to God's providence. Aquinas thinks that God through his intellect is responsible for how individual created causes are ordered together in the universe.[40] When one natural efficient cause impedes another, it may seem to an observer as a chance event that these two causes intersected. Yet, Aquinas thinks that any intersection between created causes is part of God's order for the course of events in the universe. He writes the following in his *Summa Theologiae*:

> Some effect is able to happen outside of the order of some particular cause, however, not outside of the order of the universal cause [i.e. God]. The reason for this is because nothing happens outside of the order of a particular cause except by some other impeding cause, which itself must be reduced to the first universal cause ...[41]

For example, when fire is impeded from burning a log because it is wet, Aquinas thinks that it was part of God's providential ordering of the universe that the log was wet at that time. Aquinas thinks that it is good for natural causes not to be impeded and when he discusses divine providence in his works, he is concerned with explaining why God would allow natural causes to be impeded at times.[42] Since it is good for natural causes to act and God wills the good of his creatures, God's providence orders natural causes in such a way that for the most part they are unimpeded and perform their proper actions.[43] Though he does not explicitly say so, Aquinas would likely think that it would be at odds with

---

[40] See for example, *ST* I q. 22 and q. 103; *De ver.* q. 5; *ScG* III c. 76.

[41] *ST* I q. 103, a. 7 (ed. Leon., vol. 5, 461): "praeter ordinem alicuius particularis causae, aliquis effectus evenire potest; non autem praeter ordinem causae universalis. Cuius ratio est, quia praeter ordinem particularis causae nihil provenit nisi ex aliqua alia causa impediente, quam quidem causam necesse est reducere in primam causam universalem ..." See also *ST* I q. 22, a. 2 ad 1.

[42] Aquinas refers to the impediment of natural causes as evil (*malum*). See for instance *In I Sent.* d. 39, q. 2, a. 2 ad 4.

[43] Aquinas's view that God wills for natural causes to perform their proper operations is revealed in *De ver.* q. 5, a. 5 ad 2 where he claims that there are fewer failures in natural operations, as opposed to in the operations of voluntary causes, since natural causes are provided for by God alone.

God's goodness for him to order the natural causes in the universe in such a way that they are regularly impeded.

As mentioned in the introduction to this chapter, there has been debate among contemporary scholars about Aquinas's views on the modality by which natural causes operate.

Scholars of early modern philosophy have shown interest in Aquinas's views on the modal relationship that obtains between a natural efficient cause and its effect. As mentioned in Chapter 1, Hume argued against the view that there is a necessary connection between causes and their effects.[44] Early modern scholars have questioned whether Hume's late medieval Aristotelian targets truly believed that there was a necessary connection between causes and their effects. Steven Nadler has claimed that, in fact, Aquinas denies that there is a logically necessary connection between natural efficient causes and their effects. According to Nadler, Aquinas and some other medieval figures distinguish logical necessity from nomological or causal necessity.[45] If something is logically necessary, it cannot be otherwise absolutely. However, if something is nomologically necessary, it cannot be otherwise only given the set of laws that are contingently in place. The latter form of necessity is a weaker form of necessity that is relative to a non-necessary set of laws. That which is nomologically necessary can be otherwise given that the laws of nature can be otherwise. According to Nadler, Aquinas denies that the connection between a natural cause and its effect is absolutely necessary. On Nadler's interpretation of Aquinas, the necessity which obtains between a natural cause and its effect is best characterized as nomological necessity since "God, in his absolute power, could have established a different natural order."[46] If a cause would not have produced its effect under a different natural order, then the connection between the cause and its effect is not one of absolute necessity. Nadler's interpretation of Aquinas has important historical significance. If Nadler is correct that Aquinas and other medieval Aristotelians did not believe that the connection between a natural cause and its effect is one of absolute necessity, then it seems that later figures such as Nicholas Malebranche and David Hume made the mistake of

---

[44] See Section 1.2.
[45] Steven Nadler, "No Necessary Connection: The Medieval Roots of the Occasionalist Roots of Hume," *The Monist* 79:3 (1996): 448–66, at 462–63. See also Nadler, "Malebranche on Causation," in *The Cambridge Companion to Malebranche*, ed. Steven Nadler (Cambridge: Cambridge University Press, 2000), 112–38, at 114.
[46] Nadler, "No Necessary Connection," 463.

conflating causal necessity with absolute necessity and thus attacked a position not actually held by their opponents.

I believe that Nadler's interpretation of Aquinas has some shortcomings. First, Nadler sets up a false dichotomy between two types of necessity: absolute necessity and nomological necessity. As we have seen above, Aquinas acknowledges that terrestrial natural efficient causes do not produce their effects with absolute necessity since the agent or its patient can possibly lose the dispositions required for action. Aquinas claims, as we have seen, that the necessity that obtains between terrestrial natural efficient causes and their effects is conditional or suppositional necessity. This type of necessity cannot be likened to nomological necessity. According to Aquinas, if it is assumed that there are no impediments then a terrestrial natural efficient cause will necessarily produce its effect. On the assumption that a natural cause and its patient have the dispositions required for action, the connection between a natural cause and its effect is one of absolute necessity.[47] There is no set of natural laws that could be otherwise and thereby undo the connection between a natural cause and its effect. If a natural cause and its patient have the dispositions required for action, then it is simply not possible for the natural cause not to produce its effect. The connection between a natural efficient cause considered just in itself and its effect is not absolutely necessary because individual natural causes can be impeded – not because there is a set of laws which could be otherwise. When a lack of impediments is built into the circumstances under which a natural cause operates, then there is a connection of absolute necessity between a natural efficient cause and its effect. As we have seen, there are celestial natural causes which cannot be impeded. Between these efficient causes, considered solely in themselves, and their effects, there is a connection of absolute necessity. Likewise, the same sort of necessity obtains between an impedable terrestrial natural cause when it is assumed that such a cause is not impeded.

According to Nadler's interpretation, Aquinas believed that "God, in his absolute power, could have established a different natural order."[48] Here arises the second difficulty with his interpretation. There is an ambiguity in what it means for God to establish a different natural order. First, this could mean that God could have ordered the particular natural causes which exist in the world differently so that they would intersect with each other in ways different from how they do in the actual world. For instance, God could have made a world in which the branches that are now in my

---

[47] See *ScG* II, c. 30 which is quoted in fn. 30.   [48] Nadler, "No Necessary Connection," 463.

fire pit got rained on last night and therefore, could not now be burned by fire. Natural laws, such as "fire burns wood," would still be the same in this differently ordered world. However, some of the actions of particular natural causes which obtain in the actual world might not happen in a differently ordered world since there would be different impediments under a different order of natural causes. Second, the claim that God could have established a different natural order could be interpreted to mean that God could have established different natural laws, namely different truths about how natural causes regularly behave. For instance, on this interpretation, God could have established a world in which it is false that "fire burns wood." It is not entirely clear whether Nadler has the first or the second interpretation in mind when he claims that Aquinas thinks that God could have established a different natural order. The second interpretation, however, fits better with Nadler's claim that the connection between a natural cause and its effect is nomologically, rather than absolutely, necessary. Distinguishing nomological necessity from absolute necessity itself presupposes that the natural laws could have been otherwise. I do not think that Aquinas, however, would agree that the laws of nature could be different. In his view, laws of nature are true in virtue of the powers of natural substances. For example, it is true that "fire burns wood" because fire has an active power to burn and wood has a passive power to undergo burning. As we saw above, Aquinas thinks that natural substances have their proper powers of necessity.[49] Though a fire may not burn anything because it is impeded, it is absolutely necessary for it to have the powers that it does. Natural causes have their proper powers in virtue of their natures. Even God could not make a fire which lacked the power to burn things since having such a power is part of the very nature of being fire. It is clear that Aquinas thinks that God could have established a different order in the first sense of making a world in which natural causes intersect in different ways from how they do in the actual world. Any particular natural cause could have not done the actions that it does if had been impeded under a different order. However, it does not follow that the necessity which obtains in nature must, therefore, be distinguished from absolute necessity. Rather, according to Aquinas, it follows that we must recognize that absolute necessity only obtains in nature on the supposition that natural causes are not impeded.

In addition to scholars of early modern philosophy, contemporary philosophers who defend real causal powers have also shown interest in

---

[49] See, for example, the text in fn. 26.

Aquinas's views on the modal connection between natural efficient causes and their effects. Among contemporary power theorists there has been debate about whether natural causal powers are necessarily manifested when they are in appropriate circumstances. Stephen Mumford and Rani Lill Anjum defend the view that powers, even when they are in appropriate conditions, are manifested only for the most part. According to their view, a natural power may fail to manifest without any impediment or explanation. They call the modality that obtains between a power and its manifestation "dispositional modality" and they characterize it as a modality that stands between necessity and contingency.[50] Though the manifestation of a power may fail to occur even when all conditions needed for its manifestation obtain, powers are not nevertheless related to their manifestations by mere contingency since more often than not powers are manifested when requisite conditions obtain. Powers have a tendency toward their manifestation. Mumford has claimed that "it is perhaps Aquinas who was the greatest advocate of dispositional modality."[51] It is easy to see why Mumford and Anjum would think that Aquinas defends a view like dispositional modality. We have seen that Aquinas claims throughout his works that natural efficient causes produce their effects for the most part and they fail to produce their effects in a minority of cases.[52] Claims such as these, which Aquinas frequently makes, might lead a reader to think that he holds that "dispositional modality" characterizes the relationship between a natural cause and its effect. However, I believe that upon further analysis it becomes clear that Aquinas was no defender of dispositional modality in the realm of natural causes.

Causes which act according to "dispositional modality" may fail to produce their effects without any impediment or explanation. Put otherwise it is possible that such causes might not produce their effects without any determining factor. By contrast, Aquinas thinks that whenever a natural efficient cause fails to produce its effect there is always a

---

[50] See Stephen Mumford and Rani Lill Anjum, "The Irreducibility of Dispositionalism," in *New Scholasticism Meets Analytic Philosophy*, ed. Rafael Hüntelmann and Johannes Hattler (Heusenstamm: Editiones Scholasticae, 2014), 105–28.

[51] Stephen Mumford, "The Power of Power," in *Powers and Capacities in Philosophy*, ed. Ruth Groff and John Greco (New York: Routledge, 2013), 9–24, at 19. Ben Page critiques their interpretation of Aquinas in his "Thomas Aquinas, 'the Greatest Advocate of Dispositional Modality'," *Studia Neoaristotelica* 14:2 (2017): 167–88.
  It should be noted that in later work Anjum and Mumford revise their assessment of Aquinas. They write in *What Tends to Be: The Philosophy of Dispositional Modality* (London and New York: Routledge, 2018), 37: "It looks, therefore, as if Aristotle, Aquinas and Geach had a conditional necessity view rather than allowing a dispositional modality."

[52] See texts in fn. 36.

determinant which explains why the cause failed. We saw above that Aquinas identifies several different types of impediments which might prevent a natural cause from acting. Furthermore, Aquinas claims that natural causes produce their effects "for the most part" not because he thinks they can fail without explanation, but rather because he thinks that for the most part natural causes are unimpeded. Impediments are rare. Some historical scholars have claimed that Aquinas held that natural causes operate in an indeterministic way such that even in the absence of impediments, it is still possible for a natural cause not to produce its effect.[53] Thus, it may be worthwhile to present some further textual support for my interpretation.

There are several passages in Aquinas's works which clearly demonstrate that he did not hold that natural causes operate in such a way that they might not produce their effects even when no impediments stand in the way. Aquinas claims that it is characteristic of natural causes to act in a uniform way. This is to say that if the same set of circumstances obtain, a natural cause will produce the same effect. This is what differentiates natural causes from voluntary ones. Aquinas writes:

> This is the difference between a natural agent and a voluntary agent: a natural agent acts in the same way as long as it is in the same condition. It does certain kinds of things because it is a certain way. However, a voluntary agent does the sort of things it wills.[54]

This passage denies that natural causes operate in an indeterministic way. In the absence of impediments, natural causes produce their effects without fail. According to Aquinas, this is because natural causes are determined to one effect by their nature. They are not open to producing or not producing their effects. Aquinas writes: "The power of every agent which acts by necessity of nature is determined to one effect. Thus, it is the case that all natural things happen always in the same way unless there is an impediment."[55] In the cases in which a natural cause does not produce its effect, there is always some factor (i.e. an impediment) that explains why

---

[53] Stephen Brock summarizes and responds to this literature in his "Causality and Necessity in Thomas Aquinas," *Quaestio* 2:1 (2002): 217–40.

[54] *Compend. Theo.* I c. 97 (ed. Leon., vol. 42, 116): "Haec est enim differentia inter agens naturale et agens uoluntarium, quod agens naturale eodem modo agit quamdiu eodem modo se habet, eo quod quale est, talia facit; agens autem voluntarium agit qualia uult."

[55] *ScG* II c. 23 (ed. Marietti, 134, n. 990): "Omnis enim agentis per necessitatem naturae virtus determinatur ad unum effectum. Et inde est quod omnia naturalia semper eveniunt eodem modo, nisi sit impedimentum . . ."

the effect failed to happen. These impediments might be features of the patient that make it unsuitable for receiving the agent's action or a stronger agent that interferes with the impeded agent's action. However, as we have seen, an impediment can also be a lack of a disposition necessary for action in the agent itself. For example, a fire may not be able to burn something because its own heat is weak.[56] Even though the weakness is a feature of a particular agent itself, it is extrinsic to the nature of the fire by which the agent has the power to heat. Heat by its nature heats when in the appropriate circumstance. If a cause with this nature does not heat something else when in the right circumstances due to some other feature of the agent that weakens its heat, this other feature of the agent is an impediment to the action of heating. Although the impediment inheres in the agent, it is extrinsic to the nature of the power. The power of heat is not of itself open to heating or not heating. But when it is instantiated in a particular agent, it is possible that heat may not heat because another form of this agent weakens it. Aquinas holds that in any case in which an agent fails to produce its effect, there is some prior factor that determines it to this failure. Aquinas writes: "For a natural agent produces an effect which is similar to itself unless it is impeded by something extrinsic, and this is a certain defect in it. Hence there never follows error in the effect, unless there pre-exists some other error [i.e. an impediment] in the agent or matter ..."[57] According to this passage, natural causes do not randomly fail to produce their effects. Rather, there is some prior factor determining them to this outcome. Furthermore, in every instance in which a similar impediment is present, the effect will similarly not obtain. Natural causes are not indeterministic causes, nor do they relate to their effects by "dispositional modality." Natural causes are such that in similar circumstances, they act a similar way. The reason why Aquinas says that natural causes only produce their effects for the most part is because in a minority of cases there are impediments which prevent the cause from doing so. Put otherwise, the claim that natural causes produce their effects "for the most part" is a claim about how they act across a variety of different circumstances (i.e. some with impediments and some without), rather than a claim about how they might behave in the very same circumstance in which no impediments are present.

---

[56] See fn. 27.

[57] *ST* I q. 49, a. 1 ad 3 (ed. Leon., vol. 4, 500): "Agens enim naturale producit effectum suum talem quale ipsum est, nisi impediatur ab aliquo extrinseco, et hoc ipsum est quidam defectus eius. Unde nunquam sequitur malum in effectu, nisi praeexistat aliquod aliud malum in agente vel materia ..."

Though Aquinas did not hold to "dispositional modality" regarding natural causes and their relationship to their effects, I do think it is nevertheless possible to regard him as a historical precursor to the notion of "dispositional modality," which Mumford and Anjum develop in their work. If one looks beyond the realm of natural causes, one can find in Aquinas's thought certain dispositions which he thought related to their manifestations by "dispositional modality," namely moral virtues which are manifested in virtuous action. Aquinas developed a very interesting position about how moral virtues, such as generosity, related to virtuous actions, such as giving money to someone in need. As others have noted, Aquinas rejected Aristotle's view that those with moral virtues could not fail to act virtuously when in appropriate circumstances for manifesting the virtue.[58] In an effort to make room for a more robust notion of freedom, Aquinas maintained that the moral virtues disposed an agent toward virtuous actions without determining the agent to such actions. As Aquinas, writes: "someone possessing a habit might not use it or even perform a contrary action . . ."[59] For example, though a generous person is more likely to behave generously since the virtue of generosity confers a tendency toward generous actions, nevertheless, it remains possible for her not to perform an act of generosity or to even act against her virtue by doing something stingy. In Aquinas's view, through the power of will an agent can choose not to act on a virtuous tendency since he thinks that the exercise of any habit is in the power of the human will.[60] While scholars of Aquinas's ethics and anthropology have discussed the implications of this view for his moral psychology and account of human freedom, the implications for his modal theory have yet to be noted. On Aquinas's view, moral virtues relate to virtuous actions by the modality which Anjum and Mumford label as "dispositional modality." Moral virtues do not necessitate that their bearers perform virtuous actions when in the appropriate circumstances. Yet, moral virtues do not have a merely contingent relationship to virtuous actions. Agents with moral virtues tend to perform virtuous actions. Though failure is always possible even in identical circumstances, it is more likely than not that an agent with a moral virtue will

---

[58] See Bonnie Kent, "Dispositions and Moral Fallibility: The UnAristotelian Aquinas," *History of Philosophy Quarterly* 29 (2012): 141–57 and "Losable Virtue: Aquinas on Character and Will," in *Aquinas and the Nicomachean Ethics*, ed. Tobias Hoffmann, Jorn Muller and Matthias Perkams (Cambridge: Cambridge University Press, 2013), 91–109.

[59] *ST* I-II q. 52, a. 3 (ed. Leon., vol. 6, 336): "aliquis habens habitum non utitur illo, vel etiam agit actum contrarium . . ."

[60] *ST* I-II q. 52, a. 3 (ed. Leon., vol. 6, 336): "usus habituum in voluntate hominis consistit . . ."

manifest that virtue in action. It should be noted, however, that Aquinas thinks that there is always an explanatory factor behind whether or not a virtue is manifested in virtuous action, namely an exercise of free will. By contrast, contemporary advocates of "dispositional modality" think that a natural cause might fail without any explanation or determining factor.

Now that we have seen Aquinas's views on the temporal and modal relationship between efficient causes and their effects, we can move on to examine two conditions which he thought must be met in order for an efficient cause to act.

2.4 Agent and Patient Must Be Other: No Self-Motion Even among Equivocal Causes

As is well known, Aquinas upheld the Aristotelian principle that "everything which is moved must be moved by another." This is to say that nothing that is being changed is being changed by itself.[61] The goal of this section is to explain Aquinas's rationale for accepting this position, which was controversial in the medieval period, and to address a significant question that has arisen in the secondary literature about the soundness of Aquinas's favored proof of the principle.[62] Before discussing Aquinas's defense of the principle, it is worth emphasizing its proper interpretation. What Aquinas upholds is that no being can reduce itself from a state of potentiality to actuality. Put otherwise, it cannot be that which transitions itself from not moving to moving. The principle does not, however, imply that an object already set in locomotion requires a mover constantly acting upon it to keep it moving. As we will see further on, Aquinas maintains that heavy bodies naturally move downwards and light bodies naturally move upwards, yet they do not require an agent constantly conjoined with them to keep them in locomotion.[63] Moreover, the principle "everything which is moved must be moved by another" does not require that the mover and the moved must be distinct substances. Aquinas believes that

---

[61] There has been some debate among Aquinas's commentators regarding the meaning and most accurate translation of the axiom *omne quod movetur ab alio movetur*. The debate arises because *movetur* can be translated into English passively as "whatever is moved" or intransitively as "whatever is in motion." For a summary of the debate and arguments for interpreting *movetur* passively see Wippel, *Metaphysical Thought of Thomas Aquinas*, 414–15.

[62] For literature on medieval figures who accepted self-motion, see Vucu, "Henry of Ghent and John Duns Scotus on Self-agency and Self-motion," King, "Scotus on Self-Change," and Kim, "Why Does the Wood Not Ignite Itself?"

[63] See Section 3.9. For secondary literature, see James Weisheipl, "The Principle *omne quod movetur ab alio movetur* in Medieval Physics," *Isis* 56 (1965): 36–45.

some animate substances can move themselves. Yet, a necessary condition is that it have at least two distinct parts, so that one part can be a mover and the other moved.[64] So, why does Aquinas think that what moves must be other than what is moved?

Aquinas's most extensive discussions of the "motion principle," as it has become known in the secondary literature, occur in his commentary on Aristotle's discussion of the principle in the *Physics* and in the context of his proof of a first mover in the *Summa contra Gentiles* and *Summa theologiae*.[65] Aquinas endorses Aristotle's arguments in the *Physics* and repeats them in these other works. In the *Summa contra Gentiles*, Aquinas relies on three arguments taken from Aristotle to prove that everything that is moved is moved by another.[66] The first two arguments apply only to corporeal beings, divisible into parts, while the third argument has a universal applicability to all movers. This third argument is the only one he offers in the *Summa theologiae* proof for a first mover and there he expands upon it. Since it is outside the scope of this study to go into the details of all these arguments, I will focus on just this one argument, which Aquinas seems to have regarded as the most important. He writes:

> Everything which is moved is moved by another. For nothing is moved except insofar as it is in potency with respect to that to which it is moved. But something moves insofar as it is in act. To move is nothing other than to draw something from potency to act. Something in potency is not able to be reduced to act except through something in act, just as something hot in act, such as fire, makes wood, which is potentially hot, to be actually hot, and through this it moves and changes it. It is not possible that the same thing be at once in act and potency in the same way, but only according to diverse ways. For that which is hot in act is not able to be at the same time hot in potency, but it is at the same time cold in potency. It is impossible therefore that, according to the same thing and in the same way, something is both mover and moved or that it moves itself. Therefore, everything which is moved must be moved by another.[67]

---

[64] See, for instance, *In VIII Phys.* lec. 4, n. 7. For discussion of Aquinas's views on organic self-motion see Cory, "Thomas Aquinas on How the Soul Moves the Body." For a discussion of bodily human actions in Aquinas, see Löwe, *Thomas Aquinas on the Metaphysics of the Human Act.*
[65] See *In VII Phys.* lec. 1, *In VIII Phys.* lec. 7, *ScG* I c. 13, and *ST* I q. 2, a. 3.   [66] *ScG* I c. 13.
[67] *ST* I q. 2, a. 3 (ed. Leon., vol. 4, 31):

> Omne autem quod movetur, ab alio movetur. Nihil enim movetur, nisi secundum quod est in potentia ad illud ad quod movetur: movet autem aliquid secundum quod est actu. Movere enim nihil aliud est quam educere aliquid de potentia in actum: de potentia autem non potest aliquid reduci in actum, nisi per aliquod ens in actu, sicut calidum in actu, ut ignis, facit lignum, quod est calidum in potentia, esse actu calidum, et per hoc movet

This argument presupposes Aquinas's commitments about active power, which will be discussed in more detail in Chapter 3.[68] As we will see, Aquinas believes that agents act insofar as they are actual. The very forms through which they are actualized in various ways are the powers through which they make other things actual in the same ways. Aquinas conceives of action as the communication of a form from agent to patient. No agent can communicate a form which it does not have. The argument also presupposes Aquinas's views about how patients undergo action. In order to undergo an action and be moved, a patient must have a potentiality for receiving the type of form which the agent causes. If the patient already has the form, it is not in potentiality for receiving it. The reception of a form removes the potentiality for receiving that form. Put otherwise, a substance cannot be changed to have a certain form if it already has it. With this background in place, the argument from self-motion can be reconstructed as follows: Being a mover with respect to a form f requires having f in actuality. Being moved with respect to f requires having f in potentiality. Since nothing can have a form f both actually and potentially in the same respect and at the same time, nothing can move itself. The argument appears straightforward. Yet, contemporary commentators have noted a difficulty with it.

According to Aquinas, there are certain causes known as "equivocal causes." These causes are able to actualize a type of form in their patient which they do not possess in themselves.[69] The sun is a favorite medieval example of an equivocal cause. Following Aristotle, the medievals believed that the sun was not itself hot, and yet, it caused heat in terrestrial bodies. Thus, the sun is an example of an efficient cause that actualizes a form in its patient which it does not possess itself. Given that Aquinas recognizes equivocal causes, commentators suggest that his claim "something moves insofar as it is in act" should not be interpreted strictly to mean that an agent must be f in actuality to move another to be f. Rather, we should interpret that claim to mean that an agent must be either f in actuality or virtually f (i.e. in possession of a power to cause f).[70] This move to amend

---

et alterat ipsum. Non autem est possibile ut idem sit simul in actu et potentia secundum idem, sed solum secundum diversa, quod enim est calidum in actu, non potest simul esse calidum in potentia, sed est simul frigidum in potentia. Impossibile est ergo quod, secundum idem et eodem modo, aliquid sit movens et motum, vel quod moveat seipsum. Omne ergo quod movetur, oportet ab alio moveri.

[68] See especially Sections 3.3 and 3.4.   [69] Equivocal causality is also discussed in Section 3.5.
[70] See Timothy Pawl, "The Five Ways," in *The Oxford Handbook of Aquinas*, ed. Brian Davies and Eleonore Stump (Oxford: Oxford University Press, 2012), 115–31, at 118 and Scott MacDonald,

the argument has the advantage of making Aquinas's premise more plausible insofar as it accounts for cases in which a cause produces an effect that differs from its own forms. However, another difficulty arises with the reinterpreted premise. Once it is admitted that some causes do not instantiate the very forms which they cause, it is not clear why these causes cannot be in the right state of potentiality to undergo their own causality. Timothy Pawl writes: "But now one wonders why it is that something cannot be virtually F and potentially F . . . Perhaps Aquinas would maintain that the only way something can be virtually F is if it cannot be potentially F. But now we need an argument for that claim."[71] The problem is that being virtually f (i.e. having a power to cause f) is not logically incompatible with being potentially f in the same way that being actually f is. Thus, once equivocal causes are acknowledged it is not clear that Aquinas's favored argument against self-motion works. At least the argument must be supplemented with an explanation for why equivocal causes cannot move themselves. Figures after Aquinas who rejected the "motion principle" generally construed self-moving causes as reducing themselves from being virtually f to actually f.[72] They realized that no cause could be actually f and potentially f at once. But they thought it possible for a cause to be both virtually f and potentially f. Thus, understanding Aquinas's reasons for rejecting self-motion even among equivocal causes is all the more significant.

So far as I know, Aquinas never explains why equivocal causes cannot actualize their own potentiality. However, I believe we can reconstruct his reasoning based on his general views about equivocal causes.[73] Aquinas thinks that there is an important constraint on the nature of the difference which obtains between the effect of an equivocal cause and the form through which the equivocal cause acts. Aquinas thinks that equivocal causes produce effects which are generically similar to themselves, but yet of a different species.[74] The species of the effect is always a less perfect species than the species of the power by which the equivocal cause acts. Aquinas thinks that an effect of a different and lower species results when

"Aquinas's Parasitic Cosmological Argument," *Medieval Philosophy and Theology* 1(1991): 119–55, at 134.
[71] Pawl, "The Five Ways," 118. This objection is also discussed in MacDonald, "Aquinas's Parasitic Proof," fn. 29.
[72] On Henry of Ghent, see Wippel, *Metaphysical Thought of Thomas Aquinas*, p. 448, n. 19. On Scotus, see King, "Scotus on Self-Change," 245–47 and Kim, "Why Does the Wood Not Ignite Itself?" 60–63.
[73] On equivocal causes see also Section 3.5.   [74] See *ST* I q. 4, a. 3.

there is a lack of proportion between the agent and its patient.[75] According to Aquinas, there is nothing intrinsic to the equivocal cause which accounts for why it does not produce an effect of the same species as itself. Like other active causes, equivocal causes have an inclination to produce an effect of their same species. Sometimes, however, a patient is not able to receive the full extent of the perfection that the agent communicates. The agent acts in the same way whether it produces an equivocal or univocal effect, namely an effect that is of the same species as the cause itself. The patient's characteristics and specifically their ability or inability to receive the agent's power determine whether the effect which results is of the same species as the agent or of a lower species.

In light of these details, we can now understand why an equivocal cause which is virtually f cannot move itself to be actually f. It might be that there is no formal incompatibility in the notion of a substance being both virtually f and potentially f. Rather, the difficulty lies in the notion of a cause moving itself from being virtually f to actually f. An equivocal cause has the power to cause f in virtue of some form f^* which is of a different and higher species than f. F^* is not of itself a power to cause f. It only produces f by acting on a patient which is incapable of receiving the higher form f^*. The equivocal agent, however, does not fit this description because it is already F^*. On the basis of his understanding of actuality and active power, Aquinas thinks that active powers aim at making effects of their same species. It is only accidental that an active power causes an effect of a different, lower species due to a higher agent acting on a lower patient. Thus, an agent cannot produce an equivocal effect in itself because there would be identity, and thus no lack of proportion, between the agent and the patient.

Before moving on to examine Aquinas's views on the next condition for efficient causation, it is worth noting that Aquinas's rejection of self-motion played an important role in his reasoning for the reality of efficient causation. The contemporary reader who is familiar with Hume's denial of real causation and causal powers will naturally wonder whether Aquinas has some way of verifying his beliefs in production and power.[76] Aquinas explicitly acknowledges, like Hume, that we are unable to grasp the reality of causation through sense perception.[77] All we can see, for example, is the

---

[75] *In II Sent.* d. 1, q. 2, a. 2.   [76] On the Humean view, see Section 1.2.
[77] *In VI Meta.* lec. 1 (ed. Marietti, 295, n. 1146): "Cognitiones ... quae sunt sensitivae tantum non sunt per principia et causas ... Discurrere enim a causis in causata, vel e contrario, non est sensus, sed solum intellectus."

conjunction of the efficient cause and the motion which we attribute to it. We cannot see the cause's production of the motion. In Aquinas's view, however, this does not constitute a reason to be skeptical about the reality of efficient causation since we can apprehend through reason that efficient causation must be real. Aquinas understands motion to be the process whereby a substance's potentiality is actualized. He maintains that since nothing in potentiality can actualize itself, the reality of motion implies that there is an agent cause which initiates it. Aquinas writes: "that which reason apprehends about motion ... implies the notion of cause and effect, for it is not the case that something is reduced from potency to act except by some agent cause."[78] If we observe that wood is burning, for example, we can reason to the conclusion that something is the agent cause of the burning because otherwise the burning could not be happening. Wood's potential for burning cannot actualize itself. Something else must actualize it. According to Aquinas, from our observation of change and our reasoning that it must have an origin, we can infer that there must be productive efficient causality.

2.5   Agent and Patient Must Be in Contact: No Action at a Distance

Following Aristotle, Aquinas rejected the possibility of action at a distance.[79] He writes: "No agent's action, no matter how powerful, proceeds to something distant except insofar as it acts in it through a medium."[80] In Aquinas's view, an agent must be touching that upon which it acts. There cannot be a physical gap between an agent and a patient unless there is an intervening medium. When an agent A acts on patient B through some medium C, C must touch both A and B. An example is a flame on the stove which heats water contained in a pot. The flame is not immediately touching the water. Its action passes through the metal pot that intervenes between the water and

---

[78] *In III Phys.* lec. 5 (ed. Leon., vol. 2, 115): "id quod ratio apprehendit circa motum ... implicatur ratio causae et effectus: nam reduci aliquid de potentia in actum, non est nisi ab aliqua causa agente." See also *De prin. nat.* 3 (ed. Leon., vol. 43, 42):

> Quod enim est in potentia, non potest se reducere ad actum: sicut cuprum quod est potentia idolum, non facit se idolum, sed indiget operante, qui formam idoli extrahat de potentia in actum. Forma etiam non extraheret se de potentia in actum ... Oportet ergo praeter materiam et formam esse aliquod principium quod agat, et hoc dicitur esse efficiens, vel movens, vel agens ...

[79] For a taxonomy of medieval and early modern positions on action at a distance, see Kovach, "Aquinas's Theory of Action at a Distance," 150, nn. 4 and 5. Among those who accept action at a distance are Duns Scotus, William of Ockham, Francis Bacon and John Locke.

[80] *ST* I q. 8, a. 1 ad 3 (ed. Leon., vol. 4, 82): "nullius agentis, quantumcumque virtuosi, actio procedit ad aliquid distans, nisi inquantum in illud per media agit."

the flame.[81] Though the concern of this study is action between material substances, it is worth noting that Aquinas upheld something similar to the "contact" condition even in the case of spiritual agents. Though spiritual agents cannot touch physical substances through bodily contact, Aquinas holds that angels and God must be present wherever their power acts.[82] Put otherwise, their power cannot be active at a place at which they are not.

One of the main arguments that Aquinas relies on to show that an agent must be in contact with the patient upon which it acts is drawn from Aristotle's *Physics*. Aquinas comments on and endorses this argument in his own *Physics* commentary and cites it elsewhere in his works.[83] The argument goes through the various types of motions (locomotion, quantitative and qualitative change) and argues that in all cases the agent that causes a change must be in contact with the patient upon which it acts.[84] It is outside the scope of this chapter to go through the lengthy details of this argument. However, it is worth noting that the argument is not merely an inductive one based on our observation of contact between agent and patient. Rather, at many points, the argument appeals to the very natures and definitions of the types of motion in question to show that they can only be caused by an agent which is in contact with the patient. For example, Aquinas reasons, following Aristotle, that all locomotion happens through an agent pushing or pulling on the patient. He then goes on to argue that pushing and pulling, by definition, involve contact with a mover. In pushing, the mover repels something from itself and in pulling the mover draws something to itself.[85] Throughout the *Physics* VII

---

[81] Aquinas notes that the medium may not be affected in the same way by the agent's action as the ultimate patient. This is because the final patient and the medium may have different passive powers, which would cause their reception of the agent's action to differ. One example he provides is the torpedo fish, which shocks a hand through a net without shocking the net. See *In VII Phys.* lec. 3.

[82] *Quodl.* XI q. 1, a. 1 (ed. Leon., vol. 25/1, 152): "spiritualia dicuntur esse in loco, non quidem per contactum magnitudinis, sed virtutis ..." *ST* I q. 8, a. 2 ad 2 (ed. Leon., vol. 4, 86): "incorporalia non sunt in loco per contactum quantitatis dimensivae, sicut corpora: sed per contactum virtutis."

[83] *In VII Phys.* lec. 3 & 4. Aquinas cites this argument when he aims to prove God's omnipresence. See, for instance, *In I Sent.* d. 37, q. 1, a. 1 (ed. Mandonnet-Moos, vol. 1, 857): "Primo, quod movens et motum, agens et patiens, et operans et operatum, oportet simul esse, ut in 7 Physic. probatur."

[84] *In VII Phys.* lec. 3 (ed. Leon., vol. 2, 331): "Sicut igitur tres sunt species motus, ita tres sunt species mobilium, et etiam moventium; et in omnibus est verum quod dictum est, scilicet quod movens et motum sint simul, ut ostendetur in singulis."

[85] *In VII Phys.* lec. 3 (ed. Leon., vol. 2, 333):

　　Prima autem ratio sumitur ex definitione utriusque motus: quia pulsio est motus ab ipso movente vel ab aliquo alio in aliquid aliud; et sic oportet quod saltem in principio motus pellens sit simul cum eo quod pellitur, dum pellens id quod pellitur removet a se vel ab alio.

argument against action at a distance, Aquinas also considers and refutes various counterexamples, such as magnetism.[86]

There are a couple of texts in which Aquinas provides his own argument against action at a distance. This argument is based on his view that agents act through their inherent forms. Aquinas reasons that forms which are received in matter are limited and contracted and thus, they can only be active at the place of the body in which they inhere. He writes:

> Acting, which is nothing other than to make something in act, is proper to act through itself insofar as it is act. Thus, every agent makes something similar to itself. Therefore, from the fact that something is a form not determined by matter subject to quantity, it is an agent indeterminate and universal, and from the fact that an agent is determined to this matter, it is a contracted and particular agent ... This form of fire which is in this corporeal matter is the cause of this ignition, which is from this body and into that body. Hence it happens that such action is through the contact of two bodies.[87]

According to this passage, the reason why fire can only burn things that are in contact with it is because the form by which fire is active is determined and contracted to the matter of that particular fire. The fire's form is in no way outside of the fire. Since the fire's form is contracted to the matter of the fire, the power possessed through that form does not extend beyond the body of fire. In order for something to be transformed by the power of the fire, it must come into contact with the fire because the fire's power is only located in its material body. Aquinas explains this quite clearly in his *De potentia* when he writes: "active forms received in matter subject to quantity receive a certain limited being individuated to that matter, such that through action they do not

---

> Sed tractus est motus ad ipsum vel ad alterum, ut dictum est; et quod non separatur trahens ab eo quod trahitur. Ex quo manifestum est in his duobus motibus, quod movens et motum sint simul.

[86] For an extensive discussion of apparent counterexamples and Aquinas's analysis of them, see Kovach, "Aquinas's Theory of Action at a Distance," 156–62.

[87] *ST* I q. 115, a. 1 (ed. Leon., vol. 5, 539):

> Agere autem, quod nihil est aliud quam facere aliquid actu, est per se proprium actus, inquantum est actus: unde et omne agens agit sibi simile. Sic ergo ex hoc quod aliquid est forma non determinata per materiam quantitati subiectam, habet quod sit agens indeterminatum et universale: ex hoc vero quod est determinata ad hanc materiam, habet quod sit agens contractum et particulare ... haec forma ignis quae est in hac materia corporali, est causa huius ignitionis quae est ab hoc corpore in hoc corpus. Unde et fit talis actio per contactum duorum corporum.

extend themselves to another matter."[88] The active power of material substances is localized in their own bodies and does not radiate beyond them because that is where their forms are. Thus, for one material body to be impacted by the active power of another material body it must come into contact with it.

There is one common type of motion in the natural world, which deserves some further comment in connection with Aquinas's rejection of action at a distance. Projectile motions, such as the trajectory of a ball thrown by a pitcher, seem to involve action at a distance insofar as the launcher of the projectile remains in its place while the projectile, once it loses contact with the projector, moves forward to a new place. Projectile motion may initially look like a case of action at a distance insofar as Aquinas maintains that the projector is the agent responsible for the projectile's effects even when the projectile and projector cease to be in contact. For example, when a child throws a baseball through a window, Aquinas thinks we can attribute the change in the window to the child's agency even though the child was not in physical contact with the window at any time. How does this not violate the prohibition on action at a distance? Aquinas himself considered and addressed this worry in the context of addressing a parallel concern which arises in the case of the generation of an animal through the father's agency. Aquinas thought that in generation the male's semen acted on the female menstrual blood in the womb to transform it into the new organism. The objection arises of how the father can be considered the generator of the child if the father himself is not in contact with the menstrual blood which is transformed into the child.[89]

In response to this worry, Aquinas appeals to the notion of an instrument that can be separated from its corresponding principal cause. An instrumental cause is a cause which aids another cause, known as a principal cause, in accomplishing its action. Instrumental causes will be discussed in greater detail in Chapter 8.[90] One important point to note for now is that on Aquinas's view, instrumental causes receive the power through which they act from their correlative principal causes. The instrument must be in contact with the principal cause to receive the principal cause's power. A separate instrument is one that is able to retain the power

---

[88] *De pot.* q. 3, a. 7 (ed. Pession, 57): "formae activae in materia subiecta quantitati receptae, esse quoddam limitatum recipiunt et individuatum ad materiam illam, ut sic per actionem in aliam materiam non se extendat."

[89] *De pot.* q. 3, a. 11, arg. 5.   [90] See especially Section 8.1.

of the principal cause which is impressed upon it by the principal cause
even after it ceases to be in contact with the principal cause. As long as the
separate instrument retains the power impressed upon it by the principal
agent, it is considered an instrument of this agent. The separate instrument
effectively brings the principal agent's power into contact with patients
that are spatially separated from the principal cause itself. Aquinas writes:

> the instrument is understood to be moved by the principal agent while it
> retains a power impressed by the principal agent. Thus, the arrow is moved
> by the archer as long as the power impressed by the archer remains ...
> Likewise the semen is understood to be moved by the soul of the generator
> as long as the power impressed by the soul remains there, although it is
> physically separated. It is necessary for the mover and moved to be together
> at the beginning of a motion, not, however, for the entire motion as is
> apparent in projectiles.[91]

The fact that a principal agent can impress a transitory form in its
instrument which remains even after contact with the principal is lost
makes it possible for the principal to act through the instrument at places
at which it (i.e. the principal) is not. For example, the baseball player is
able to break a window at a different place from himself because the ball is
able to retain the baseball player's power. As Aquinas notes in this passage,
there must be contact between the principal and the instrument at the
beginning of the motion. This is because the principal cannot transfer a
form to the instrument without contact with it. Furthermore, the instrument can only act upon a patient with which it is in contact. For example,
the semen can only act on menstrual blood when it is in contact with it
and the baseball can only break the window where it touches it. The

---

[91] *De pot.* q. 3, a. 11 ad 5 (ed. Odetto, 75):

> instrumentum intelligitur moveri a principali agente, quamdiu retinet virtutem a principali
> agente impressam; unde sagitta tamdiu movetur a proiciente, quamdiu manet vis impulsus
> proicientis ... unde et semen tamdiu intelligitur moveri ab anima generantis quamdiu
> remanet ibi virtus impressa ab anima, licet corporaliter sit divisum. Oportet autem movens
> et motum esse simul quantum ad motus principium, non tamen quantum ad totum
> motum, ut apparet in proiectis.

It should be noted that there are other texts in which Aquinas seems to endorse Aristotle's account
of projectile motion according to which the projector impresses a force onto the air rather than onto
the projectile. See *In VIII Phys.* lec. 22 and *In III de Caelo et Mundo* lec. 7. Even if the projector
impresses the force onto the air, the motion of the projectile can still be attributed to the projector
instrumentally insofar as the projectile is moved by the impressed force in the air. On scholastic
theories of projectile motion see Rega Wood, "The Influence of Arabic Aristotelianism on
Scholastic Natural Philosophy," in *The Cambridge History of Medieval Philosophy*, ed. Robert
Pasnau and Christina Van Dyke (Cambridge: Cambridge University Press, 2009), 247–66.

separated instrument functions as a vehicle for taking a form from the principal to the place of the patient, which undergoes the final effect.[92]

The reader might wonder whether Aquinas's views on projectile motion reveal that instead of accepting the thesis that there is no action at a distance, he rather accepted the weaker thesis that there is no initiation of action at a distance. If, for example, a ball-throwing boy can be considered the agent which causes a window to break even when he is not in physical contact with the window, it looks like Aquinas accepts that an agent can act from a distance, albeit by having initial contact with an instrument (e.g. the ball) to initiate action at a distance. I think that this is a mistaken way to interpret Aquinas's views on action at a distance. Rather, I think the special case of projectile motion reveals that when Aquinas claims that action requires contact, that which must be in contact with the patient is not necessarily the agent itself, but rather the agent's power. The agent's power might be present where the agent is not by means of a separable instrument. As we will see in Chapter 8, Aquinas thinks that the principal cause truly imparts its own power to the instrument. Accordingly, the agent's power can be carried to locations where the agent is not. But that power nevertheless acts only upon that with which it is in contact. The claim that there is no action at a distance is essentially a claim that a power must be in contact with a patient to initiate a change in it. The power, however, may pass through a medium or be carried to a new location by a separable instrument.

2.6 Conclusion

In this chapter, we first saw Aquinas's views on the defining features of *per se* instances of efficient causation. While Aquinas acknowledges that there

---

[92] One implication of this view of projectile motion is that a projector can continue to act through its instrument even after it passes out of existence. For example, if a pitcher were to die after throwing a ball, but prior to the breaking of the window, the action of breaking the window could still be attributed to him since the ball acted through the power which he impressed upon it. This objection was discussed up through the early modern period by figures such as Descartes and Gassendi. On their positions, see my "What Is an Action? Peter Auriol vs. Thomas Aquinas on the Metaphysics of Causality," n. 41. Though it may seem counterintuitive to attribute an action to a substance which no longer exists, this is not as problematic as it seems. We will see in Chapter 6 that Aquinas maintains that an agent's action is the motion which its patient undergoes. The patient is the substance in which the motion of the action exists. Furthermore, even if the principal agent no longer exists, it nevertheless does seem correct to still attribute the action done through the instrument to the principal agent since the principal is responsible for the power by which the instrument acts. For example, the ball would have no power to sail through the window if the pitcher had not thrown it.

are other instances of efficient causation besides *per se* causation, instances
of *per se* causation are especially important because they are fundamental
insofar as they do not occur in virtue of prior exercises of efficient
causation and they are paradigm insofar as they involve all of the ontological elements Aquinas postulates to explain efficient causation. We saw that
per se instances of efficient causation are those in which an efficient cause
produces an effect through a power which is specifically a power for that
specific effect and furthermore, in *per se* causation the efficient cause has an
inclination for producing the particular type of effect.

We then examined Aquinas's views on the temporal and modal
features of efficient causal interactions. We saw Aquinas's view that
efficient causes in actuality are simultaneous with their effects. An efficient cause is an efficient cause in actuality just as long as motion is
arising from its power. Aquinas does, however, make room for other
respects in which efficient causes can be viewed as prior to their effects.
For example, he thinks that efficient causes are prior to the end result of
their actions. For instance, though a builder in actuality does not exist
prior to the motion of building which arises through his power, he
nevertheless exists temporally prior to the house which he causes through
the motion of building.

We also saw Aquinas's views on the modal relationship between *per se*
efficient causes and their effects. Aquinas denies that terrestrial natural
causes necessitate their effects by logical or absolute necessity since such
causes can be impeded. If lack of impediments is assumed as a condition,
then Aquinas thinks that natural causes necessitate their effects. Thus,
Aquinas claims that terrestrial natural efficient causes produce their effects
by conditional or suppositional necessity. In Aquinas's view, terrestrial
natural causes uniformly produce the same effects as long as they are
not impeded.

In the second half of the chapter, we examined Aquinas's views on some
important conditions that must be met for efficient causal interactions. We
first saw Aquinas's rationale for rejecting self-moving causes and thus,
maintaining that an agent must be other than its patient. A cause cannot
produce in itself an effect which is the same species as the power by which
it acts because this would imply that the same substance is both in actuality
and in potentiality with respect to the same form. Furthermore, causes
cannot produce effects of a different, lower species as the power by which
they act in themselves because such effects only result when there is a lack
of proportion between agent and patient. An agent cannot have this lack of
proportion with itself.

Lastly, we saw why Aquinas thought that agents must be present where they act, and thus, physical agents must be in contact with their patients. Agents act through the very forms by which they are actual and thus their power is located where they exist. In the special case of projectile motion, an instrument takes on the form which is the principal agent's power and carries it to the location of the patient which is acted upon. Thus, even in this case, the agent's power is in contact with that upon which it acts.

CHAPTER 3

Active Powers

Aquinas, like Aristotle, recognizes several different types of cause. Each species of cause is distinguished from the others according to how the cause influences the being of its effect. Action is the distinctive way in which efficient causes influence their effects.[1] Active powers are the features of agents which enable them to perform actions. Aquinas writes: "For every action, there are two things to consider, namely the thing itself which acts, and the power (*virtutem*) by which it acts, just as fire heats through heat."[2] Experience shows that not just any type of substance can engage in any type of action. For example, a carrot cannot perform the action of heating. Furthermore, not every feature of a substance is relevant to explaining how it is able to act in a certain way. For instance, the red-orange color of fire is not that which explains why it can heat things and the carrot cannot. To fully understand how substances act in certain ways, we must isolate the features of substances through which they act. The main goal of this chapter is to reconstruct the central aspects of Aquinas's conception of active powers.

The chapter begins with an overview of Aquinas's understanding of the distinction between potentiality and actuality. As we saw in Chapter 1, Aquinas uses a number of Latin terms to refer to active powers.[3] The Latin term *potentiae* is the one which he uses most often to refer to active powers in general, as opposed to a specific type of active power. For example, he writes: "active potentiality is the principle of acting on another."[4] In the

---

[1] See Section 1.1.
[2] *ScG* III c. 70 (ed. Marietti, 99, n. 2464): "In quolibet enim agente est duo considerare, scilicet rem ipsam quae agit, et virtutem qua agit: sicut ignis calefacit per calorem." See also *ST* I q. 36, a.3 ad 1.
[3] See Section 1.5.
[4] *ST* I q. 25, a. 1 (ed. Leon., vol. 4, 290): "potentia activa est principium agendi in aliud"; see also *De operat. occult.* (ed. Leon., vol. 43, 184): "dicimus potentiam principium intrinsecum quo agens agit, uel patiens patitur."

first section, we will see how Aquinas understood the notion of a potentiality, as well as where active power fits into his division of types of
potentialities. Next, we will examine the criteria he proposes for distinguishing between diverse active powers. It is clear that there are many
different types of action which occur in the natural world. The question
arises of whether diverse types of power are required to explain how
substances engage in different kinds of action. Put otherwise, can multiple
types of action arises through one and the same active power? After
examining Aquinas's views on this topic, we will move to consider his
views on what active powers are ontologically. We will see that Aquinas
identifies active power with form. Forms are both that by which a
substance is actual in a determinate way and that through which a
substance is capable of communicating the same type of form to another
substance. We will examine Aquinas's rationale for this view, as well as its
implications. Though Aquinas thinks that active powers are forms, we will
see that he denies that every form is an active power which enables its
bearer to communicate a form of the same type to another by material
change. For example, the form of redness is not an active power for making
other substances red. In the final sections of the chapter, we will examine
Aquinas's views about which forms are and are not active powers for
initiating material change.

3.1 The Twofold Distinction between Potentiality and Actuality

Since Aquinas appeals to the distinction between potentiality and actuality
to understand causal powers, it is useful to first begin with an overview of
this distinction. Aquinas's most extensive discussion of potentiality and
actuality occurs in his commentary on book IX of Aristotle's *Metaphysics*.
There he explains, following Aristotle, that potentiality and actuality are
basic notions which cannot be defined. Yet, also like Aristotle, he thinks
that we can come to an understanding of the difference between potentiality and actuality through examples and analogies. He writes:

> For example, we might consider the proportion that exists between the one
> who is building and the one who is capable of building; the one who is
> awake to the one who is sleeping; and of him who sees to him who has his
> eyes closed although he has a power to see; and of that which has been
> separated from unformed matter, namely that which is formed through
> the operation of nature or art, to what is unformed; and similarly that which
> is through the separation of it prepared to that which is not prepared;

or that which is elaborated to that which is not elaborated. But in each of these different pairs one member will be actual and the other potential.[5]

A being which is in potentiality is one which is incomplete in a given way, but yet it is able to be completed in that same way. It is imperfect in a certain respect, but yet it is able to be perfected in that same respect. The incompleteness and imperfection of being-in-potentiality is what sets it apart from being-in-actuality. The one who has his eyes shut is not in the same state as the one who is seeing. The materials which have not been worked on or prepared are not the same as the final product. Yet, a being-in-potentiality's capability for being perfected and completed distinguishes it from a pure non-being. The one who can see, but has his eyes shut is in a different state with respect to seeing than the one who is not only not seeing, but also physically incapable of seeing. Bricks and planks are not an actual house, but yet they are in a different state with respect to being a house than sand or water is – the bricks are capable of being made into a house, while sand and water is not. These examples illustrate what Aquinas means by the claim that "a being in potentiality is midway between a pure non-being and a being-in-actuality."[6] A non-being simply is not. A being in potentiality is something which exists. It is that which is capable of being perfected, determined, or completed. Yet, it differs from a being-in-actuality because it is *not* perfected and completed. In this way, beings-in-potentiality share features of beings-in-actuality, namely existence in reality, and features of non-beings, namely incompleteness and imperfection. From Aquinas's discussion of potentiality and actuality, we can conclude that potentialities and actualities come in pairs. For every potentiality there is a corresponding actuality. To describe something as an actuality or a potentiality is to state whether it is the complete and fulfilled member of a pair or the or incomplete or unfulfilled one.

As is well known, Aquinas appeals to the distinction between potentiality and actuality to describe the functional relationship between matter and form with respect to material substances. Matter is that which is able

---

[5] *In IX Meta.* lec. 5 (ed. Marietti, 437, n. 1827):

> Ut si accipiamus proportionem aedificantis ad aedificabile, et vigilantis ad dormientem, et eius qui videt ad eum qui habet clausos oculos cum habeat potentiam visivam, et eius quod segregatur a materia, idest per operationem artis vel naturae formatur, et ita a materia informi segregatur; et similiter per separationem eius quod est praeparatum, ad illud quod non est praeparatum, sive quod est elaboratum ad id quod non est elaboratum. Sed quorumlibet sic differentium altera pars erit actus, et altera potentia.

[6] *In I Phys.* lec. 9 (ed. Leon., vol. 2, 28): "Ens enim in potentia est quasi medium inter purum non ens et ens in actu."

to take on form and be perfected by it, while form is that which perfects matter. In substantial change, prime matter is perfected by a substantial form to compose an actual substance of a determinate species. In accidental change, the substance itself functions as matter and it is perfected by an accidental form and exists in a new way through it. For example, water comes to exist as hot through the form of heat and water is itself the matter which is perfected by the form of heat. Aquinas claims that "matter and form relate to each other as potentiality and actuality."[7] It is important to note that form is not itself a being-in-actuality. Rather, it is that which perfects and completes matter to compose a being-in-actuality.[8] The form of heat, for example, is not itself a being-in-actuality, but rather it is an actuality through which water is a hot being in actuality. Matter is a potentiality for being. It is that which is able to be perfected and completed by form to compose a being-in-actuality. The potentiality for being is essentially a potentiality for receiving form.

In a number of texts, Aquinas states that there is another sort of potentiality in addition to the potentiality for being. He writes: "[P]otentiality is twofold, namely the potentiality for being and the potentiality for acting . . ."[9] In addition to the potentialities for being which are actualized by form to compose a being-in-actuality, there are potentialities which are realized by action. These are active causal powers. Like potentialities for being, potentialities for acting have a midway status between complete nothingness and actuality. Just as the matter which can take on the form of the house stands midway between nothingness and an actually existing house, so too do dormant active potentialities stand midway between the complete absence of causality and actual causal activity. For example, there is something really different between the fire which is not burning anything right now and a brick. Though both may not be actually burning anything at an instant, there is something within the fire which is at present unfulfilled or unmanifested at that instant. There is something real within the fire through which it is ordered to the further perfection of actual causal activity and through which it could give rise to burning. In this regard, active potentialities are like potentialities for being. Both sorts

---

[7] *ScG* II c. 71 (ed. Marietti, 206, n. 1480): "materia et forma habent se ut potentia et actus." See also *In II Sent.* d. 1, q. 2, a. 4 ad 3 and *De ver.* q. 8, a. 9.

[8] For discussion of this point and Aquinas's comparison of matter and form and potentiality and actuality, see Brower, *Aquinas's Ontology of the Material World*, 67–69.

[9] *ST* I-II q. 55, a. 2 (ed. Leon., vol. 6, 351): "duplex sit potentia, scilicet potentia ad esse et potentia ad agere . . ." See also *De pot.* q. 1, a. 1 (ed. Pession, 9): "Unde et similiter duplex est potentia"; *De malo* q. 1, a. 5; *ST* I, q. 48, a. 5; and *ST* I q. 105, a. 5.

of potentialities are incomplete or unfulfilled realities that are proportioned to a further actuality or perfection.

Just as Aquinas identifies two different types of potentialities, the potentiality for being and the potentiality for action, he likewise identifies two different sort of actualities which correspond to each. He writes: "Act is twofold, first and second. First act is the form and integrity of a thing and second act is its operation."[10] As already discussed, form is that which completes or perfects the potentiality for being. Action is the fulfillment and completion of active potentiality. Aquinas writes: "the action of anything is a certain completion of its potentiality."[11] Just as the form of fire completes or perfects the matter out of which the fire is composed, in a similar way the action of burning is the corresponding realization or fulfillment of the fire's active potential to burn something.

Though action is like form insofar as it is the completion or fulfillment of a corresponding potentiality, Aquinas explains in his commentary on Aristotle's *Metaphysics* that there are different ways in which an actuality can fulfill or realize a potentiality.[12] The first way in which an actuality can complete or perfect a potentiality is by inhering in it. This is the way in which form, namely first actuality, perfects or completes matter. Through inhering in it, form actualizes its corresponding potentiality, namely potentiality for being, to compose a being-in-actuality. In the case of active potentialities, the relevant actuality completes or perfects its corresponding potentiality in a different way. The actualities of active potentialities do not inhere in the active potentiality. Rather the act of an active potentiality arises from it. Unlike potentialities for being, active potentialities are not in

---

[10] *ST* I q. 48, a. 5 (ed. Leon., vol. 4, 496): "Actus autem est duplex: primus, et secundus. Actus quidem primus est forma et integritas rei: actus autem secundus est operatio." In the following text he explicitly traces the distinction to Aristotle: *In II de caelo* lec. 4 (ed. Leon., vol. 3, 136): "dictum est enim in II de anima quod forma est actus primus, operatio autem est actus secundus, tanquam perfectio et finis operantis ..."

[11] *ScG* II c. 9 (ed. Marietti, 120, n. 900): "Actio alicuius rei est complementum quoddam potentiae eius ..."

[12] *In IX Meta.* l. 5 (ed. Marietti, 437, n. 1828–29):

> *diversimode dicatur actus.*.. non omnia dicimus similiter esse actu, sed hoc diversimode. Et haec diversitas considerari potest per diversas proportiones. Potest enim *sic* accipi proportio, ut dicamus, quod sicut hoc est in hoc, ita hoc in hoc ... Et per hunc modum proportionis accipitur comparatio substantiae, idest formae, ad materiam; nam forma in materia dicitur esse. *Alius modus* proportionis est, ut dicamus quod sicut habet se hoc ad hoc, ita hoc ad hoc; puta sicut se habet visus ad videndum, ita auditus ad audiendum. Et per hunc modum proportionis accipitur comparatio motus ad potentiam motivam, vel cuiuscumque operationis ad potentiam operativam.

On this passage and the topic of how actualities can perfect potentialities in different ways, see also Section 6.3.

need of an actuality to inhere in them in order to be perfected as beings. Fire's potentiality to heat, for example, is not an incomplete or imperfect way the fire itself is which can be perfected by a form. Rather, an active potentiality is incomplete in the sense that it has not fulfilled the function to which it is ordered, that is, it has not manifested itself in activity. The actuality which corresponds to an active potentiality is the activity or operation which it is for. When this operation or activity arises from an active potentiality, that potentiality is fulfilled or complete in the sense that it has achieved its purpose. Consider again a fire's active potentiality to heat. This potentiality has not fulfilled the function of an active potentiality until it gives rise to heating. The action of heating is the actuality of the potentiality to heat insofar as this action is the goal or purpose of the potentiality.

As we saw in Chapter 1, in addition to distinguishing between the potentiality for being vs. the potentiality for acting, Aquinas draws a distinction between active vs. passive potentialities.[13] An active potentiality is the principle in the agent through which it acts, while a passive potentiality is that in the patient through which it undergoes action. Before moving on to the question of what active potentialities are in themselves, it is worth explicitly noting the relationship between Aquinas's two sets of distinctions (i.e. potentiality for being vs. for acting and active vs. passive potentiality). It is clear that the potentiality for action coincides with active potentialities since active potentialities are by definition potentialities through which an agent acts. In Chapter 5, I will argue that for Aquinas passive potentialities are the same in reality as potentialities for being.[14] Thus, the distinction between the potentiality for being and the potentiality for action is equivalent to the distinction between active and passive potentiality.

3.2 The Conditions for Positing and Defining a Distinct Active Power

Many agents in the physical world can perform multiple different types of action. For example, fire is able to heat and illuminate. Water is able to cool and to moisten. This raises the question of how many active potentialities should be attributed to a substance in order to explain how it is able to perform all of its actions. Must a distinct active potentiality be posited to account for every action which a substance is able to perform?

[13] See Section 1.1.   [14] See Section 5.4.

Aquinas's views on how active powers are individuated and distinguished from one another rely heavily on his understanding of the relationship between potentiality and actuality.

Aquinas offers the following principle to explain when there is justification for positing a distinct potentiality in a substance:

> [P]otentiality, according to what it is, is described with reference to act. Therefore, act must be that through which a potentiality is defined and potentialities must be diversified according to the diversity of acts.[15]

Aquinas states in this passage that since potentialities depend on a corresponding actuality to be defined, there must be an actuality which corresponds to every potentiality. As we have seen, a potentiality is a reality which is in some respect incomplete, imperfect or unrealized. It can only be posited that there is some incomplete, imperfect or unrealized reality by making reference to its corresponding actuality. The active potentiality to heat, for example, can only be defined in reference to the action of heating, which is its fulfillment and manifestation. Without reference to the activity of heating, there is no way to identify or describe the active potentiality from which this act arises. Thus, there cannot be a potentiality without a corresponding actuality.

Aquinas recognizes that it is important to understand how actualities themselves are distinguished into different types in order to fully understand when there are grounds to posit a distinct type of active potentiality. Regarding how different types of acts are distinguished, he writes: "An act, however, has its species from its object ... In the case of active potentialities, the objects [of their acts] are their ends."[16] According to this passage, actions are distinguished from one another in virtue of their objects. In scholastic terminology the term "object" derives from the Latin verb *obiicio*, which means to "to throw or put before" or "to be situated near or opposite (to)."[17] By their very nature, acts are placed or situated with reference to some other reality. Every action of an active power has an order to some end state and the end state is its object. Accordingly, actions of active powers are categorized into types according to the particular end

---

[15] *Q.D. de anima* 13 (ed. Leon., vol. 24/1, 115): "[P]otentia, id quod est, dicitur ad actum. Vnde oportet quod per actum definiatur potentia, et secundum diuersitatem actuum potentie diuersificentur." See also *ST* I q. 54, a. 3 and *De ver.* q. 15, a. 2 ad 12.

[16] *Q.D. de anima* 13 (ed. Leon., vol. 24/1, 115): "Actus autem ex obiectis speciem habet ... [S]i autem sunt actiuarum potentiarum, obiecta sunt ut fines."

[17] My discussion of the meaning of "object" is indebted to Joseph Pilsner, *The Specification of Human Actions in St. Thomas Aquinas* (Oxford: Oxford University Press, 2006), 73–74. He cites the *Oxford Latin Dictionary* for these definitions.

or term to which they are directed. For example, an action of heating is an act of heating, rather than an act of cooling, because it results in heat rather than coolness.

So far it is clear that Aquinas thinks that there can be no active potentiality in a substance that lacks a corresponding actuality, since it is on the basis of distinct actualities that we are able to define and distinguish potentialities. Yet, the question remains of whether there are any potentialities from which two different types of action can arise. For example, could it be the case that water both cools and moistens through one and the same active potentiality? Aquinas thinks that natural active powers are determined to produce only one type of action. He contrasts natural active powers with rational powers, which are open to contrary actions, such as medicine and the power to build.[18] Aquinas thinks that something further, namely a choice, is required to determine which of the two possible acts proceeds from a rational power.[19] Since natural substances lack intellect and will, their active powers are of themselves determined to one action. Accordingly, in the case of natural active powers, there is a one-to-one correspondence between active powers and the actions that immediately arise from them. He writes:

> Natural active principles are determined always to the same act. Therefore, the diverse species in natural actions are not only according to the objects, which are the ends or terms, but also according to the active principles; just as to heat and to cool are distinguished according to species by heat and cold.[20]

Since each type of natural active power is a power for producing a single determinate act, there is a diverse active power for each different type of action. As Aquinas explains in this passage, this implies that natural actions differ in kind from one another based both on the active power from which they arise and on the object (i.e. end state) in which they result. For

---

[18] *In IX Meta.* lec. 2, n. 1788.

[19] *In IX Meta.* lec. 4 (ed. Marietti, 435, n. 1820): "sequitur quod necesse est, praeter potentiam rationalem, quae est communis ad duo contraria, poni aliquid, quod appropriet eam ad alterum faciendum ad hoc quod exeat in actum. Hoc autem est appetitus aut prohaeresis, idest electio quorumcumque, idest electio quae pertinet ad rationem."

[20] *ST* I-II q. 72, a. 3 (ed. Leon., vol. 7, 15): "Nam principia activa naturalia sunt determinata semper ad eosdem actus: et ideo diversae species in actibus naturalibus attenduntur non solum secundum obiecta, quae sunt fines vel termini, sed etiam secundum principia activa; sicut calefacere et infrigidare distinguuntur specie secundum calidum et frigidum." See also *De pot.* q. 6, a. 8. Aquinas goes on to explain that the species of a voluntary action cannot similarly be known by knowing the active potentiality from which the act arose. This is because unlike in the case of natural principles, the will is not determined to one type of act.

example, the action of heating differs from the act of cooling both because it results in coolness rather than heat and because it arose from an active power for heating, rather than an active power for cooling. Since each natural active power is determined toward one act, each natural action arises from a distinct type of active power.

Based on Aquinas's claim that natural active powers are ordered toward a single type of action, it would seem that he denies that there are natural active powers from which multiple different types of actions can arise. While this describes his position in general, there is one exception. Aquinas thinks it is possible for some natural active potentialities to give rise to multiple different types of action as long as those actions have a certain relationship to one another. He writes:

> When all acts follow from one another, proceeding from the agent according to the same nature, every act proceeds from one power (*virtute*). They do not each have a separate power from which they may proceed. This is evident in corporeal things: since fire, by heating, liquifies and rarifies and yet, there is not in fire some liquifying power and another rarifying one. Rather, all of these acts are done by fire through its one power to heat.[21]

In a text just prior to this passage Aquinas explained that when a type of action arises in virtue of a prior type of act, just as the melting of the wax follows from its being heated, it is not necessary that a diverse active potentiality be posited to account for the origin of each of these actions. The potentiality from which the prior act (e.g. heating) proceeded is sufficient to account for the acts which arise from it (e.g. melting). Aquinas claims that when a multitude of acts follows from one active potentiality in virtue of one arising from another, the potentiality is properly defined only in terms of the act which follows immediately from the potentiality.[22] For example, the power through which fire heats and liquefies is properly defined as an active potentiality to heat because this is the act which immediately arises from the active potentiality. The power gives rise to other acts in virtue of the act of heating.

---

[21] *ST* II-II q. 29, a. 4 (ed. Leon., vol. 8, 238–39):

> cum omnes actus se invicem consequuntur, secundum eandem rationem ab agente procedentes, omnes huiusmodi actus ab una virtute procedunt, nec habent singuli singulas virtutes a quibus procedant. Ut patet in rebus corporalibus: quia enim ignis calefaciendo liquefacit et rarefacit, non est in igne alia virtus liquefactiva et alia rarefactiva, sed omnes actus hos operatur ignis per unam suam virtutem calefactivam.

[22] *ST* II-II q. 28, a. 4 (ed. Leon., vol. 8, 234): "Et quia posteriores actus non procedunt ab habitu virtutis nisi per actum priorem, inde est quod virtus non definitur nec denominatur nisi ab actu priori, quamvis etiam alii actus ab ea consequantur."

3.3 The Identification of Active Potentiality with Form

Above we saw that Aquinas maintained that there were two different actuality–potentiality pairs, namely potentiality for being and form which actualizes it *and* active potentiality and action.[23] We can gain further insight into Aquinas's views about what active potentialities are in themselves by examining some texts in which Aquinas explains the relationship between these two different actuality-potentiality pairs. Aquinas claims that first actuality (i.e. form) which actualizes matter is in fact the same reality as active potentiality. He writes: "The imperfect is always for the sake of the more perfect. Just as matter is for the sake of form, which is first actuality, first actuality is for the sake of its operation, which is second actuality."[24] Aquinas claims here that just as matter is a potentiality for form, so too is form a potentiality for action. Elsewhere he similarly writes: "But first act is said to be in potentiality with respect to second act which is operation."[25] On Aquinas's view, the forms that are active powers are both actualities and potentialities. They are actualities with respect to matter and potentialities with respect to action. Aquinas conceives of these forms as both that which confers being-in-actuality and that through which a substance acts. Even as such a form is actualizing matter to constitute a being-in-actuality, the form remains unrealized when compared with the action which is able to arise from it.[26] The form has not fulfilled its purpose until action arises from it.

---

[23] See Section 3.1.

[24] *ST* I q. 105, a. 5 (ed. Leon., vol. 5, 475): "Semper enim imperfectum est propter perfectius: sicut igitur materia est propter formam, ita forma, quae est actus primus, est propter suam operationem, quae est actus secundus . . ." See also *ST* I q. 76, a. 4 ad 1 (ed. Leon., vol. 5, 224): "Sed actus primus dicitur in potentia respectu actus secundi, qui est operatio." *ST* III q. 13, a. 1 (ed. Leon., vol. 11, 171): "Potentia autem activa cuiuslibet rei sequitur formam ipsius, quae est principium agendi. Forma autem vel est ipsa natura rei, sicut in simplicibus: vel est constituens ipsam rei naturam, in his scilicet quae sunt composita ex materia et forma. Unde manifestum est quod potentia activa cuiuslibet rei consequitur naturam ipsius."

[25] *ST* I q. 76, a. 4 ad 1 (ed. Leon., vol. 5, 224): "Sed actus primus dicitur in potentia respectu actus secundi, qui est operatio."

[26] See for instance *De malo* q. 1, a. 5 (ed. Leon., vol. 23, 24): "Actu autem primo inhaerente adhuc adest potentia ad actum secundum . . ." Contemporary philosophers have made some attempt to incorporate the Aristotelian language of potentiality and act into their discussions of causal powers. Yet, many have not been sensitive enough to the distinction between first act and second act. This distinction is required to understand how forms (or properties in contemporary parlance) can be both actual qualities of objects and yet in potential to operation. Overlooking the twofold character of act and potentiality leads David Oderberg to writes in *Real Essentialism* (New York: Routledge, 2007), 139: "[I]t is hard to see what could be meant [i.e. to maintain that there is a potential and actual aspect to each property], since actuality and potentiality are distinct and *incompatible* . . . [I]nsofar as something is in act, it is not in potentiality, and insofar as it is in potentiality, it is not in

Aquinas routinely identifies form as first actuality and action as second actuality. Yet, it is important to clarify the respect in which form has priority over action. Form, as first actuality, is naturally prior to action, as second actuality, since actions arise from an agent in virtue of form. To say that form is naturally prior to action is to say that action ontologically depends on form. Substances cannot act without form. However, Aquinas considers action to be more perfect than form insofar is it is the perfection or fulfillment to which form is ordered. Furthermore, though Aquinas calls form "first act," he notes that the term "act" was first used to refer to the operation (i.e. the action) of a thing. The name "act" was then by analogy applied to form since form is both the principle through which substances act and the goal of the substance's action is to transmit a form to another (as will be discussed below).[27]

While Aquinas thinks that "first act" (i.e. form) is in potentiality to "second act" (i.e. operation), he believes the substance in which the form inheres, rather than the form itself, is the agent which performs the action.[28] Aquinas writes:

> [T]he act of a form is twofold. One is an operation, such as to heat, which is second act; and this act of the form is attributed to the supposit. The other act of a form is to inform matter, which is first act; for instance, to enliven the body is the act of the soul; and this act of the form is not attributed to the supposit.[29]

To say that "first act" is attributed to the form is to say that the form itself is what actualizes matter. For example, a soul (i.e. a form of a living thing) is that which makes a living body alive. To say that "second act" is not attributed to the form, but rather to the supposit, means that the whole material substance is the agent which acts upon other material bodies in the world. Aquinas explains this further in the following passage:

---

act ..." Aquinas by contrast explicitly claims that "active potentiality is not divided from act, but rather it is founded upon it ..." See *ST* I q. 25, a. 1 ad 1.

[27] *De pot.* q. 1, a.1 (ed. Pession, 9): "nomen actus primo fuit attributum operationi: sic enim quasi omnes intelligunt actum; secundo autem exinde fuit translatum ad formam, in quantum forma est principium operationis et finis." Elsewhere, however, Aquinas cites a different reason for why forms are called "act": *De prin. nat.* c. 1 (ed. Leon., vol. 43, 39): "Et quia forma facit esse in actu, ideo forma dicitur esse actus ..."

[28] See Section 1.1, esp. fn. 13.

[29] *De ver.* q. 27, a.3 ad 25 (ed. Leon., vol. 22 3/1, 801): "duplex est actus formae: unus qui est operatio, ut calefacere, qui est actus secundus, et talis actus formae supposito attribuitur; alius vero actus formae est materiae informatio, quae est actus primus, sicut vivificare corpus est actus animae, et talis actus supposito formae non attribuitur."

[P]otentiality is nothing other than the principle of something's operation, either an action or passion. Indeed it is not the principle which is the acting or suffering subject, rather it is that by which the agent acts or the patient suffers. Just as the building art is a potentiality in the builder who builds through it, and heat is a potentiality in the fire which heats through heat, and dryness is a potentiality in wood because in virtue of it wood is combustible.[30]

Forms are principles in virtue of which substances exist in a determinate way. They are principles which explain why subsistent beings have the attributes that they actually do have. They are not themselves subjects of change and bearers of accidents. Thus, forms do not have the right sort of ontological status to impact material objects in the world by efficient causation. Forms cannot touch, bump, or scratch material substances. Only complete substances can act upon and react to one another. For example, the form of heat can actualize a substance to be hot, but it cannot heat something according to efficient causation. Only the complete substance actualized by heat can touch another substance and efficiently cause it to have a form of heat inherent in it.

3.4 Form Is Active Potentiality Because Goodness and Perfection Are Diffusive

In Aquinas's system, forms have two ontological roles: First, they are that through which a substance exists in a determinate way in first actuality. Second, they are that by which substances are in potentiality to second actuality. The form of heat, for instance, makes fire both hot and able to heat another. Aquinas himself explicitly recognizes that not every form is an active power for affecting material change.[31] Nevertheless, he thinks that all forms as such are principles of some type of activity. Forms which are not principles for changing matter, nevertheless, are principles of action upon the senses and intellects of cognizant beings. A sweet cake, for example, cannot make a fork sweet by touching it, yet it can actualize

---

[30] *Q.D. de anima* q. 12 (ed. Leon., vol. 24/1,108): "potentia nichil aliud est quam principium operationis alicuius, siue sit actio siue passio; non quidem principium quod est subiectum agens aut patiens, set id quo agens agit aut patiens patitur: sicut ars aedificativa est potentia in edificatore qui per eam edificat, et calor in igne qui calore calefacit, et siccum est potentia in lignis quia secundum hoc sunt combustibilia."

[31] See for instance *ST* I q. 78, a. 3 (ed. Leon., vol. 5, 254): "non omnia accidentia habent vim immutativam secundum se; sed solae qualitates tertiae speciei, secundum quas contingit alteratio."

sweetness in the sense of taste. A red thing cannot make another object red by touching it, but through its form of redness it can actualize redness in the power of vision.[32] Furthermore, with the cooperation of the active power of intellect, any form can communicate itself to an intellect.[33] For instance, though a triangular-shaped piece of wood cannot make another piece of wood into a triangle by touching it, nevertheless, with the agent intellect cooperating, a triangle can actualize a thought about a triangle in my intellect. Thus, while only some forms are active powers that enable their bearer to transmute matter, every form enables its bearer to cause some form of change in another. The goal of this section is to understand why Aquinas thinks that forms are not merely the actuality of matter but also active potentialities for affecting change in another.

The first step to understanding Aquinas's rationale for why forms are principles of action is grasping the connection between form and goodness. Forms are principles of action insofar as they are principles of goodness. Aquinas thought that forms were principles of goodness since they are principles of actuality. It is through their inherent forms that substances exist with various perfections and by having various perfections, substances are good. Aquinas writes that: "To be in act, therefore, constitutes the nature of the good . . ."[34] Given that forms are principles of actuality, they are also principles of goodness.

In Aquinas's view, there is an important connection between goodness and causal activity. Through reading and commenting on works such as Pseudo-Dionysius's *Divine Names*, Aquinas encountered the idea that good things seek to spread their goodness to others. Pseudo-Dionysius writes the following in his *Divine Names*: "The Good by being extends its goodness to all things. For as our sun, not by choosing or taking thought but by merely being, enlightens all things, so the Good . . . by its mere

---

[32] See for instance *Quodl. VIII* q. 2, a. 1 (ed. Leon., vol. 25/1, 56): "Dicendum quod anima humana similitudines rerum, quibus cognoscit, a rebus accipit illo modo accipiendi quo patiens accipit ab agente. Quod non est intelligendum quasi agens influat in patiens eamdem numero speciem quam habet in seipso, set generat sui similem, educendo de potencia in actum. Et per hunc modum dicitur species coloris deferri a corpore colorato ad uisum."

[33] In *De ver.* q. 10, a. 6, Aquinas explains that the active intellect is the primary agent and the phantasms (i.e. the likenesses of individual things) are the secondary agents which act upon the passive intellect. For a helpful discussion of how the agent intellect cooperates with the likenesses of sensible things in cognition, see Therese Scarpelli Cory, "Rethinking Abstractionism: Aquinas's Intellectual Light and Some Arabic Sources," *Journal for the History of Philosophy* 53:4 (2015): 607–46. For a very brief overview of Aquinas's cognition theory, see Cory, *Aquinas on Human Self-Knowledge*, 9–12.

[34] *ScG* I c. 37 (ed. Marietti, 47, n. 306): "Esse igitur actu boni rationem constituit . . ."

existence sends forth upon all things the beams of its goodness."[35] In several texts, Aquinas himself endorses the idea that goodness is self-diffusive. For example, he writes: "Goodness, therefore, seeks to communicate perfection because the good is diffusive of its being."[36] Elsewhere he states, "Communication of being and goodness arises from the good. This is evident from the very nature of the good and from its definition (*ratione*)."[37] In Aquinas's view, good things do not stay self-contained. Rather it is of their very nature to go beyond themselves to make other things good. From the passage quoted from Pseudo-Dionysius, it might seem that the "diffusiveness of goodness" means that good things quite literally emit little bits of their goodness as the sun beams out rays of light. Aquinas, however, explicitly rejects this model. He explains that the diffusiveness of goodness does not describe the mechanism whereby substances act, but rather it tells us about the goal for which substances act. He writes: "When it is said that the good is diffusive by its nature, diffusion should not be understood in a manner which implies the operation of an efficient cause, but rather as implying the having of a final cause."[38] According to Aquinas's understanding of the Dionysian axiom, good things do not emit their goodness by efficient causality, but rather

---

[35] I quote this translation from Arthur Lovejoy, *The Great Chain of Being: The Study of the History of an Idea* (Cambridge, MA: Harvard University Press, 2009), 68. For the original, see ch. 4.1 of Pseudo-Dionysius, *De divinis nominibus*, in *Patrologiae cursus completus, Series Graeca*, ed. J. P. Migne, vol. 3 (Paris: Garnier, 1857), col. 693. For the notion of the diffusiveness of goodness in Plato, see his *Timaeus* 29e–30a where he claims that insofar as the demiurge is good it desires to make others things good like itself.

[36] See for instance *In IV Sent.* d. 46, q. 2, a. 1, qc. 2 (ed. Parma, vol. 7/2, 1143): "Bonitas ergo respicit communicationem perfectionis, quia bonum est diffusivum sui esse." For relevant literature see Julien Péghaire, "L'axiome 'bonum est diffusivum sui' dans le néoplatonisme et le thomisme," *Revue de l'Université d'Ottawa* 1 (1932): 5–30. As Péghaire notes, Aquinas attributes the axiom to Pseudo-Dionysius. For discussion of Aquinas's views on causality as the diffusiveness of goodness, see also De Finance, *Être et agir dans la philosophie se Saint Thomas*, 62–68.

[37] *ScG* I c. 37 (ed. Marietti, 47, n. 307): "Communicatio esse et bonitatis ex bonitate procedit. Quod quidem patet et ex ipsa natura boni, et ex eius ratione."

[38] *De ver.* q. 21, a. 1 ad 4 (ed. Leon. vol. 22 3/1, 594): "Cum autem dicitur quod bonum sit diffusivum secundum sui rationem, non est intelligenda diffusio secundum quod importat operationem causae efficientis, sed secundum quod importat habitudinem causae finalis . . ." Aquinas's interpreters agree that he understands the Dionysian principle according to final causality. See, for example, Péghaire, "L'axiome 'bonum est diffusivum sui' dans le néoplatonisme et le thomisme" ; John Wippel, "Aquinas on God's Freedom to Create or Not," in *Metaphysical Themes in Thomas Aquinas II* (Washington, DC: The Catholic University of America Press, 2007), 218–39, esp. 237–39; and Norman Kretzmann, "A General Problem of Creation," in *Being and Goodness: The Concept of the Good in Metaphysics and Philosophical Theology*, ed. Scott MacDonald (Ithaca, NY: Cornell University Press, 1991), 208–28, at 220. Kretzmann claims that Aquinas's interpretation of the Dionysian principle is "wrongheaded" and "counterintuitive" and Wippel admits that Aquinas's interpretation of the principle may not express its original author's understanding of it.

they have as their final cause, namely their end or goal, spreading their goodness to another. Put otherwise, "diffusing goodness" is not a description of how the agent acts, but rather it is a description of the goal toward which the agent acts. Substances which are in act are ordered toward making other substances actual in similar ways. Thus, it is through being actualized by a form that a substance has an aptitude for causing that form in another. Aquinas writes: "To act toward some effect is proper to a being-in-act: for each one acts insofar as it is in act. Therefore, every being in act is apt to make something existing in act."[39] It is the nature of actual beings to act toward producing certain effects beyond themselves.

Forms do not merely confer on their bearers an order toward actualizing a form of the same kind in another. They are also the very power by which the form is caused by its bearer in another. Aquinas claims that forms, by their nature as actualities, must be the sort of reality that can be caused by one substance that bears the form in another. He writes: "communication follows upon the nature of act: hence every form, insofar as it is a form, is communicable. . ."[40] Since actuality is a good which by its nature is diffusive, forms must be the sort of reality which is such that its bearer can induce it in another. Put otherwise, if a bearer of a form could not make that same form in another, then act would not be communicable, and this would be at odds with the notion that goodness is diffusive. Thus, since act is a diffusive good, forms must empower their bearer to make the same form to another.

As should be clear by now, Aquinas's conception of form as a diffusive good both explains why agents are able to act and what sort of effect each agent produces. Through their forms, substances are ordered toward the goal of making another have the same form. Aquinas writes: "The proximate end of each agent is to induce a similitude of its form in another, just as the end of fire's heating is to induce a similitude of its heat in the patient."[41] The fact that each agent strives to make another

---

[39] *ScG* II c. 6 (ed. Marietti, 118, n. 881): "Agere autem aliquem effectum per se convenit enti in actu: nam unumquodque agens secundum hoc agit quod in actu est. Omne igitur ens actu natum est agere aliquid actu existens." For discussion of Aquinas's use of the principle "everything acts insofar as it is in act," see Kendall Fisher, "Thomas Aquinas on Hylomorphism and the In-Act Principle," *British Journal for the History of Philosophy*, 25:6 (2017): 1053–72.

[40] *In I Sent.* d. 4, q. 1, a. 1 (ed. Mandonnet-Moos, vol. 1, 132): "communicatio enim consequitur rationem actus: unde omnis forma, quantum est de se, communicabilis est . . ." See also *De pot.* q. 2, a.1.

[41] *ST* II-II q. 123, a. 7 (ed. Leon., vol. 10, 16): "Finis autem proximus uniuscuiusque agentis est ut similitudinem suae formae in alterum inducat: sicut finis ignis calefacientis est ut inducat similitudinem sui caloris in patiente . . ."

actual in the same ways as itself is what explains why the powers of natural agents are ordered toward the production of a single effect. Aquinas writes: "every natural agent acts toward a determinate species because every agent makes its like."[42] On Aquinas's view, active powers are not powers for a generic type of causal influencing. Nor are they "multi-track" powers which can immediately lead to a number of different types of action. Rather, each active power is a power for immediately causing a single action, namely the one which terminates in a form of the same species as itself.

Because each agent acts through one of its inherent forms to produce a form of the same kind in another, Aquinas thinks that an agent's effects can be said to pre-exist in it. Aquinas writes: "The similitude of an effect to an agent cause is attained through the form of the effect which preexists in the agent. For an *agent makes something similar* in form *to itself* insofar as it acts. For the form of the agent is received in the effect ..."[43] Since the form by which the natural agent acts is of the same species as the effect it produces, there is a sense in which the natural agent's specific types of effect preexist in it. Just as the carpenter's idea of the bench has the same formal features as the bench which he makes, so too does a fire have the same formal features as the effect which it produces. The forms which a natural cause possesses are likenesses according to species of the effects which it is able to produce through these forms. Since agents make effects like themselves, we can know the natures of agents through their effects. For Aquinas, an agent's effects reveal its own nature.[44]

---

[42] *In X Meta.* lec. 11 (ed. Marietti, 503, n. 2134): "omne agens naturale agit ad determinatam speciem, quia agit sibi simile." See also *ST* I q. 44, a. 4 ad 2 (ed. Leon., vol. 4, 461–2): "forma generati non est finis generationis nisi inquantum est similitudo formae generantis, quod suam similitudinem communicare intendit." *ScG* II c. 79 (ed. Marietti, 230, n. 1600): "Operatio enim rei demonstrat substantiam et esse ipsius: quia unumquodque operatur secundum quod est ens, et propria operatio rei sequitur propriam ipsius naturam."

[43] *In II ScG* c. 46 (ed. Marietti, 167, n. 1233): "Similitudo effectus ad causam agentem attenditur secundum formam effectus quae praeexistit in agente: *agens* enim *agit sibi simile* in forma secundum quam agit. Forma autem agentis recipitur quidem in effectu ..." Aquinas clarifies in *De malo* q. 1, a. 3 ad 2 that the claim that effects preexist in their causes only applies to *per se* causes.

[44] On this topic see Norris Clarke, "Action as the Self-Revelation of Being: A Central Theme in the Thought of St. Thomas," in *Explorations in Metaphysics* (Notre Dame, IN: University of Notre Dame Press, 1994), 45–64. For a thorough and insightful discussion of Aquinas's understanding and use of the principle "every agent makes its like," see Daniel Pierson, "Thomas Aquinas on the Principle *omne agens agit sibi simile*," PhD diss., Catholic University of America, 2015, ProQuest Dissertations Publishing, 3705731. Aquinas's position is also discussed along with earlier ancient and medieval authors in Philip Rosemann, *Omne agens agit sibi simile: A "Repetition" of Scholastic Metaphysics* (Leuven: Leuven University Press, 1996).

In this section we have seen the connection between form and activity in Aquinas's thought. Before moving on, it is worth noting that Aquinas explicitly denies that material substances have any active potentialities through their matter. He writes: "active power is not from the part of matter, but rather from the part of form."[45] As we have seen, for Aquinas being actual constitutes the good of any substance and the good, as such, is diffusive. Thus, forms are principles of action because they are principles of actuality. Matter, by contrast, is the principle through which a material body is in potentiality to existing in different ways from how it actually is. Matter as a principle of potentiality is imperfect and in need of completion. Thus, it is not a diffusive good as form is. Aquinas explains: "It is manifest that a body cannot act through its whole self since it is composed of matter which is being in potentiality, and from form which is act: for each thing acts insofar as it is in act."[46] Although matter is not a principle of activity, we will see in the subsequent chapter on passive potentialities that it nevertheless has an important function in accounting for the possibility of causal interactions between material substances. Matter is that in virtue of which material substances undergo action.

3.5   The Similitude Principle and Equivocal Agents

A contemporary reader might worry about the empirical plausibility of Aquinas's conception of forms as active powers for making forms of the same kind in another and its implication that effects resemble their causes. In reproduction, generated offspring are of the same species as their parents. In the case of accidental change, there are some clear cases of causation in which effects resemble their causes. For instance, hot substances make other substances hot. However, in many other cases of efficient causation it seems that the qualities of the produced effect do not perfectly align with the qualities of the agent that produced it. In response to this concern, one can find in Aquinas's theories some explanations for why the resemblance between an agent and its effect is often obscured.

---

[45] *In II Sent.* d. 30, q. 2, a. 2 (ed. Mandonett-Moos, vol. 2, 791): "virtus activa non est ex parte materiae, sed magis ex parte formalis . . ."
[46] *ScG* III c. 69 (ed. Marietti, 98, n. 2496): "Manifestum est enim quod corpus non potest agere se toto, cum sit compositum ex materia, quae est ens in potentia, et ex forma, quae est actus: agit enim unumquodque secundum quod est actu."

First, the forms that already actualize the patient determine how it receives the agent's causality.[47] As will be discussed in more detail in Chapter 5, Aquinas thinks that the forms that inhere in a patient dispose it toward receiving certain further forms.[48] For example, a dry substance will be more susceptible to receiving heat than a wet one. Because the forms that inhere in a patient will often differ from the other forms which inhere in the agent, the patient might receive the form communicated by the agent to a less perfect degree than it has in the agent. Secondary qualities arise in a patient through its possession of various degrees of primary qualities. Thus, given that the patient might receive the agent's form to a lesser degree due to its differing dispositions, the change might induce secondary qualities in the patient which differ from the agent's own secondary qualities. For instance, heating wax with a hot iron also melts it. The softness of the wax which is caused through heating it, however, is unlike the hardness of the iron. The difference in secondary qualities can obscure the resemblance to the agent which results in the patient.

Furthermore, Aquinas recognized that many effects are caused through the joint operation of agents acting through several different types of active power. In these cases, the effect will bear some similarity to each agent which produced it, and thus, it will resemble none of the individual agents perfectly.[49] In addition to ordered cooperation between distinct agents, there are cases of causation in which the patient substance is being acted upon by several conflicting powers. An ordinary example would be dropping ice cubes into water that is being heated on a stove. The action of the ice and the action of the fire work against each other. Thus, the water becomes neither hot like fire, nor cold like the ice. By its self-diffusive character, each form tends toward actualizing another form like itself. However, sometimes conflicting powers impede this result from being perfectly achieved or the contribution of cooperating powers to the final effect might obscure the resemblance between the final effect and any single cooperating cause.

In addition to these cases, Aquinas acknowledges that there is a type of causation called equivocal causation in which a single agent produces an

---

[47] *De malo* q. 7, a. 2 (ed. Leon., vol. 23, 162): "Alio modo ex parte subiecti, quod quidem perfectius recipit formam ex actione agentis quanto melius fuerit dispositum, sicut lignum siccum magis calescit quam uiride et aer quam aqua ab eodem igne."
[48] See Section 5.1.
[49] Aquinas's views on how agents cooperate in various ways to produce joint effects are discussed in Chapters 7 and 8.

effect which is not of the same species as itself.[50] Examples of this are when God creates creatures or when the heavenly bodies cause effects in earthly material substances.[51] Aquinas claims that created equivocal causes are always of higher species than the effects that they cause. Yet, the equivocal cause and its effect always belong to the same genus. Thus, Aquinas concludes that there is similarity between an equivocal cause and its effect, yet it is according to genus, rather than species.[52] For example, when the sun generates material bodies on earth, although they are not suns, they nevertheless are material bodies as the sun is a material body. According to Aquinas, there is nothing intrinsic to the equivocal cause which accounts for why it does not produce an effect of the same species as itself. Like other active causes, equivocal causes are inclined toward producing another of their same species. Aquinas thinks that it is the relationship between the agent and the patient which accounts for why the effects of certain agents are of a different and lower species than the agent's own species. In his view, an effect of a different and lower species results when there is a lack of proportion between the agent and its patient. He writes: "A certain agent is not proportioned to the recipient of its effect. Thus the effect does not follow the species of the agent, but it has some similitude with it to the

---

[50] On equivocal causality, see also 2.4. For an extensive study of the texts in which Aquinas discusses equivocal causality see Christopher Decaen, "An Inductive Study of the Notion of Equivocal Causality in St. Thomas," *The Thomist* 79:2 (2015): 213–63.

[51] Aquinas's favorite example of equivocal causality is the sun, which he thought was not hot in itself, but nevertheless caused heat in other things. This example is, of course, based on an outdated cosmology. I suspect that some contemporary readers may wonder if equivocal causality is itself an outdated conception of how causes can function if we now know that the sun does not function as assumed in the example. Though the sun is probably Aquinas's most oft-repeated example of equivocal causality, he does provide some other examples of this type of causality occasionally in his works. For the example of motion (e.g. when two sticks are rubbed together) as an equivocal cause of heat, see *In VII Meta.* lec. 8 (ed. Marietti, 354, n. 1448): "Et iste calor in motu existens virtute, facit calorem in corpore, non quidem generatione univoca, sed aequivoca; quia calor in motu, et in corpore calido, non est unius rationis." In *ST* I q. 27, a. 2 he mentions an animal body's production of hair. For an attempt to supply other examples of equivocal causality based on contemporary science, see Decaen, "An Inductive Study of Equivocal Causality in St. Thomas," 253–62.

[52] *ST* I q. 4, a. 3 (ed. Leon., vol. 4, 54):

> Cum enim omne agens agat sibi simile inquantum est agens, agit autem unumquodque secundum suam formam, necesse est quod in effectu sit similitudo formae agentis. Si ergo agens sit contentum in eadem specie cum suo effectu, erit similitudo inter faciens et factum in forma, secundum eandem rationem speciei; sicut homo generat hominem. Si autem agens non sit contentum in eadem specie, erit similitudo, sed non secundum eandem rationem specie, sicut ea quae generantur ex virtute solis, accedunt quidem ad aliquam similitudinem solis, non tamen ut recipiant formam solis secundum similitudinem speciei, sed secundum similitudinem generis.

extent that it is able, as is the case with all equivocal agents ..."[53] Sometimes a patient is not able to receive the full extent of the perfection which the agent communicates. In identifying the recipient's lack of proportion to the agent as the reason for why the effects of equivocal causes fall short in perfection, Aquinas is applying the neo-Platonic axiom, which he invokes throughout his works, that everything is received according to the mode of the receiver.[54] The patient's characteristics play a role in determining how the perfection which the agent communicates is manifested. When the agent far surpasses the patient in ontological perfection, an effect of a different and lower species results.

3.6 Action as the Communication of Form and the Agent's Educing of Form from Matter

As we have seen, Aquinas believes that forms are principles of action because they are principles of actuality. Act, insofar as it is good, is diffusive. Thus, each form is such that its bearer must be able to induce that same form in another. Aquinas's views about why forms are active powers supports a particular conception of what action is. According to Aquinas, what it is for an agent to act is for it to communicate its form to another. He writes: "To act is nothing other than to communicate that by which the agent is in act insofar as it is possible."[55] Throughout his works, Aquinas repeatedly describes an agent's action as a making of its form in another. For example, in the early *Sentences*, he writes: "[I]n any alteration or generation the agent multiplies its form in matter."[56] Later in the *Summa contra Gentiles*, he writes: "The form which belongs to any being does not come to be in another except through its [i.e. the agent's] action: For the *agent* makes another *like itself* insofar as it communicates its form

[53] *In II Sent.* d. 1, q. 2, a. 2 (ed. Mandonnet-Moos, vol. 2, 48): "Quoddam vero agens non est proportionatum recipienti suum effectum. Unde effectus non consequitur speciem agentis, sed aliquam similitudinem ejus quantum potest, sicut est in omnibus agentibus aequivoce ..." In *De malo* q. 16, a. 9, Aquinas explains that there is a hierarchy of substantial forms and the operations of causes are more excellent in accord with the excellence of the agent's form. The higher beings move the lower ones and the lower ones are disposed to receive the universal effects of the higher beings in a more particular way.

[54] For a study on Aquinas's use of this axiom see Wippel, "Thomas Aquinas and the Axiom 'What Is Received Is Received According to the Mode of the Receiver'."

[55] *De pot.* q. 2, a. 1 (ed. Pession, 25): "Agere vero nihil aliud est quam communicare illud per quod agens est actu, secundum quod est possibile."

[56] *In II Sent.* d. 30, q. 2, a. 1 (ed. Mandonnet-Moos, vol. 2, 780): "in qualibet alteratione et generatione, quod agens multiplicat formam suam in materia."

to another."[57] From these passages it is clear that Aquinas conceives of natural action as involving a form which the agent transmits to the patient. Yet, Aquinas's conception of action as the communication of form can be easily misunderstood.

One might imagine a model upon which forms are like metaphysical bullets that shoot out from the agent and into the patient. One might even assume that the agent gives its own form to the patient. Aquinas, however, explicitly denies that this happens when he writes: "For a natural agent does not hand over its own form to another subject, but rather it reduces the patient from potency to act."[58] Elsewhere he makes the more general point that agents do not deposit anything whatsoever into the matter of the patient upon which they act. He writes: "[I]t is evident that the existence of a form in matter is not perfected by the addition of something extrinsic, which was not in the potential of matter."[59] Although Aquinas writes of the agent "communicating" a form to the patient, this should not be understood as a description of the mechanism by which the agent changes the patient. It is clear that Aquinas denies that the agent deposits or injects anything into the patient when it acts upon it. The claim that an agent communicates a form when it acts should be interpreted as a claim about the type of change which the agent produces in its patient. As we saw in the section above, each agent makes its patient to have a form of the same species as its own. For example, hot substances make other substances hot and human beings generate human beings. Agents communicate their forms insofar as they make qualities like their own in their patients, yet the mechanism of their action does not involve passing over a form from themselves to their patient.

---

[57] *ScG* III c. 52 (ed. Marietti, 71, n. 2292): "Forma alicuius propria non fit alterius nisi eo agente: *agens* enim facit *sibi simile* inquantum formam suam alteri communicat."

[58] See, for instance, *ScG* III c. 69 (ed. Marietti, 98, n. 2458): "Agens enim naturale non est traducens propriam formam in alterum subiectum: sed reducens subiectum quod patitur, de potentia in actum." The lines which immediately proceed this line are also very instructive:

> Ridiculum autem est dicere quod ideo corpus non agat quia accidens non transit de subiecto in subiectum. Non enim hoc modo dicitur corpus calidum calefacere quod idem numero calor qui est in calefaciente corpore, transeat ad corpus calefactum: sed quia virtute caloris qui est in corpore calefaciente, alius calor numero fit actu in corpore calefacto, qui prius erat in eo in potentia.

See also *De spirit. creat.* a. 2 ad 8. Aquinas explains why it is metaphysically impossible for numerically the same form to passed from one substance to another in *ST* III q. 77, a.1.

[59] *De pot.* q. 3, a. 8 ad 10 (ed. Pession, 62): "patet enim quod non perficitur esse formae in materia alio exteriori addito, quod in potentia materiae non esset."

Aquinas describes what the agent does when it actualizes a form in a patient as "educing a form" or "reducing the patient from potency to act." He writes: "Every form which is educed into being by the transmutation of matter is a form educed from the potentiality of matter; for what it is to transmute matter is to reduce it from potentiality to actuality."[60] The Latin term "educere" means to lead forth or draw up. "Reducere" means to lead back or restore. Yet, the reader must avoid taking Aquinas's use of these terms too literally. There were other medieval figures who maintained that matter pre-contained all forms in an "inchoate" or "latent" way. Agent causes were seen as fully actualizing forms which were to some extent already actually present in the patient's matter. Aquinas explicitly rejects the "latent form" theory. He claims that such a position rests on ignorance about the distinction between potentiality and actuality.[61] The theory mistakenly reasons from the fact that forms are *potentially* in matter prior to their being actualized, that the forms are in matter *simply* prior to their actualization. According to Aquinas's view, when a subject has a form potentially there is no sense in which the form is there in actuality. For example, prior to fire's act of heating water, the form of heat is only potentially in the water, and by fire's action the status of the form of heat in fire goes from potentiality to actuality. Aquinas sees potentiality and actuality as two contradictory states which a form can have in a subject. A suitable agent can immediately effect a transition between these states. Aquinas writes: "[N]othing is able to be reduced from potentiality to actuality, except through some being in act. For example, a hot thing in actuality, such as fire, makes wood, which is hot in potentiality, to be actually hot, and through this, it moves and changes it."[62] In Aquinas's view, actuality and potentiality fit together in such a way that agents which are actualized in a certain way can actualize corresponding potentialities in other substances. Aquinas's use of the terms "to educe" and "to reduce" are best understood as metaphors to describe the agent's effecting a change of state from potentiality to actuality with respect to a form in a patient.

An objector might worry that it is impossible for an agent to actualize a potentiality in a patient without first separately causing or uncovering a

---

[60] *ScG* II c. 86 (ed. Marietti, 248, n. 1709): "Omnis forma quae educitur in esse per materiae transmutationem, est forma educta de potentia materiae: hoc enim est materiam transmutari, de potentia in actum reduci."

[61] See for example *ST* I q. 45, a. 8, co.

[62] *ST* I q. 2, a. 3 (ed. Leon., vol. 4, 31): "de potentia autem non potest aliquid reduci in actum, nisi per aliquod ens in actu: sicut calidum in actu, ut ignis, facit lignum, quod est calidum in potentia, esse actu calidum, et per hoc movet et alterat ipsum."

form in the patient since form is the principle by which potentialities are
actualized. For instance, it is through having a form of heat that water is
actually (rather than potentially) hot. How then can fire actualize water's
potentiality for heat without first depositing or uncovering a form of heat
in the water? In response to such a worry, Aquinas thinks that the agent's
active power is that through which the transition from potentiality to
actuality is initiated. The new form in the patient is the result of the
transition from potentiality to actuality, which the agent initiates through
its active power. Put otherwise, a new form is not what starts a change
from potentiality to actuality. Rather, the new form is the end-point of the
change. In Aquinas's view, agents cause forms indirectly by changing
substances. Put otherwise, a form of x is caused to be by making some
substance exist as an actual, rather than potential, x.[63] For example, when a
sculptor makes a lump of clay into a statue she causes the form of a statue
to be in the clay as a consequence of her manipulating the clay so that it is
shaped as a statue. It is not a pre-condition for beginning to change the
clay into a statue to cause the form of a statue to be in the clay, as if it were
something coming to it extrinsically. Rather, the statue form results as the
endpoint of the sculptor's changing of the clay into a statue. Similarly, fire
does not heat water by first causing an extrinsic form of heat to come into
the water. Rather, the form of heat is the end of the change of heating. Fire
causes the form of heat indirectly in water by changing the state of the
water, through its active power to heat, until it is finally actually hot. To
"educe" a form x from a patient's matter is to act upon it until it is changed
into an x.

3.7 Not Every Form Is an Active Principle for Transmuting Matter

As already mentioned, Aquinas himself explicitly recognizes that not every
form is an active power for affecting material change.[64] Some forms are
active powers for communicating their likenesses to the senses and intellect
alone. From Aquinas's various principles and commitments, we can piece
together his rationale for why only some forms are powers for transmuting
matter, while others are not. As we have already seen, Aquinas thought
that all natural, qualitative changes to material substances were brought

---

[63] See for example *ST* I q. 75 a. 6 co.
[64] See for instance *ST* I q. 78, a. 3 (ed. Leon., vol. 5, 254): "non omnia accidentia habent vim
immutativam secundum se; sed solae qualitates tertiae speciei, secundum quas contingit alteratio."

about through the primary elemental qualities of hot, cold, wet and dry.[65]
These are the only forms which are immediate principles for affecting
change to a material substance's qualities. Aquinas thought that the higher-
level powers of substances, such as the power to grow and reproduce,
operate in virtue of the elemental powers.[66] This view will be discussed in
detail in Chapter 8.[67] It is obvious from experience that the secondary
qualities, such as colors, textures and tastes, which are possessed in virtue
of the primary ones, are not active principles for changing matter. For
example, red things do not make other things red. But is there some
rationale for why this is so? The very status of a secondary quality as
secondary provides an explanation. Secondary qualities, as we have seen,
are acquired and lost in virtue of changes to primary qualities. Thus, the
active power required for changing a material substance's secondary quality
turns out to be the active quality needed to change the primary qualities
which give rise to it. It follows from the relationship between primary and
secondary qualities in material substances that secondary qualities are not
changed immediately. For example, a substance cannot be turned red
without making a more basic change to its elemental qualities. It is not
possible to communicate the form of redness without communicating
some more primary forms. Because they cannot be immediately communicated, secondary qualities are not active principles for communicating
themselves in matter. The form of redness cannot make another substance
red by touching it since things do not become red by immediately
receiving the form of redness. Something becomes red in virtue of transmuting its primary qualities.[68]

Aquinas explains that the primary qualities are active on material bodies
because they are the cause of other qualities. He writes: "[T]he tangible
qualities are the cause of other sensibles and therefore they have more with
regard to active power and are able to act in any body ..."[69] The tangible

---

[65] See Sections 1.1 and 2.1.   [66] See for instance *ST* I, q. 78, a. 1.   [67] See Section 8.2.

[68] Still, one may wonder why the primary qualities which underly secondary qualities do not cause the
same primary qualities in other bodies, thereby causing them to have the same secondary qualities.
For example, why is it that the primary qualities through which a substance has the secondary
quality of redness induce the same primary qualities in a patient thereby making it red? As explained
above in Section 3.5, primary qualities are often received in a patient with a degree different from
the degree to which they exist in the agent due to the differing qualities of the patient. Thus, the
secondary qualities of the agent are often not communicated to the patient along with the
primary qualities.

[69] *In II De anima* c. 24 (ed. Leon., vol. 45/1, 171): "qualitates tangibiles sunt causae aliorum
sensibilium, et ideo habent plus de virtute activa, et possunt agere in quaecumque corpora ..."
He goes on to write: "set alia sensibilia, quia habent minus de virtute activa, non possunt agere nisi
in corpora valde passibilia ..."

qualities can communicate themselves to other material substances upon contact because they are the most basic qualities from which other qualities arise. Secondary qualities, inasmuch as they are qualities that are caused by other qualities, cannot act upon material bodies. Secondary qualities can, however, immediately communicate their likenesses in the senses. For example, redness is an active principle of its likeness in the sense of sight. One does not need to see a substance's primary qualities in order to see its secondary qualities.

In addition to their qualitative forms, Aquinas maintains that material substances have quantitative forms, such as heights, lengths, and weights. In Aquinas's view, quantitative forms are not of themselves active, yet they make a difference to the manner in which an agent acts through other forms that are active as such. First, let us see why Aquinas denies that quantitative forms are active of themselves. Aquinas writes: "Since quantity is had from the part of matter, and quality from the part of form, therefore quantity does not act except as mediated through quality, which is a *per se* principle of action ..."[70] In this passage, Aquinas says that quantity is not active through itself because substances have quantity in virtue of their matter. This claim is initially confusing because Aquinas believes that substances are characterized by quantities in virtue of an inherent accidental form. For example, Socrates is six feet tall in virtue of an inherent form of six feet. So, what can it mean to say that substances possess quantity through their matter? In Aquinas's view, all material substances have certain types of accidents solely because they have prime matter as a component. For example, material substances have length, width and depth, and consequently occupy space just because they are material bodies in virtue of being composed of prime matter.[71] Furthermore, quantitative forms are not those which differentiate the basic elements from one another. It is possible for elements of different kinds to have the same quantities. Because quantities do not differentiate one type of elemental substance from another, they cannot be that whereby substances are active. Action, as we have seen, is a communication of form and substances communicate their forms in order to make others like

[70] *In IV Sent.* d. 12, q. 1, a. 2, qc. 1 (ed. Mandonnet-Moos, vol. 4, 508): "Et quia quantitas se tenet ex parte materiae, et qualitas ex parte formae; ideo quantitas non agit nisi mediante qualitate, quae est per se actionis principium ..."
[71] *ST* I q. 76, a. 6 ad 2 (ed. Leon. vol. 5, 229): "Ad secundum dicendum quod dimensiones quantitativae sunt accidentia consequentia corporeitatem, quae toti materiae convenit"; *In II De Trin.* q. 4, a. 3 (ed. Leon. vol. 50, 128): "secundum quam dicitur esse in loco simpliciter, et haec comparatio sequitur corpus ex ipsa natura corporeitatis, non propter aliquid additum ..."

themselves. Thus, an agent can only act upon a patient through those forms whereby it differs from it. Forms which elements of different types share in common cannot be that in virtue of which such elements seek to conform one another to themselves. The reason that qualities are active through themselves is because they are that in virtue of which bodies differ in type from one another.[72]

Aquinas thought that quantitative forms even relied on qualitative forms to be sensed. Quantitive dimensions, for instance, are only seen in virtue of the active character of the color that inheres in them. If *per impossibile* color could not actualize the sense of sight, the dimensions of the colored body could not be seen.[73] Aquinas's view that quantitative forms were not active of themselves leads him to maintain that artificial forms, such as the form of a saw or hammer, are also not active of themselves. From an ontological perspective, the form of artifact is a figure, namely a shape. A figure is a quality, but a quality which is possessed in virtue of quantities. A figure is the end-point of a substance's quantity. For example, metal is made to have the shape of an axe by changing the dimensions of its surfaces. Aquinas thinks that since quantities are not of themselves active, the very shapes by which a substance, such as metal, is constituted as a certain kind of artifact, such as an axe, are not active powers.[74] Like other substances, the artificial instrument is active through its primary elemental qualities. Aquinas's view that artificial forms are not active powers was controversial. His teacher Albert, for example, held that artificial forms were active powers for causing locomotion.[75]

Although Aquinas rejects the view that quantities are of themselves principles of motion, he nevertheless acknowledges that these forms

---

[72] *In II De anima*, lec. 23 (ed. Leon. vol. 45/1, 166): "tangibiles qualitates sunt differentiae corporis, secundum quod est corpus; idest differentiae, quibus elementa distinguuntur abinvicem, scilicet calidi, frigidi, humidi et sicci ..." See also *In III De anima*, lec. 1.

[73] See for instance *ST* I q. 78, a. 3 ad 2 (ed. Leon. vol. 5, 254):

> Quantitas autem est proximum subiectum qualitatis alterativae, ut superficies coloris. Et ideo sensibilia communia non movent sensum primo et per se, sed ratione sensibilis qualitatis; ut superficies ratione coloris. Nec tamen sunt sensibilia per accidens: quia huiusmodi sensibilia aliquam diversitatem faciunt in immutatione sensus. Alio enim modo immutatur sensus a magna superficie, et a parva: quia etiam ipsa albedo dicitur magna vel parva, et ideo dividitur secundum proprium subiectum.

[74] *ST* II-II q. 96, a. 2 ad 2 (ed. Leon., vol. 9, 332): "Sed corporum artificialium formae procedunt ex conceptione artificis: et cum nihil aliud sint quam compositio, ordo et figura, ut dicitur in I Physic., non possunt habere naturalem virtutem ad agendum."

[75] On the debate about whether artificial forms are active see Dennis Des Chene, *Physiologia: Natural Philosophy in Late Aristotelian and Cartesian Thought* (Ithaca, NY: Cornell University Press, 1996), 114–20.

make a difference to causal interactions in the material world. It is through quantitative forms that active qualities are extended in space.[76] Because of this, a substance's quantity can determine the manner in which it acts through its active qualities. Aquinas writes: "The larger a hot body is, supposing an equal intensity of heat, the more it heats; and supposing equal weight, the larger a body is, the more quickly it will move with natural motion, and its larger size is the reason it will be moved more slowly by unnatural motion."[77] As we have seen, Aquinas thinks that an agent must be in contact with its patient in order to act upon it.[78] Thus, a larger hot body makes contact with more places of its patient than a smaller one. Thus, it acts on it more vigorously. It should be noted that Aquinas does not think that quantity was the only, or perhaps even the most important, factor in determining the strength of a power's operation. He maintains that substances can "participate" more or less perfectly in qualitative forms.[79] The degree to which a substance participates in a form impacts the strength of its action through the form.[80]

3.8   Non-elemental Powers of Mixed Substances and Substantial Form as Active Power

In addition to the basic powers which substances have in virtue of the elements (e.g. the power to heat), medieval thinkers held that some higher substances which were generated from mixing the elements together also have higher powers not possessed by any of the elements. For example, plants have the power to grow and take in nutrients and animals have powers for sensation. None of the elements have such powers. In the medieval period, there was much debate about what the non-elemental powers of higher substances were in themselves. Are such

---

[76] See, for instance, the text in note 28, in which Aquinas claims that quantity is the proximate subject for quality.

[77] *ScG* III, c. 69 (ed. Marietti, 98, n. 2455): "Nam quanto corpus calidum fuerit maius, supposita aeque intensa caliditate, tanto magis calefacit; et supposita gravitate aeque intensa, quanto maius fuerit corpus grave, tanto velocius movebitur motu naturali; et inde est quod tardius movetur motu innaturali." See also *De pot.* 3.7.

[78] See Section 2.5.

[79] For Aquinas's views on how substances participate more or less in their inherent forms, see Gloria Frost, "Aquinas on the Intension and Remission of Accidental Forms," *Oxford Studies in Medieval Philosophy* 7 (2019): 116–46.

[80] *De virt.* Q. 1, a. 11 (ed. Odetto, 739): "Ex hoc autem ipso quod subiectum magis participat qualitatem, vehementius operatur; quia unumquodque agit in quantum est actu; unde quod magis est reductum in actum, perfectius agit." See also *ST* I, q. 25, a. 1 and *ScG* II, c. 8.

powers to be identified with the substance's substantial form or are they distinct accidental forms? The debate pertained specifically to the human being and its vital and intellectual operations. Some medieval thinkers maintained that the human substantial form was the immediate active power through which human beings performed all of their higher-level operations.[81] On this view, the human substantial form is identical with powers such as the power of intellect and the power of will. However, Aquinas rejects this position, maintaining instead that higher-level mixed substances have powers distinct from their substantial forms through which they carry out their non-elemental operations. On Aquinas's view, for example, a human being has a power of intellect and a power of will and a power of growth which is distinct from its substantial form.[82] Though explicit discussions of this problem in the Middle Ages focused particularly on the relationship between the human substantial form and distinctively human powers, Aquinas's position has implications for all higher-level substances and their non-elemental powers.

Before examining Aquinas's rationale for his views on what higher-level powers are, it is helpful to first see his views on how higher-level mixed substances come to possess powers which none of the elements have. In his view, mixed substances are not merely elements that are juxtaposed together in various shapes. Rather, when the elements act upon each other, their qualities are gradually transformed in such a way that the elements themselves go out of existence and a new substance comes into being in their place. This is to say that the substantial forms that actualized the matter composing the elements are replaced by a new substantial form through which the mixed substance has existence.[83] Aquinas writes: "[F]lesh is not only fire and earth, nor the hot and cold whose power is that by which the elements are mixed, but there is also something else by

---

[81] See Section 1.4 and for secondary literature fn. 57 of Chapter 1.
[82] It has been claimed in the secondary literature that Aquinas abandoned this position later in his career. Wippel has responded to this interpretation by demonstrating the consistency of Aquinas's views across time. See Wippel, *Metaphysical Thought of Thomas Aquinas*, 275–94.
[83] *De mixt. element.* (ed. Leon., vol. 43, 157): "Sunt igitur formae elementorum in corporibus mixtis non quidem actu, sed uirtute." For literature on Aquinas's views on the presence of elements in compounds, see the introduction to Joseph Bobik, *Aquinas on Matter and Form and the Elements: A Translation and Interpretation of the* de Principiis Naturae *and the* de Mixtione Elementorum *of St. Thomas Aquinas* (Notre Dame, IN: University of Notre Dame Press, 1998); Christopher Decaen, "Elemental Virtual Presence in St. Thomas," *The Thomist* 64:2 (2000): 271–300; and Michael Hector Storck, "Parts, Wholes, and Presence by Power: A Response to Gordon P. Barnes," *Review of Metaphysics* 62:1 (2008): 45–59.

which flesh is flesh."[84] According to Aquinas, there are some substantial forms which by actualizing matter also actualize in them certain novel causal powers that are not possessed by any of the elemental substances.[85] For instance, the substantial form of a tree actualizes matter to compose a tree and actualizes in the tree the powers of growth and nutrition. To be clear, the substantial form is not an agent that educes these powers in the tree by efficient causality. Rather, the vital powers of the tree naturally result from its substantial form since having these powers is part of what it is to be a tree.[86]

Aquinas makes a number of arguments to support his rejection of the view that the substantial form itself is the immediate power by which a substance acts. The arguments are intended to show why it is necessary to posit that there are distinct powers, which are accidental forms, that follow from the substantial form. Here I will focus on Aquinas's arguments that apply to all created substances and their powers, rather than the arguments that are specific to the case of the human being.[87] In various works, Aquinas advances an argument for the distinction between a substantial form and the powers that flow from it which rests on correspondence between potentiality and actuality. We have seen that Aquinas conceives of powers as potentialities that are ordered toward the actuality of action. As we saw, potentialities are distinguished and defined by the corresponding actualities that are their completion and fulfillment. It follows from the correlative nature of potentiality and actuality that a potentiality must be in the same genus as the actuality to which it corresponds. If a potentiality and an actuality are of different genera, then there would be no basis of similarity to consider one as the completion and fulfillment of the other. He writes in his *Summa theologiae*:

> since potentiality and actuality divide being and every genus of being, it is
> necessary that a potentiality and actuality are referred to the same genus.

---

[84] *In VII Meta.* lec. 17 (ed. Marietti, 398, n. 1674): "[C]aro non solum est ignis et terra, aut calidum et frigidum, per quorum virtutem elementa commiscentur, sed etiam est aliquid alterum per quod caro est caro."

[85] Though Aquinas thinks that the substantial form is that in virtue of which the substance has non-elemental powers, he nevertheless maintained that the material substance (i.e. the composite of matter and substantial form) is the agent that acts through the powers. See, for instance, *ST* I q. 75, a. 2 ad 2.

[86] *ST* I q. 77, a. 7 ad 1 (ed. Leon., vol. 5, 247): "[P]otentia animae ab essentia fluit, non per transmutationem, sed per naturalem quandam resultationem, et est simul cum anima ..." See also ST I q. 77, a. 6 ad 3.

[87] Aquinas is careful to note which of his arguments are proper to the soul and which apply to all created substances. See especially *De spirit. creat.* a. 11. After making an argument which applies to all created substances, he prefaces his next set of arguments with this line, *De spirit. creat.* a. 11 (ed. Leon., vol. 24/2, 118): "Secundo impossibile apparet hoc speciali ratione in anima, propter tria ..."

Therefore, if an act is not in the genus of substance, the potentiality which is said with respect to that act is not able to be in the genus of substance.[88]

According to this passage, an actuality that is an accident cannot be the actuality that corresponds to a potentiality that is in the category of substance. Thus, Aquinas reasons that since the actions of creatures are not substances, therefore, the potentiality from which they arise cannot be a form in the genus of substance, namely a substantial form. For example, the actions of knowing, willing or growing are accidents. They are changes which exist in a substance as their subject. Thus, according to Aquinas's principles, these actions must be actualities which correspond to a potentiality that is in an accidental category rather than a substantial one. Put otherwise, creatures must act through accidental forms, rather than their substantial forms, because their actions are accidents rather than substances.

In his *Disputed Questions on the Soul*, Aquinas advances a slightly different line of reasoning to support the principle that the forms by which creatures act must be accidents since creaturely actions are accidents.[89] There he refers to some of his other views, which we saw above, about why forms, as principles of actuality, are principles of activity.[90] He reminds that every agent acts insofar as it is in act. Fire heats, for example, insofar as it is hot. Thus, there must be a similarity between the effect which an agent produces and the power by which it acts. If an agent does not produce a substance as its effect, then it does not act through a substantial form. Aquinas claims that it is obvious in the case of natural substances that their powers do not produce substances immediately. Even when one substance generates another substance, it does so by gradually transforming its patient's matter. Only after a series of accidental changes does a substantial change result. The immediate effects of created agency are accidental changes, thus we can conclude that creatures operate through accidental forms that resemble the accidental changes which they cause.[91] They do not operate immediately through their substantial forms.

---

[88] *ST* I q. 77, a. 1 (ed. Leon., vol. 5, 236): "cum potentia et actus dividant ens et quodlibet genus entis, oportet quod ad idem genus referatur potentia et actus. Et ideo, si actus non est in genere substantiae, potentia quae dicitur ad illum actum, non potest esse in genere substantiae." See also *In I Sent.* d. 3, q. 4 a. 2.

[89] *Q.D. de anima* q. 12.   [90] See Section 3.4.

[91] *Q.D. de anima* q. 12 (ed. Leon., vol. 24/1, 109):

> unumquodque agit secundum quod actu est illud scilicet quod agit. Ignis enim calefacit non in quantum actu est lucidum, sed in quantum est actu calidum. Et exinde est quod omne agens agit sibi simile. Vnde oportet quod ex eo quod agitur consideretur principium quo agitur: oportet enim utrumque esse conforme. Vnde in II Physicorum dicitur quod forma et generans sunt idem specie. Quando igitur id quod agit non pertinet ad esse substantiale rei,

Aquinas acknowledges that substantial forms are active powers for producing another being of the same substantial kind. Given the principles we have discussed in this section, it is necessary to posit an active power in the genus of substance in order to explain how one creature can generate another. For instance, if a potentiality must be in the same genus as its act, then the production of new substance demands a potentiality in the genus of substance. For instance, when a frog generates another frog, its action terminates in a substance, thus it must have an active power in the genus of substance for producing the frog's substantial kind. Thus, Aquinas claims that the substantial forms of living beings are active powers for producing another substance of the same kind. Yet, he denies that substantial forms are active powers that can act immediately on matter.[92] Substantial forms operate through the active qualities of the elements. He writes: "[I]n natural actions, substantial forms are not the immediate principle of action, but they act mediately using active and passive qualities as their proper instruments."[93] This is to say that any substantial change will be the result of changes of hot, cold, wet and dry. It is the substantial form that explains why these elemental changes terminate in a new substance, but the substantial form does not effect any change which is not also a change of an elemental quality effected by a similar elemental quality. In Chapter 8, we will examine Aquinas's views on how higher powers use elemental powers as instruments for carrying out their operations.[94]

Though Aquinas argues that substances do not operate immediately in virtue of their substantial forms throughout his career, there are passages in his corpus in which he refers to the power by which a living body engages in a certain vital action simply as the "soul." For example, when arguing

> impossibile est quod principium quo agit sit aliquid de essentia rei. Et hoc manifeste apparet in agentibus naturalibus. Quia enim agens naturale in generatione agit transmutando materiam ad formam – quod quidem fit secundum quod materia primo disponitur ad formam, et tandem consequitur formam, secundum quod generatio est terminus alterationis –, necesse est quod ex parte agentis id quod immediate agit sit forma accidentalis correspondens dispositioni materiae . . .

See also *In I Sent.* d. 3, q. 4, a. 2.

[92] *Q.D. de anima* q. 12 (ed. Leon., vol. 24/1, 109): "set oportet ut forma accidentalis agat in uirtute formae substantialis, quasi instrumentum eius, alias non induceret agendo formam substantialem. Et propter hoc in elementis non apparent aliqua principia actionum nisi qualitates actiue et passiue, que tamen agunt in uirtute formarum substantialium; et propter hoc earum actio non solum terminatur ad dispositiones accidentales, set etiam ad formas substantiales . . ." See also *In I Sent.* d. 3, q. 4, a. 2.

[93] *In IV Sent.* d. 12, q. 1, a. 2, qc. 2 (ed. Mandonnet-Moos, vol. 4, 509): "[I]n actionibus naturalibus formae substantiales non sunt immediatum actionis principium, sed agunt mediantibus qualitatibus activis et passivis, sicut propriis instrumentis . . ."

[94] See Section 8.2.

that the power of heat cannot alone carry out the act of nutrition, he identifies the further power responsible for nutrition simply as the "soul" (*anima*).[95] He does not speak there of a "nutritive power" as he does in other works.[96] This might lead a reader to wonder whether Aquinas really thought that the operations of living organisms which transmute matter, namely nutrition, growth and reproduction, required separate powers of soul, such as a reproductive power, over and above the substantial form and the elemental powers. Elsewhere, however, Aquinas explains that the name "soul" can be predicated of the soul's powers.[97] The soul can be considered a certain whole which is comprised of its powers as parts. Just as the name of a whole material substance can be predicated of one of its integral parts, as for example when a hand is said to be "human," the powers of the soul can be referred to as "soul." So, the nutritive power can be referred to as the "soul" since it is one of the parts comprising the soul, yet this is not what the nutritive power is properly in itself.

3.9   Locomotion and Aquinas's Model of Power and Action

As we have seen in this chapter, Aquinas thinks that forms are principles of action because they are principles of goodness and goodness is diffusive. Aquinas conceives of action as a communication of form by the agent to the patient. While this model may apply well to qualitative changes, such as when a hot substance heats another, it is difficult to apply it to locomotive changes in which an agent moves a patient from one place to another. Aquinas himself recognized that locomotions do not involve an agent communicating a form to a patient or making it to be like itself. He writes: "In virtue of that which is received in the patient, the patient is assimilated [i.e. made like] the agent ... [I]n locomotion nothing is received in the mobile, but rather the mobile itself is received in

---

[95] *In II De anima* lec. 8.
[96] For instance, in *ST* I q. 78, a. 1, he explicitly refers to a genus of powers which are the "vegetative powers" and in the following article he identifies three distinct powers: nutritive, growth and reproductive.
[97] *Quodl.* X q. 3, a. 1 (ed. Leon., vol. 25/1, 131):

> Alio modo possumus loqui de anima secundum quod est quoddam totum potenciale; et sic diuerse potencie sunt partes eius, et ita anima praedicatur de potenciis uel e conuerso, abusiua praedicatione, sicut totum integrale de suis partibus uel e conuerso, quamuis minor sit abusio in toto potenciali quam integrali, quia totum potenciale secundum suam substanciam adest cuilibet parti, non autem integrale.

some place."[98] According to Aquinas, when a substance is moved to a different place, it does not acquire an intrinsic form.[99] Rather, in changes which are locomotion what is varied is a substance's order to an external place.[100] In this final section we will see Aquinas's views on the active powers by which substances cause locomotions.

Following Aristotle, Aquinas thought that there were two types of locomotion, natural and violent. Each of these motions is caused in a different way. To understand the difference between these two types of motions, it is necessary to begin with the Aristotelian doctrine of natural place. Aristotle thought that each of the four elements had a natural place in the cosmos. Earth's natural place was in the center. Water's natural place was in the circle surrounding earth since earth sinks in water. Since air bubbles rise in water, air's natural place was in the circle surrounding water. Lastly, since fire rises, its natural place was in the highest circle, surrounding air.[101] A natural motion is a locomotion that moves a thing toward its natural place, while a violent motion is one that takes it away from where it is naturally apt to be. Aquinas thought that the secondary qualities of lightness and heaviness were especially important in explaining the natural motions by which substances tend to their natural places. Aquinas conceives of heaviness as a natural aptitude to be below, while lightness is a natural aptitude to be above. Yet, in his view, heaviness and lightness are not active principles that move the bodies that have these qualities upwards or downwards. Rather, following Aristotle, he conceives of heaviness and lightness as passive potentialities for being upward or downward.[102] According to Aquinas, the agent cause that efficiently causes a body to move upwards or downwards is the agent that caused the body to be light or heavy, namely the generator of the body. He writes:

---

[98] *De ver.* q. 26, a. 1 (ed. Leon. 22 3/1, 747): "Secundum hoc autem, quod recipitur in patiente, patiens agenti assimilatur ... [I]n motu locali non recipitur aliquid immobile, sed ipsum mobile recipitur in aliquo loco."

[99] *ScG* III c. 82 (ed. Marietti, 117, n. 2577): "motus localis non variat rem secundum aliquid ei inhaerens, sed solum secundum aliquid extrinsecum; et propter hoc est rei iam perfectae." *In II Sent.* d. 8, q. 1, a. 2 (ed. Mandonnet-Moos, vol. 2, 206): "sed quantum ad motum localem, per quem nulla forma ponitur in re mota ..."

[100] *De pot.* q. 6, a. 3 (ed. Pession, 166): "nam motus localis est primus et perfectissimus motuum, utpote qui non variat rem quantum ad rei intrinseca, sed solum quantum ad exteriorem locum ..." See also passage in note above.

[101] Aristotle, *On the Heavens* II c. 13–14. For Aquinas's commentary see, *In II de caelo*, lec. 12.

[102] By contrast, Anneliese Maier claims that many scholastics regarded heaviness and lightness as active qualities on par with hot, cold, wet, and dry. See Maier, "Causes, Forces and Resistance," in *On the Threshold of Exact Science*, trans. Steven Sargent (Philadelphia: University of Pennsylvania Press, 1982), 40–60, at 44.

What it is to be light is to have an aptitude toward that which is above, and the nature of heaviness is to have an aptitude toward that which is below. Hence it is nothing other to seek why a heavy thing moves downward than to seek why it is heavy. Thus, the same thing that makes it heavy, makes it move downward.[103]

Through inducing the quality of heaviness in a thing (in virtue of causing the primary qualities upon which heaviness follows), the generating agent moves the heavy body downwards.[104] It should be noted that the action by which the generator generates a light or heavy body itself conforms to Aquinas's basic model of efficient causation. For example, when fire generates fire, this is an instance in which an agent communicates its form and makes another like itself. Through this act of generation, a light thing is caused to exist and made to move upward. Thus, natural motions are caused in virtue of a standard *per se* instance of efficient causation in which a form is communicated from agent to patient. Aquinas thinks that violent motions are caused through natural ones.[105] Inanimate objects that are moving by natural motion can collide and one might move the other to a non-natural place. Self-moving animals can also move other substances to new places. Though Aquinas has a theory about the immediate causes of violent motions, namely they are caused through natural motions, the causation of a violent motion cannot be analyzed using his model of active power and action. Violent motion does not involve any communication of form and the agent does not make the patient like itself. It seems that Aquinas's model of active

---

[103] *In VIII Phys.* lec. 8 (ed. Leon., vol. 2, 392): "Hoc enim est esse leve, habere aptitudinem ad hoc quod sit sursum: et haec est etiam ratio gravis, habere aptitudinem ad hoc quod sit deorsum. Unde nihil est aliud quaerere quare grave movetur deorsum, quam quaerere quare est grave. Et sic illud idem quod facit ipsum grave, facit ipsum moveri deorsum."

[104] Aquinas recognizes that sometimes substances are prevented from moving toward their natural places, as when a pillar holds a heavy object up. Aquinas says that the agent which removes such an impediment can be considered a *per accidens* cause of the object's movement toward its natural places. But nevertheless, the generator remains the *per se* cause. *In VIII Phys.* lec. 8 (ed. Leon, vol. 2, 392):

> Sic ergo patet quod illud quod *movet*, idest removet hoc quod est prohibens et *sustinens*, idest detinens, quodammodo movet et quodammodo non movet: puta si columna sustineat aliquod grave, et sic impediat ipsum descendere, ille qui divellit columnam, quodammodo dicitur movere grave columnae superpositum; et similiter ille qui removet lapidem qui impedit aquam effluere a vase, dicitur quodammodo movere aquam ... Sic igitur generans est per se movens gravia et levia, removens autem prohibens, per accidens.

[105] *In IV Phys.* lec. 11 (ed. Leon., vol. 2, 182): "Motus naturalis est prior violento, cum motus violentus non sit nisi quaedam declinatio a motu naturali. Remoto ergo motu naturali, removetur omnis motus; cum remoto priori, removeatur posterius."

power and action is incompatible with postulating active powers for immediately causing violent motions since these motions do not involve reception of form.[106]

3.10 Conclusion

In this chapter we have seen that Aquinas's account of active power is inextricably bound up with his understanding of potentiality and actuality. His preferred way of describing active powers is as "potentialities." Active potentialities are realities that stand mid-way between inertness and actual causal activity. Even when they are inactive, substances are poised and primed for action through their active powers. Since active powers are potentialities, they are defined and distinguished from one another in virtue of the actions that are their corresponding actualities. One active power differs from another through the different actions that arise from each. We saw that active potentialities are in themselves forms. Forms are both the actuality of matter and potentiality for action. Aquinas's neo-Platonic conception of goodness as diffusive offers a metaphysical reason for why forms do not merely characterize their bearers, but also dispose their bearers toward causal activity. Good things by their nature seek to spread their goodness beyond themselves and being actual is a good. Since forms are that by which substances are actual, they are also that through which substances have active power. Possession of a form enables that bearer to realize that form in another. On Aquinas's view, active powers do not enable a generic sort of causal influencing. Rather, each active power is a power for inducing a form of its same species in

---

[106] A contemporary reader may find it problematic that Aquinas has no conception of active powers for immediately causing violent motions since changes such as these are the ones that contemporary science tends to regard as most important and fundamental. While Aquinas conceives of qualitative changes as irreducible, contemporary science tends to reduce qualitative changes to changes of locomotion. Consider the case of a person who walks outside on a cold day and quickly loses body heat. Aquinas, following Aristotle, would view this case as a two-way qualitative change. The body acts through its heat on the surrounding air to make heat in it, while the air acts through its coolness on the body to make cool in it. Both the air through its coolness and the body through its heat make the other like itself. By contrast, modern physics would explain the loss of body heat in terms of an exchange of energy between the body and the air. On this conception of the change, no entity makes another like itself. Rather particles, change according to place. Thus, if the change is caused through an active power, such a power must be a power for causing locomotive changes.

another substance. While not every form is an active power for inducing a form like itself in matter, every form enables its bearer to communicate that same form in some way, such as in sensation or intellection. Aquinas thinks that all material changes happen in virtue of the elemental qualities. Living substances have higher powers which operate through the elemental qualities and Aquinas maintains that such powers are distinct forms from substantial form.

CHAPTER 4

Natural Inclination and Final Causality

Consider fire and its active power to burn. Aquinas thinks that fire's power to burn explains why it is able to burn flammable objects. Yet, he thinks that the presence of this power in fire does not alone explain why fire actually does burn flammable things whenever it comes into contact with them. Aquinas thinks that we must posit something further in a natural agent to account for why it exercises its power whenever it is in contact with an appropriate patient. According to him, natural things have an inclination within them that determines them to perform their proper actions whenever they are in contact with a suitable patient. Aquinas writes: "In each thing there is a natural inclination for accomplishing the action commensurate with its power, as is evident in all natural things, both animate and inanimate."[1] In Aquinas's view, an agent's natural inclination toward its action explains why it consistently exercises its power whenever it is in the right circumstances, as well as why it exercises its power to the fullest extent possible. The goal of this chapter is to examine Aquinas's understanding of natural inclination and the role it plays in efficient causation.

In the first section, we will see Aquinas's views on what natural inclinations are and why he posits them. Aquinas thinks that powers are of themselves open to being exercised or not exercised and something must determine a power toward exercise. Natural inclination is that which determines a natural agent toward exercising its power. We will also see Aquinas's view that natural inclination follows from a natural being's form. In the next section, we will examine the connection between Aquinas's views on natural inclinations and his views on how ends, namely final causes, function as causes. By its natural inclination, the agent tends

---

[1] *ST* II-II q. 133, a. 1 (ed. Leon., vol. 10, 86): "Inest autem unicuique rei naturalis inclinatio ad exequendam actionem commensuratam suae potentiae: ut patet in omnibus rebus naturalibus, tam animatis quam inanimatis."

toward its end and Aquinas claims that the end is a cause of an agent's action insofar as it is something toward which the agent tends. Fire, for instance, tends toward generating fire by its natural inclination and the end of generating fire causes fire's action insofar as it is that toward which fire tends. In Aquinas's view, natural inclinations enable beings which lack cognition to act for the sake of goals. In the final section, we will examine Aquinas's views on the relationship between natural inclinations and God's cognition. Aquinas maintains that it is possible for natural beings to act for ends even though they lack cognition. He nevertheless thinks that natural inclinations, and the natures upon which they follow, must have their ultimate causal source in a being with cognition, namely God. We will analyze Aquinas's rationale for this view.

4.1 The Role of Natural Inclinations and Their Relationship to Form

In Aquinas's view, a natural inclination is an impetus that a substance has for engaging in a determinate action or producing a determinate effect.[2] The determinate action or effect which the inclination regards is described as an "end."[3] Aquinas claims that the natural inclination of a natural being is akin to will in rational agents. Aquinas writes: "In natural things there is a certain impetus or inclination for some end, which corresponds to will in a rational nature, hence this natural inclination is also called appetite."[4] In a rational being, the will has the role of determining whether an agent exercises a power to perform an action or produce an effect. For example, a builder's power to build is only a principle from which the action of house building follows if the builder wills to build. Aquinas claims that through

---

[2] For a helpful discussion of natural inclination see Brock, *Action and Conduct*, 115–17.

[3] Aquinas says that if the agent's action terminates in something which is made, such as a house in the case of building, then the impetus of the agent tends toward the product. If the action does not result in something made then the agent tends toward the action itself. *ScG* III c. 2 (ed. Marietti, 3–4, n. 1869):

> Actio vero quandoque quidem terminatur ad aliquod factum, sicut aedificatio ad domum, sanatio ad sanitatem: quandoque autem non, sicut intelligere et sentire. Et si quidem actio terminatur ad aliquod factum, impetus agentis tendit per actionem in illud factum: si autem non terminatur ad aliquod factum, impetus agentis tendit in ipsam actionem. Oportet igitur quod omne agens in agendo intendat finem: quandoque quidem actionem ipsam; quandoque aliquid per actionem factum.

[4] *In V Meta.* lec. 6 (ed. Marietti, 226, n. 829): "In naturalibus quidem est impetus, sive inclinatio ad aliquem finem, cui respondet voluntas in natura rationali; unde et ipsa naturalis inclinatio appetitus dicitur."

will a rational agent inclines itself toward an end and this inclination toward an end is required for its power to be exercised.[5] If a builder had no inclination toward the goal of building a house, he would not build. Aquinas thinks that natural agents likewise require an inclination toward some end in order to exercise their power in action. He writes the following in his *Summa theologiae*:

> If an agent were not determined toward some effect, it would no more act toward one effect than another. In order that it might produce a determinate effect, it is necessary that an agent be determined toward something certain, which has the nature of an end. Just as this determination happens in rational nature through rational appetite, which is called will; so too in others it happens through natural inclination, which is called natural appetite.[6]

In this passage, Aquinas claims that without a determination toward some determinate type of effect, an agent would not act. It would be indeterminate between different types of actions, and thus would do none of them. Put otherwise, in order for an agent to act, it must do some specific type of act. Some factor must determine which specific type of act it does. Aquinas explains at the end of the passage that natural inclination or appetite is that which determines a natural being toward doing something certain, namely toward a determinate end. Thus, natural inclinations in non-rational substances play a similar role to will in rational substances.

According to Aquinas, the specific ends toward which a natural inclination determines a natural substance is the distinctive actions which their form enables. He writes elsewhere in the *Summa*: "Each thing is naturally inclined toward the operation which is fitting to it according to its form, just as fire is to heating."[7] It is not a toss-up whether a natural agent will act through its distinctive powers. Rather, in each natural substance there

[5] See, for instance, *ST* I q. 14, a. 8.
[6] *ST* I-II q. 1, a. 2 (ed. Leon., vol. 6, 9): "Si enim agens non esset determinatum ad aliquem effectum, non magis ageret hoc quam illud: ad hoc ergo quod determinatum effectum producat, necesse est quod determinetur ad aliquid certum, quod habet rationem finis. Haec autem determinatio, sicut in rationali natura fit per rationalem appetitum, qui dicitur voluntas; ita in aliis fit per inclinationem naturalem, quae dicitur appetitus naturalis." See also *ScG* III c. 2 and *In II Sent.* d. 25, q. 1, a. 1. Note that in the latter text Aquinas attributes this argument to the "Commentator," namely Averroes. For other discussions of this argument, see Stephen Makin, "Aquinas, Natural Tendencies, and Natural Kinds," *New Scholasticism* 63.3 (1989): 253–74 and Paul Hoffman, "Does Efficient Causation Presuppose Final Causation? Aquinas vs. Early Modern Mechanism," in *Metaphysics and the Good: Themes from the Philosophy of Robert Merrihew Adams*, ed. L. Jorgensen and S. Newlands (Oxford: Oxford University Press, 2009), 297–312.
[7] *ST* I-II q. 94, a. 3 (ed. Leon., vol. 7, 170): "Inclinatur autem unumquodque naturaliter ad operationem sibi convenientem secundum suam formam: sicut ignis ad calefaciendum."

is something within their very being that skews them toward their characteristic activity. In addition to having the power for their proper operations, natural beings have an impetus toward those operations.

In Aquinas's view, natural beings do not only have an inclination toward exercising their proper powers, but they also have an inclination toward exercising those powers to the greatest extent possible. Natural agents do not cease to exercise their powers until they have made their patient as perfect as possible. Aquinas writes: "Natural beings ... have a natural inclination ... to diffuse their own good in another as much as possible. Hence we see that every agent insofar as it is actual and perfect makes another like itself."[8] Fire, for example, does not cease to heat water until it has realized in water the greatest degree of heat of which it is capable. A fire which is 600 degrees hot will not stop heating water when the water is any temperature lower than 600 degrees. Fire keeps heating the water until the water reaches its same temperature or the water can no longer receive a higher degree of heat. Aquinas writes:

> from an agent which acts by necessity of nature, an effect is only able to follow according to the mode of its active power: hence an agent which has very great power is not able to immediately produce a little effect, but rather it produces an effect proportionate to its power ...[9]

Natural inclination is not only that which explains why agents exercise their powers at all, but it also explains why they exercise their powers to produce the greatest effect of which they are capable. Since natural agents do not cease acting when it is still within their power to perfect their patient further, there must be something within them that determines them to act to the greatest extent possible. Natural inclination is what drives a natural agent to keep acting until it is not possible for it to perfect its patient any further.

---

[8] *ST* I q. 19, a. 2 (ed. Leon., vol. 4, 233): "Res enim naturalis... habet naturalem inclinationem ut ... proprium bonum in alia diffundat, secundum quod possibile est. Unde videmus quod omne agens, inquantum est actu et perfectum, facit sibi simile." See also *ST* I q. 80, a. 1 (ed. Leon., vol. 5, 282): "Ad cuius evidentiam, considerandum est quod quamlibet formam sequitur aliqua inclinatio: sicut ignis ex sua forma inclinatur in superiorem locum, et ad hoc quod generet sibi simile." *ST* I q. 60, a. 4 (ed. Leon., vol. 5, 103): "Et ideo dilectione naturali quaelibet res diliget id quod est secum unum secundum speciem, inquantum diligit speciem suam. Et hoc etiam apparet in his quae cognitione carent: nam ignis naturalem inclinationem habet ut communicet alteri suam formam, quod est bonum eius: sicut naturaliter inclinatur ad hoc quod quaerat bonum suum, ut esse sursum."
[9] *ScG* III c. 99 (ed. Marietti, 151, n. 2747): "ab agente secundum necessitatem naturae effectus non potest sequi nisi secundum modum virtutis activae: unde agens quod est maximae virtutis, non potest immediate producere effectum aliquem parvum, sed producit effectum suae virtuti proportionatum ..."

Natural inclinations play an important role in explaining the regularities that we observe in the natural world. Natural agents exercise their powers according to regular patterns because their natural inclinations determine them toward a single end. Aquinas writes: "The power of every agent acting by necessity of nature is determined toward one effect. Thus, it is the case that all natural things always happen in the same way, unless there is an impediment . . ."[10] Without natural inclination determining creatures toward their proper actions, they would be indeterminate between exercising their powers or not and we would not observe regular patterns in nature. It does sometimes happen that natural agents do not exercise their powers even though they are determined toward this end. But as we saw in Chapter 2, whenever a natural thing fails to act, it is always due to some impediment.[11]

As we saw earlier in Chapter 1, later figures such as Ockham claimed that the removal of an impediment or contact with a suitable patient is alone sufficient to explain why natural active powers are exercised.[12] According to this view, natural inclinations are unnecessary to explain why natural agents exercise their proper powers whenever they are able. Aquinas would certainly agree that there is a lack of impediments and a suitable patient whenever active powers are exercised. However, in his view, these factors do not explain why natural agents exercise their powers. Voluntary agents also require a lack of impediments and a suitable patient to act. Yet, they do not exercise their active powers without fail and to the greatest extent possible whenever these conditions are met. Voluntary agents only act when the further factor of will determines them toward action. Aquinas thinks that there likewise must be something further within the agent that explains why it acts whenever it is possible for it to do so. This is the role of natural inclination.

Now that we have seen Aquinas's views on the role that natural inclinations play in explaining natural agents' activities, as well as natural necessities, we can move on to see how natural inclinations arise in natural agents. Aquinas claims that the source of natural agents' natural inclinations is their forms. He writes in his *De malo*: "in natural things there is found form, which is a principle of action, and an inclination following from form, which is called natural appetite, from which action

---

[10] *ScG* II c. 23 (ed. Marietti, 134, n. 990): "Omnis enim agentis per necessitatem naturae virtus determinatur ad unum effectum. Et inde est quod omnia naturalia semper eveniunt eodem modo, nisi sit impedimentum . . ."

[11] See Section 2.3.   [12] See Section 1.4.

follows . . ."[13] Forms actualize substances in such a way that they are inclined toward certain actions. For example, in virtue of its form of heat, fire not only has a power to heat, but also an impetus toward heating. Aquinas writes, "we see in natural bodies that the inclination which is toward the being of a thing is not in virtue of something superadded to its essence . . . Rather . . . the inclination . . . for making something similar to itself is through its active qualities."[14] According to this passage, a natural inclination is not something superadded to a substance in addition to its form. Rather, it is an impetus that a substance has in virtue of its form. For example, heat and the natural inclination to heat are not two separate forms in fire. Rather, natural inclination is an impetus toward heating which a fire has through its form of heat. Elsewhere Aquinas writes: "From form, follows an inclination to an end or toward action or toward something of this kind since each one, insofar as it is in act, acts and tends toward that which is fitting to it according to its form."[15] In Aquinas's view, forms do not merely enable action. In addition to enabling a determinate type of activity, forms also bestow on substances a tendency toward performing that activity. So long as they are in the relevant circumstances and not impeded by something external, natural causes will produce the actions of which their forms make them capable.

Given that Aquinas identifies active power with form and natural inclination follows upon form, a reader might wonder whether the attribution of natural inclination to an agent amounts to anything more than a claim that an agent has a power which is a power for some determinate action. The passages considered in this section reveal that having a natural inclination toward an action as an end is in fact something more than merely having a power to do that action. Though the inclination toward an action arises from the form which is also the power for the action, the inclination has a different function than the power: it determines an agent toward the exercise of a power. As we have seen, rational agents have powers that do not of themselves give rise to an inclination which determines their exercise. For example, the power of shipbuilding does not

---

[13] *De malo* q. 6 (ed. Leon., vol. 23, 148): "in rebus naturalibus inuenitur forma, que est principium actionis, et inclinatio consequens formam, que dicitur appetitus naturalis, ex quibus sequitur actio . . ."

[14] *ST* I q. 59, a. 2 (ed. Leon., vol. 5, 93): "videmus in corporibus naturalibus quod inclinatio quae est ad esse rei, non est per aliquid superadditum essentiae . . . Sed . . . inclinatio . . . ad faciendum sibi simile est per qualitates activas."

[15] *ST* I q. 5, a. 5 (ed. Leon., vol. 4, 63): "Ad formam autem consequitur inclinatio ad finem, aut ad actionem, aut ad aliquid huiusmodi: quia unumquodque, inquantum est actu, agit, et tendit in id quod sibi convenit secundum suam formam."

endow an agent with an inclination such that she will always exercise the power when the opportunity arises. Powers like shipbuilding are only exercised when the agent determines them to be through the power of will. Thus, Aquinas is telling us something informative about natural powers when he claims that natural inclinations follow upon them. He is telling us something more than the claim that a natural power is a power for a determinate action. A form which is a natural power does not only give an agent an ability to act and specify the type of act it will perform. The form also gives the agent an impetus which "tips the balance" between not acting and acting toward acting. A substance with a natural inclination will automatically exercise its power whenever it is in the relevant circumstances.

4.2   How Natural Agents Act for Ends without Cognition and How Ends Cause Actions according to Final Causality

In the previous section, we saw that Aquinas thinks that through their natural inclinations natural beings tend toward the end of exercising their powers to the greatest extent possible. Natural inclination is an impetus that directs them toward this end. In several passages throughout his works, Aquinas addresses the question of how it is possible for a natural agent to tend toward a goal if it lacks cognition of that goal. For example, how can fire tend toward heating its patient as much as possible if fire lacks cognition? It might seem that in order for a being to tend toward some action or effect, it would need knowledge of that action or effect. In response to such a worry, Aquinas writes the following in his early *De principiis naturae*:

> It must be known that every agent whether natural or voluntary intends an end, it does not follow nevertheless that every agent knows the end or deliberates about the end. For to know the end is necessary in those whose actions are not determined, but regard opposite acts, just as voluntary agents find themselves, therefore it is necessary that they know the end for which they determine their actions. But in natural agents the actions are determined, hence it is not necessary to choose those things which are for the end.[16]

---

[16] *De prin. nat.* c. 3 (ed. Leon., vol. 43, 42):

> Et sciendum, quod omne agens tam naturale quam uoluntarium intendit finem; non tamen sequitur quod omne agens cognoscat finem, uel deliberet de fine. Cognoscere enim finem est necessarium in his quorum actiones non sunt determinatae, sed se habent ad opposita, sicut se habent agentia uoluntaria; et ideo oportet quod cognoscant finem per quem suas actiones determinent. Sed in agentibus naturalibus sunt actiones determinatae, unde non est necessarium eligere ea quae sunt ad finem.

See also *ST* I-II, q. 12, a. 5 and *De ver.* q. 25, a. 1.

In this passage, Aquinas claims that knowledge of the end is only necessary for an agent to tend toward that end when the agent is not determined to that end. If the agent has something within it that inclines it toward a single act, it need not know its end because it does not need to determine itself to it. Aquinas goes on to give an example from Avicenna of a harpist who plays chords without deliberating about the notes. This is supposed to show that it is possible even for a rational agent, which has the capacity for deliberation, to act for an end without deliberating.[17] The harpist plays the chord for the sake of making music and thus acts for an end. Yet, she does this action which tends toward an end without thinking about it. This demonstrates that it is possible for agents to act for ends without thinking about those ends. At the end of the passage, Aquinas states that "to intend is nothing other than to have a natural inclination toward something."[18] In contemporary language, "intentionality" is usually reserved to refer to the directedness that a mind can have toward objects of thought, and the term "intentional" is usually used to describe actions that are deliberately chosen by a rational being. Thus, a reader may assume that "to intend" something is proper to cognitive beings. Aquinas, by contrast, writes the following: "'intention,' just as its name sounds, signifies *to tend toward something*."[19] Natural beings can intend ends because they are determined by natural inclination to tend toward an end.

In his *Physics* commentary, Aquinas again compares the natural inclinations of creatures with human arts. An art is a habit which a human being acquires through repeated action. Arts enable their possessors to act well with regard to certain objects, such as medicine, music, and the building of artifacts. Aquinas gives the example of a writer who is able to form letters well through the art of writing without thinking about how to form the letters. The art directs her toward right action in an effortless way. If one needs to think through one's movements, this is usually a sign that one is still learning the art and does not yet possess it. The true artisan acts without deliberation because the internalized principles of the art are themselves sufficient for proper action. The artisan's intellect has been

[17] *De prin. nat.* c. 3 (ed. Leon., vol. 43, 42): "Et ponit exemplum Avicenna de citharaedo, quem non oportet de qualibet percussione chordarum deliberare, cum percussiones sint determinatae apud ipsum: alioquin esset inter percussiones mora, quod esset absonum. Magis autem uidetur de operante uoluntarie quod deliberet quam de agente naturali: et ita patet per locum a maiori quod possibile est agens naturale sine deliberatione intendere finem ..."
[18] *De prin. nat.* c. 3 (ed. Leon., vol. 43, 42): "et hoc intendere nichil aliud erat quam habere naturalem inclinationem ad aliquid."
[19] *ST* I-II q. 12, a. 1 (ed. Leon., vol. 6, 94): "intentio, sicut ipsum nomen sonat, significat *in aliquid tendere*."

formed in such a way that the proper actions simply flow from her. Aquinas views natural inclination as akin to art insofar as it is similarly sufficient to direct the natural creature toward its proper actions without any need for thought about those actions.[20] Just as the accomplished writer has been formed in such a way that well-formed letters naturally flow from her, so too is fire constituted in such a way that it naturally tends toward heating. Fire would only need to deliberate to heat if it were indifferent toward heating or not heating. Since fire is naturally inclined toward heating, it need not deliberate between these two possibilities. As Aquinas writes elsewhere:

> Since a natural thing is determined in its natural being, and it has a single inclination toward some determinate thing, it follows that some apprehension is not required through which an appetible thing is distinguished from a non-appetible thing according to the nature of appetibility . . .[21]

Natural beings have built into them an impetus toward what is good for them. Thus, they can act for an end "mindlessly" since they need not select between what is desirable or undesirable. Their very being directs them toward the proper action for a thing of their kind.

It is important to note that in Aquinas's view it is not only the case that a natural agent's natural inclination is a cause of its action. He also thinks that the end itself toward which the natural inclination directs is a cause of a natural agent's action according to final causality.[22] Aquinas writes:

> in any action there are two things to consider: namely the agent, and the reason for acting; as in heating, fire is the agent, and the reason for acting is heat. In moving, the end is said to move as the reason for moving: but the efficient cause moves as the agent of motion, that is educing the mobile from potency to act.[23]

According to this passage, heat is a cause of fire's act of heating because fire engages in heating since heat is something it has an inclination to produce.

---

[20] *In II Phys.* lec. 14.

[21] *De ver.* q. 25, a. 1 (ed. Leon., vol. 22 3/1, 729): "Quia vero res naturalis in suo esse naturali determinata est; et una est eius inclinatio ad aliquam rem determinatam, unde non exigitur aliqua apprehensio, per quam secundum rationem appetibilitatis distinguatur res appetibilis a non appetibili . . ." See also *ST* I-II q. 12, a. 5.

[22] For a recent study of Aquinas's views on final causality see Joel Johnson, "Final Causality in the Thought of Thomas Aquinas," PhD diss., Purdue University, 2018, ProQuest Dissertations Publishing, 10840028.

[23] *De ver.* q. 22, a. 12 (ed. Leon., vol. 22 3/1, 642): "in qualibet actione duo considerentur, scilicet agens, et ratio agenda, ut in calefactione ignis est agens, et ratio agendi calor. In movendo dicitur finis movere sicut ratio movendi, sed efficiens sicut agens motum, hoc est educens mobile de potentia in actum."

In general, exercises of efficient causality depend on final causes because efficient causes only exercise their powers in action because they intend some end. Thus, action depends on an end for its being. Aquinas writes elsewhere: "but the end is said to be a cause of the efficient cause since it [i.e. the efficient cause] does not operate except through intention of an end."[24] As this passage explains, if an efficient cause does not intend an end, it will not operate. Thus, exercises of efficient causality depend on ends. In fact, Aquinas thinks that the end or final cause is the most fundamental of the four causes. He claims that the final cause is "the cause of all causality" since if it were not for the sake of the end, the agent would not act.[25] If the agent does not act, then no form is induced in matter. Thus, the other three types of causes (e.g. efficient, material and formal) all depend on final causes to exercise their causality.

The view that final causes or ends are genuine causes of actions has been the source of much controversy and objection in the history of philosophy. It is generally accepted that causes must exist temporally prior to or at least simultaneous with their effects. It is hard to see how an effect could depend for its existence on something that does not exist before or while it exists. But the end comes to be after the action that causes it. For instance, heat only comes to be in a patient consequent to the action of heating. So, how could heat be a cause of the action of heating if it does not exist until the act of heating is elicited? This worry led early modern figures to reject final causes.[26] Spinoza expresses this apparent problem with final causes when he writes:

> This doctrine concerning the end turns nature completely upside down. For what is really a cause, it considers an effect, and what is an effect it considers as a cause. What is by nature prior it makes posterior.[27]

Spinoza notes that the efficient cause's action is that which causes the end to exist. Fire's action of heating, for example, is that which causes

---

[24] *De prin. nat.* c. 4 (ed. Leon., vol. 43, 43): "sed finis dicitur causa efficientis, cum non operetur nisi per intentionem finis."

[25] *De prin. nat.* c. 4 (ed. Leon., vol. 43, 44): "Vnde dicitur quod finis est causa causarum, quia est causa causalitatis in omnibus causis." See also *ST* I, q. 105 a. 5 (ed. Leon., vol. 5, 476): "Finis vero et agens et forma se habent ut actionis principium, sed ordine quodam. Nam primo quidem, principium actionis est finis, qui movet agentem; secundo vero, agens; tertio autem, forma eius quod ab agente applicatur ad agendum (quamvis et ipsum agens per formam suam agat); ut patet in artificialibus."

[26] For a brief overview of early modern debates about final causality, see Steven Nadler, "Doctrines of Explanation in Late Scholasticism and Mechanical Philosophy," in *Cambridge History of Seventeenth Century Philosophy*, ed. D. Garber and M. Ayers (Cambridge: Cambridge University Press, 2008), 513–52, esp. section VIII.

[27] Spinoza, *Ethics*, trans. Edwin Curley (London and New York: Penguin Press, 2005), 28.

heat to exist. Thus, it seems backwards to claim that the end, such as heat, is a cause of the agent's action, namely heating. How can an end be the cause of an action if it depends on the action for its being? Aquinas himself considered this objection.[28] It is worthwhile for us to examine how he responds, as well as how his response applies to natural causes, because it will help us to understand more clearly how final causes are causes of natural actions.

Aquinas writes in response to the objection of how the end can be a cause if it only exists upon the completion of the agent's action: "[E]ven if the end is last in the order of execution, it is nevertheless first in the intention of the agent. In this way, it has the nature of a cause."[29] As the response implies, Aquinas draws a distinction between two different ways an end can be considered: as the end of execution and as the end of intention. The end of execution is the actual end-point of the agent's action, while the end of intention is the object which the agent intends to reach.[30] The end of execution is the agent's effect. The end of intention, however, is the end which functions as a final cause of the agent's action. It is through being intended by an agent that the end causes the agent's action. The end which the agent intends, not the effect which it actually produces, is that on account of which it acts. For example, when the builder builds a house, it is not the completed house made out of timbers and bricks that is the final cause of his action, but rather it is the house which he intended that moved him to act. Though the form of the house only exists in matter subsequent to the builder's action, the house exists in the builder's intellect prior to his act of building. By existing in the builder's intellect, the house causes the builder to act. Final causality does not assume that the final effect is the cause of the action that brings it about. Rather, it is the end in the agent's intention that causes the agent's act and the end exists in the agent's intention prior to its action.

---

[28] For Aquinas's consideration of the objection, see for instance, *ST* I-II q. 1, a. 1, obj. 1 (ed. Leon., vol. 6, 6): "Causa enim naturaliter prior est. Sed finis habet rationem ultimi, ut ipsum nomen sonat. Ergo finis non habet rationem causae."

[29] *ST* I-II q. 1, a. 1, ad 1 (ed. Leon., vol. 6, 6): "[F]inis, etsi sit postremus in executione, est tamen primus in intentione agentis. Et hoc modo habet rationem causae." See also *ST* III q. 61, a. 3 ad 1: "Causa autem finalis non praecedit tempore, sed solum in intentione agentis." *De pot.* q. 3, a. 16 (ed. Pession, 87): "Causae autem sunt quatuor, quarum duae, scilicet materia et efficiens, praecedunt causatum, secundum esse internum; finis vero etsi non secundum esse, tamen secundum intentionem ..." *In III Sent.* d. 23, q. 2, a. 5 ad 4 (ed. Mandonnet-Moos, vol. 3, 740): "finis est prior in intentione, et posterior in esse ..."

[30] Another text in which Aquinas draws this distinction is *Super Io.* c. 13, lec. 1.

It should be noted that the claim that the end is a cause only insofar as it exists in the intention of the agent is not original or unique to Aquinas. Prior to Aquinas, Avicenna had claimed that the end functioned as a cause insofar as it exists in the soul of the agent.[31] Some scholastics, such as Scotus, likewise followed Avicenna on this point. By contrast, Averroes contended that it was the end as it exists outside of the soul in real being that functions as a final cause and other scholastic figures, such as Ockham, adopted his view.[32]

It is natural to wonder how this view that the final cause is the end in intention can apply to natural agents. If natural agents lack cognitive capacities how could it be that their ends or goals exist in them intentionally prior to their actions? As we saw above, Aquinas thinks that causes which lack cognition can intend ends. To say that an end is in intention is just to say that there is something within the cause that is directed toward the end. Though natural beings do not have cognition, they have within them something that is directed toward an end, namely their natural inclinations. Aquinas writes: "to intend is nothing other than to have a natural inclination toward something."[33] That which is directed toward the end need not be a cognitive act. It can also be a natural inclination. A natural inclination's proportionality to an end is that which makes the inclination what it is. Thus, through its natural inclination, the end is in a natural agent according to intention.[34] For example, the end of heat is in fire according to intention since within fire there is something, namely the fire's natural inclination for heating, which is a directedness toward this end. Fire's natural inclination is intrinsic to it, yet it has its identity from the extrinsic act it regards, namely heating. The extrinsic heat that fire is inclined to produce is that which makes its natural inclination for heating what it is. Thus, the heat which fire is ordered toward producing is in it according to intention. Since natural inclination is a directedness toward a

---

[31] Avicenna, *Liber de philosophia prima*, ed. Gérard Verbeke (Leuven: Peeters, 1983), 337: "Eius autem causalitas non est causa esse earum, nisi prius sit imaginata in anima vel in alio consimili."

[32] For a discussion of the debate between Averroes and Avicenna and its influence on scholastic discussions of final causality, see Pasnau, "Intentionality and Final Causes," 312–15 and "Teleology in the Later Middle Ages," 96–98.

[33] *De prin. nat.* c. 3 (ed. Leon., vol. 43, 42): "et hoc intendere nichil aliud erat quam habere naturalem inclinationem ad aliquid."

[34] Aquinas claims that in the similar way, actions are prior in intention to powers. A power is essentially a directedness toward an action. Thus, the action is in the power according to intention. *ST* I, q. 77, a. 3, ad 1 (ed. Leon., vol. 5, 241): "dicendum quod actus, licet sit posterior potentia in esse, est tamen prior in intentione et secundum rationem, sicut finis agente. – Obiectum autem, licet sit extrinsecum, est tamen principium vel finis actionis. Principio autem et fini proportionantur ea quae sunt intrinseca rei."

determinate end, a being with a natural inclination has its end in it according to intention.

We are now in a position to understand how the final causes of natural agents can have the priority required to cause their actions. As we have seen, a natural inclination is an impetus within a natural agent which inclines it toward exercising its powers. Each natural inclination is what it is through its proportion to an end. Thus, ends have a priority over natural inclinations. Since natural inclinations are causes of natural action, so too are the ends toward which natural inclinations are proportioned properly identified as causes of action. Heat, for example, causes fire to engage in heating insofar as fire exercises its power to heat through a natural inclination toward producing heat. The inclination toward heating is what it is through its proportion to heat. In this regard, heat is a cause which explains why fire engages in heating. The fact that it has an inclination toward producing heat explains why it heats.

4.3   God as Source of Natural Inclinations and a Natural Agent's Intention of Its End

In the previous two sections, we have seen Aquinas's view that natural inclinations follow upon form and have the role of directing natural efficient causes toward their end. Furthermore, we have seen that Aquinas thinks that natural inclinations explain how natural agents are able to act for ends even though they lack cognition. By determining the agent toward one action, the inclination makes deliberation about whether to do an action unnecessary. Furthermore, since natural inclinations are a directedness toward an end, the end has a priority in intention over the agent's action and thus, functions as the final cause of the agent's action. Heat is a final cause of fire's heating, for example, because fire engages in heating because it has an intrinsic directedness toward heat. Given that Aquinas has a theory about how natural agents act for ends through natural inclinations and an account of the source of these inclinations in form, it would seem that there is nothing left to explain regarding how natural agents act for ends. However, in numerous texts we find Aquinas claiming that a natural agent's movement toward its end ultimately depends on God's cognition.[35] The goal of this section is to reconstruct Aquinas's rationale for why, in addition to forms and the natural inclinations which

---

[35] See for example *De ver.* q. 22, a. 1; *ScG* III, c. 64 and *ST* I q. 103, a. 1 ad 1.

follow from them, God's cognition is necessary to explain how natural agents act for ends. In brief, Aquinas thinks that if natural inclinations direct creatures toward ends, then natural inclinations must themselves be the work of an intelligent cause.

Aquinas reasons that if natural inclinations are to be inclinations for certain ends, then they must be caused by a cause which grasps the end toward which the inclination leads. For example, he thinks that an inclination toward heating must be caused by a cause which understands heat and understands it as an end to be sought. As we saw above, a natural inclination is a determination within a creature toward a certain end.[36] Fire's natural inclination to heat, for example, is a determination within fire toward heating. Aquinas thinks that if a cause is genuinely determined from within toward a certain end, and not merely reaching that end by chance, then the determination must be due to a cause with knowledge. Aquinas writes the following in his *Sentences* commentary:

> It is necessary that the determination come forth from intention of the end, not only from nature tending toward the end, because then everything would be by chance, just as certain philosophers posited. To intend an end, however, is impossible unless the end is known as an end as well as the proportion of those things which are for the end to the end itself.[37]

According to this passage, the reason why it is necessary for creatures which are genuinely determined toward certain ends to be fashioned by a cause with knowledge is because the cause must understand the creature's end in order to fashion the creature in such a way that it is intrinsically determined toward its end. In another passage, Aquinas makes the same point and explicitly claims that natural inclination or appetite must be bestowed on natural agents by an intelligent cause. He writes:

> [E]verything which tends toward another naturally requires that it has this from another directing it toward an end, otherwise it would tend toward it by chance. In natural things we find natural appetite by which each thing tends toward its end, hence it is necessary to posit above all natural things some intellect which has ordained natural things to their end and bestowed them with natural inclination or appetite. But a thing is not able to be

[36] See Section 4.1.
[37] *In III Sent.* d. 27, q. 1, a. 2 (ed. Mandonnet-Moos, vol. 3, 860): "Illa autem determinatio oportet quod proveniat ex intentione finis, non solum ex natura tendente in finem, quia sic omnia essent casu, ut quidam philosophi posuerunt. Intendere autem finem impossibile est, nisi cognoscatur finis sub ratione finis, et proportio eorum quae sunt ad finem in finem ipsum."

ordered to any end unless the thing itself is known together with the end toward which it is ordered . . .[38]

In Aquinas's views, a natural inclination is an impetus toward an action or effect and thus, it must be caused by a being which understands the action or effect toward which the inclination impels. For example, fire's inclination toward heating must arise from a cause which understands fire and that its end is to heat because without such a cause it could not be explained why the inclination leads to heating and not to some other outcome.

Aquinas does not deny that the natural inclination can explain how its bearer moves toward an end without cognition. Yet, he thinks that if the inclination itself is to direct toward an end, it must come from a cause that knows the end. Consider a parallel example: If a construction crew makes a road which is for the sake of travelling to Athens, then the construction crew has to know where Athens is. The travelers on the road may simply follow the path without knowing how exactly to get to the final destination. Yet, the ones who make the road for the sake of others reaching a certain destination must know where that destination is so that they can proportion the road to it. Similarly, if it is posited that natural inclinations direct creatures to their ends, then they must have been caused in creatures by a cause which has knowledge of their ends and fashions the inclination in accord with them.

As both of the passages just quoted make clear, Aquinas thinks that the alternative to positing that creatures have been determined by an intelligent cause toward certain ends is to posit that they reach their ends by chance. For example, the alternative to claiming that fire has been caused by an intelligent cause in such a way that it is intrinsically inclined toward heating is to conclude that fire heats by chance. Aquinas argues elsewhere that natural causes cannot be reaching their ends by chance because events which are due to chance do not happen with regularity.[39] For example, if it

---

[38] *De ver.* q. 2, a. 3 (ed. Leon. vol. 22 1/2, 50–51):

> [O]mne enim quod naturaliter in alterum tendit, oportet quod hoc habeat ex aliquo dirigente ipsum in finem, alias casu in illud tenderet; in rebus autem naturalibus invenimus naturalem appetitum quo unaquaeque res in finem suum tendit, unde oportet supra omnes res naturales ponere aliquem intellectum, qui res naturales ad suos fines ordinaverit, et eis naturalem inclinationem sive appetitum indiderit; sed res non potest ordinari ad finem aliquem, nisi res ipsa cognoscatur simul cum fine ad quem ordinanda est . . .

[39] See for example *In II Phys.* lec. 13 (ed. Leon., vol. 2, 93):

> Omnia quae fiunt, aut fiunt a casu, aut fiunt propter finem; quae enim accidunt praeter intentionem finis, dicuntur accidere casualiter: sed impossibile est ea quae fiunt semper vel

was due to chance that fire heated objects, rather than remaining inactive in their presence, then this occurrence would not happen with regularity. But we clearly observe that natural agents exercise their powers for their proper activities with regularity. Thus, it cannot be due to chance that they do so. They must be internally determined toward exercising their powers for their proper operations since they do this with uniformity.

A contemporary reader might wonder why it couldn't simply be a matter of necessity that creatures' natures make them a certain way and that way in which they are through their natures necessitates that they are inclined toward their proper operations. On this model, no intelligence would be necessary to explain why natural creatures are determined in such a way toward certain ends since there is only one way they can be according to their nature. By Aquinas's own principles, it would seem that the determination need not happen through knowledge if it follows from the nature since there is no other possibility about which a cognitive agent would need to deliberate.

Aquinas would likely think this approach only pushes the problem of explaining a natural creature's determination toward an end up a level. Aquinas agrees that the determination which a creature has toward its end follows from its very nature. Given that a creature is of a certain species, it follows that it has certain inclinations through its form. Yet, Aquinas thinks that natures and forms themselves must be the work of intelligence if they confer natural inclinations on creatures. Aquinas writes: "[T]he operation of nature, which is toward a determinate end, presupposes an intellect, instituting the end of nature and ordering nature to that end. For this reason, every work of nature is said to be a work of intelligence."[40] Aquinas acknowledges that it is in the nature of creatures to have certain natural inclinations. Fire, for example, is such by its nature that it has an inclination to heat. Since this inclination follows from its nature, there is no other way it could be while still being fire. Aquinas seems to think that a nature's conferral of inclinations toward ends cannot be a brute fact. In his view, the only way a nature could be ordered or proportioned to an end is if the nature itself were the product of an intelligence that grasped the end and proportioned the nature to it. In his view, anything which is intrinsically

---

frequenter, accidere a casu: ergo ea quae fiunt semper vel frequenter, fiunt propter aliquid. Sed omnia quae fiunt secundum naturam, fiunt vel semper vel frequenter, sicut etiam ipsi confitebantur: ergo omnia quae fiunt a natura, fiunt propter aliquid.

[40] *De ver.* q. 3, a. 1 (ed. Leon., vol. 22 1/2, 100): "operatio naturae, quae est ad determinatum finem, praesupponit intellectum, praestituentem finem naturae et ordinantem ad finem illum naturam, ratione cuius omne opus naturae dicitur esse opus intelligentiae."

proportioned to something extrinsic to it must be the product of an intelligence that grasps the extrinsic thing to which it is proportioned.

Throughout his works Aquinas reiterates that the forms of natural things depend on God's intelligence.[41] He writes in his *Sentences* commentary: "[T]he emanation of creatures from God is just as the emergence of artifacts from an artisan, hence just as from the art of the artisan flows the forms of artificial things in matter, so too from the ideas existing in the divine mind flow all natural forms and powers."[42] He similarly writes in the *Summa contra Gentiles*: "Hence the whole of nature is just as an artifact of divine art."[43] In later works, he repeats the analogy between God and the human artisan. He writes in the *Summa theologiae*: "Just as artificial things are compared to human art, so are all natural things compared to divine art."[44] He explains that although creation does not presuppose any prior existing realities out of which creatures are made, creation does presuppose cognition in God.[45] The natures of creatures which confer natural inclination must themselves be the product of an intellect. Let us reflect for a moment on how the analogy between God and the human artisan helps to illuminate Aquinas's reasoning for why nature must be the work of intelligence. Whenever a human artisan makes something, such as a tool, clothing or furniture, the artisan must have a grasp of the end or purpose of the artifact. It is through understanding the end that the artisan knows how to best make the artifact. For example, one who makes a hammer must have a conception of what a hammer is for, namely driving nails, in order to shape the hammer properly for this purpose. Similarly, Aquinas thinks that if created natures are that by which creatures act for ends, then these natures must be the product of an intellect which knows the ends which they are for. Aquinas thinks that God does not merely

---

[41] For a study of Aquinas's views on God's exemplars of creatures, see Gregory Doolan, *Aquinas on Divine Ideas as Exemplar Causes* (Washington, DC: Catholic University of America Press, 2008). In *ST* I 15, a. 3, Aquinas explains that God ideas are called "exemplars" insofar as they are principles for making creatures, rather than knowing them in a speculative way. Doolan discusses the texts in which Aquinas claims that God's direction of natural causes to their ends proves the existence of divine ideas, see pp. 44–64.

[42] *In II Sent.* d. 18, q. 1, a. 2 (ed. Mandonnet-Moos, vol. 2, 451): "emanatio creaturarum a Deo est sicut exitus artificiatorum ab artifice; unde sicut ab arte artificis effluunt formae artificiales in materia, ita etiam ab ideis in mente divina existentibus fluunt omnes formae et virtutes naturales."

[43] *ScG* III c. 100 (ed. Marietti, 143, n. 2761): "Unde tota natura est sicut quoddam artificiatum divinae artis."

[44] *ST* I-II q. 13, a. 2, ad 3 (ed. Leon., vol. 6, 99–100): "Sicut autem comparantur artificialia ad artem humanam, ita comparantur omnia naturalia ad artem divinam." See also *ST* I q. 91, a. 3; *ST* I q. 17, a. 1.

[45] *ST* I q. 21, a. 4 ad 4.

make natural creatures in such a way that they can be moved or used for an end by another, just as the hammer can be used by a craftsman. Rather, by giving creatures a nature, he gives them the means by which they move themselves toward their own end. Through its own nature, for example, fire heats and thereby, fulfills its purpose as fire. Aquinas likens God's giving of a nature to creatures to placing his own art in them. He writes:

> Hence it is clear that nature is nothing other than the principle (*ratio*) of a certain art, namely divine art, implanted in things by which they are moved to a determinate end. It is just as if the maker of a ship were to give to wooden boards that by which they would be moved through themselves to inducing the form of a ship.[46]

The shipbuilder uses the art in his intellect to make the ship suitable to be used by others for a certain end, namely sailing. God, however, gives the things he makes an intrinsic principle, namely a nature, which impels them toward acting for their end themselves. Human artifacts are made to reach their ends by being used by human artisans. By contrast, in giving creatures their natures and the inclinations which follow from them, God has made natural agents in such a way that they reach their ends by their own actions.

In Aquinas's view, God gives inclinations to creatures not by super-adding something which lies outside of their form or nature. Rather, he gives the inclination by giving the very form or nature to the creature. He writes: "The very nature of each one is a certain inclination put in it by the first mover, ordering each to its proper end."[47] Elsewhere he writes: "[T]he natural inclination for some end is from the one instituting nature, who gives nature such order . . ."[48] As this passage makes clear, God does not give natural inclinations to creatures as if they were something not already included in their nature. Rather, God gives natural inclinations insofar as, through his cognition, he constitutes the creature's nature in such a way that the natural inclination flows from it.[49] Aquinas writes elsewhere:

---

[46] *In II Phys.* lec. 14 (ed. Leon., vol. 2, 96): "Unde patet quod natura nihil est aliud quam ratio cuiusdam artis, scilicet divinae, indita rebus, qua ipsae res moventur ad finem determinatum: sicut si artifex factor navis posset lignis tribuere, quod ex se ipsis moverentur ad navis formam inducendam."

[47] *In XII Meta.* lec. 12 (ed. Marietti, 613, n. 2634): "Et ipsa natura uniuscuiusque est quaedam inclinatio indita ei a primo movente, ordinans ipsam in debitum finem."

[48] *In III Sent.* d. 33, q. 2, a. 4, qc. 4 (ed. Mandonnet-Moos, vol. 3, 1066): "naturalis inclinatio ad finem aliquem est ex praestituente naturam qui talem ordinem naturae tribuit . . ."

[49] Aquinas likewise thinks that God's wisdom is responsible for creature's possession of powers which are proportioned to certain actions. See *In III Sent.* d. 23, q. 1, a. 1 (ed. Mandonnet-Moos, vol. 3, 697): "Sunt autem *quaedam potentiae limitatae* ad determinatas actiones vel passiones; et secundum quod illas implent, suae regulae conformantur, quia per divinam sapientiam ad talia sunt ordinatae."

God moves all things to their actions, nevertheless they are inclined toward them by their proper forms. Therefore, it is the case that he disposes all things gently because he gives all things forms and powers inclining them toward that to which he himself moves, so that they tend toward it not by coercion, but as if spontaneously.[50]

Natural creatures' movement toward their ends is both natural and from God since God is the cause of their natures.[51] Natures are themselves a work of divine cognition. Thus, the natural inclination that directs creatures to their ends is both perfectly natural and dependent on God.

In Chapter 3, we saw that the precise end that natural agents tend to in their actions is realizing a form like their own in another; and therefore, Aquinas thinks that every agent makes an effect like itself.[52] Aquinas thinks that even this tendency which natural agents have toward making others like themselves must ultimately depend on divine cognition. He writes:

Since natural things naturally intend to induce their likenesses in generated things, it is necessary that this intention is reduced to some directing principle which is ordering each one to an end. And this cannot be anything other than an intellect which has knowledge of the end and the proportion of things to the end. Thus, the similitude of effects to natural causes is reduced, as a first principle, to some intellect.[53]

---

[50] *De virt.* q. 2, a. 1 (ed. Odetto, 755–56): "Deus movet omnia ad suas actiones, ad quas tamen inclinantur ex propriis formis. Et inde est quod omnia disponit suaviter, quia omnibus dat formas et virtutes inclinantes in id ad quod ipse movet, ut in illud tendant non coacte, sed quasi sponte." Though Aquinas often uses example of the arrow which is shot toward the target by the archer as an analogy for understanding how God directs natural causes to their ends, he clarifies in some passages that God moves natural causes in a very different way from how the archer moves the arrow. See for instance, *ST* q. 103, a. 1 ad 3: "[N]ecessitas naturalis inhaerens rebus quae determinantur ad unum, est impressio quaedam Dei dirigentis ad finem, sicut necessitas qua sagitta agitur ut ad certum signum tendat, est impressio sagittantis, et non sagittae. Sed in hoc differt, quia id quod creaturae a Deo recipiunt, est earum natura; quod autem ab homine rebus naturalibus imprimitur praeter earum naturam, ad violentiam pertinet."

[51] Some have worried that Aquinas's theory of natural inclinations involved inconsistency in this regard. Stephan Schmid articulates this objection: "If natural substances do have a natural or intrinsic inclination toward some ends as Aquinas maintains, there is no need for God to direct them towards these ends, for they intrinsically are. . . If it is indeed God who is responsible for the finality of natural things, they do have their purposes only in a derivative sense – similar to artefacts the purposes of which depend on our intentions." See Stephan Schmid, "Teleology and the Dispositional Theory of Causation in Thomas Aquinas," *Logical Analysis and the History of Philosophy* 14 (2011): 21–39, at 35–38.

[52] See especially Sections 3.4 and 3.6.

[53] *In I Meta.* lec. 15 (ed. Marietti, 68–69, n. 233): "Cum enim res naturales naturaliter intendant similitudines in res generatas inducere, oportet quod ista intentio ad aliquod principium dirigens reducatur, quod est in finem ordinans unumquodque. Et hoc non potest esse nisi intellectus cuius sit cognoscere finem et proportionem rerum in finem. Et sic ista similitudo effectuum ad causas naturales reducitur, sicut in primum principium, in intellectum aliquem."

As this passage indicates, Aquinas thinks even that inclination to make another like itself must be the result of an agent which understands the "likeness" as an end and proportions the creature's inclination to it. We saw in Chapter 3 that Aquinas also thinks that natural agents act toward making their like because goodness is self-diffusive.[54] It may seem like there would be no need for God to order creaturely natures toward self-replication if all good things naturally have the tendency toward making another like themselves. I don't know of a passage in which Aquinas makes this point, but I suspect that he might claim that while goodness specifies what creatures' ends are, namely to make another like themselves, God's cognition of goodness is required to fashion creaturely natures in such a way that non-rational creatures have an intrinsic impetus toward this end. It should be noted that Aquinas thinks that God is goodness itself.[55] Thus, the specific ends which creatures have in virtue of the nature of goodness (i.e. making another like themselves) are in fact dependent upon God since God is goodness itself.

4.4 Conclusion

From Aquinas's perspective, active powers alone cannot explain why natural agents act and why they regularly act in the same ways. In addition to powers, something else is required to explain why, as long as there is no impediment, natural agents exercise their powers and to the fullest extent possible. Natural inclination is a determination within the natural agent toward the exercise of its proper powers, to the fullest extent possible. Natural inclinations also account for how natural agents, though they lack cognition, can act for ends. Natural inclination is an impetus toward a single action or effect, and thus, the agent which possesses it need not deliberate between options. As we saw in this chapter, Aquinas thinks that natural inclination follows from the form of a natural being. Yet, God is ultimately responsible for natural inclinations insofar as both the form and the natural inclination which arises from it depend on God's cognition for their constitution.

---

[54] See Section 3.4.   [55] On divine goodness see, for instance, *ST* I, q. 6.

CHAPTER 5

Passive Powers

Aquinas thinks that if we want to understand causal interactions between material substances, we cannot focus exclusively on agents and their active powers.[1] We must also consider the substance which undergoes action as well. For example, to understand how burning happens we cannot exclusively consider fire and its active power. We must also consider the features of things which are able to be burned. Not just any type of substance can undergo burning. In Aquinas's view, there must be something real in a patient that allows it to be acted upon in a certain way. Aquinas writes that "[I]n any action there is something to consider from the part of the agent, and from the part of the patient ..."[2] Aquinas refers to that in virtue of which the patient is acted upon as passive potentiality; and he claims that to every type of active power, there corresponds a determinate type of passive power.[3] In this chapter we will consider Aquinas's views on passive powers. First, we will examine Aquinas's thinking about the constituents of material substances which give rise to their passive potentialities for being acted upon. We will see that material substances have passive potentialities in virtue of both their matter and their qualitative forms. Next, we will consider Aquinas's views on how a material substance's passive potentialities are identified and distinguished from one another. Finally, we will see Aquinas's thinking on the question of whether a substance's passive potentialities for undergoing action are the same as its potentialities for existing in determinate ways. For example, is a pot of

---

[1] Several parts of this chapter appeared earlier in my article "Aquinas on Passive Powers," *Vivarium*, 59:1–2 (2021): 33–51. I am grateful to Brill Publishing for permission to reprint material from this article.

[2] *De ver.* q. 23, a. 2 (ed. Leon., vol. 22.3/1, 656): "[I]n qualibet actione est aliquid considerandum ex parte agentis, et aliquid ex parte recipientis ..."

[3] *In IX Meta.* lec. 6 (ed. Marietti, 440, n. 1834): "Quibuslibet enim activis respondent determinata passiva."

water's potentiality for being heated the same as its potentiality for being hot? Or are these two different potentialities?

5.1 The Sources of a Material Substance's Passive Powers: Matter and Qualitative Forms

In the previous chapter on active power, we saw that Aquinas explicitly claims that substances are not active in virtue of their matter.[4] For example, he writes: "It is manifest that a body cannot act through its whole self since it is composed of matter, which is a being in potentiality, and of form, which is actuality: for any being acts insofar as it is in act."[5] Since action involves communicating the principle by which a substance is in act (i.e. form) and matter is not a principle of act, it follows that matter is not a principle of action. Rather, matter is a principle of passivity.

Texts throughout Aquinas's corpus reveal that he thought that the complementary nature of form and matter is that which makes it possible for material substances to act and be acted upon by one another. For causal interactions to occur, material substances must have both an active and a receptive component. Aquinas writes in his *De potentia*: "there is mutual action in corporeal substances because the matter of one is in potentiality to the form of the other and vice versa."[6] Similarly, he writes in the *Summa theologiae*: "But the potentiality for being is from the part of matter, which is a being in potentiality, but the potentiality for acting is from the part of form."[7] Through their matter substances have potentialities to exist in various ways and thus, they are able to receive the forms which agents communicate. Aquinas makes clear that substances receive forms through their matter. He writes: "[N]o thing, whatever its degree of materiality, receives anything according to that which is form in it, but only according to that which is material in it ... Corporeal things do not receive any

---

[4] See Section 3.4.

[5] *ScG* III c. 69 (ed. Marietti, 98, n. 2496): "Manifestum est enim quod corpus non potest agere se toto, cum sit compositum ex materia, quae est ens in potentia, et ex forma, quae est actus: agit enim unumquodque secundum quod est actu." See also *In II Sent.* d. 30, q. 2, a. 2 (ed. Mandonnet-Moos, 791): "[V]irtus activa non est ex parte materiae, sed magis ex parte formalis . . ."

[6] *De pot.* q. 3, a. 7 (ed. Pession, 57): "est mutua actio in substantiis corporalibus, cum materia unius sit in potentia forma alterius, et e converso." See also *In III Phys.* lec. 2 (ed. Leon., vol. 2, 106): "Et quia omnia corpora naturalia inferiora communicant in materia, ideo in unoquoque est potentia ad id quod est actu in altero: et ideo in omnibus talibus aliquid simul agit et patitur, et movet et movetur."

[7] *ST* I-II q. 55, a. 2 (ed. Leon., vol. 6, 351): "Sed potentia ad esse se tenet ex parte materiae, quae est ens in potentia, potentia autem ad agere se tenet ex parte formae . . ."

impression in virtue of form, but only in virtue of matter."[8] Patients are able to be acted upon by agents because they have a component, namely matter, which is able to be formed. In Aquinas's view, it is the "fit" between form as that which perfects and matter as that which can be perfected that enables agents to act and patients to suffer. Aquinas writes:

> [T]here is a proportion between matter and form because there is an order such that matter is perfected by form, and it is according to a proportionality. For *just as* form is able to give being, *so* too matter is able to receive that same being. In this way also the mover and the moved have a proportionality, and also the agent and the patient, so that *just as* an agent is able to impress some effect, *so* is the patient able to receive the same.[9]

The agent can act on a patient because the agent has something by which it can communicate form and the patient has something by which can receive form, namely matter.

The passages presented so far make clear that Aquinas held that substances undergo action in virtue of their matter. However, an important question remains about this view: Which type of matter does Aquinas have in mind when he makes these claims? As is well known to scholars of his thought, Aquinas, along with other Aristotelians, distinguishes between different types of matter.[10] One type of matter is prime matter, which, in Aquinas's view, is a principle of pure potentiality. Prime matter is that which is actualized by a substantial form to compose a material substance of a determinate substantial kind, such as a cat, a human, or a tree. In cases of substantial generation and corruption, prime matter is that which is first under one substantial form and then under another.[11] According to

---

[8] *De ver.* q. 9, a. 1 ad 12 (ed. Leon., 22 2/1, 282): "nulla res, quantumcumque materialis, recipit aliquid secundum id quod est formale in ipsa, sed solum secundum id quod est materiale in ea … res corporales non recipiunt aliquam impressionem ex parte formae, sed ex parte materiae …"

[9] *In III Sent.*, d. 1, q. 1, a.1 ad 3 (ed. Mandonnet-Moos, 10):

> Sicut dicimus esse proportionem inter materiam et formam, quia se habet in ordine, ut perficiatur materia per formam, et hoc secundum proportionabilitatem quamdam. Quia *sicut* forma potest dare esse, *ita* et materia potest recipere idem esse. Et hoc modo etiam movens et motum debent esse proportionabilia, et agens et patiens, ut scilicet *sicut* agens potest imprimere aliquem effectum, *ita* patiens possit recipere eumdem.

[10] For an overview of the different types of matter Aquinas recognizes see Matthew Kent, "Prime Matter according to St. Thomas," PhD diss., Fordham University, 2006, ProQuest Dissertations Publishing, 3201130.

[11] *In I Phys.* lec. 13 (ed. Leon., vol. 2, 46):

> Sic enim cognoscimus quod lignum est aliquid praeter formam scamni et lecti, quia quandoque est sub una forma, quandoque sub alia. Cum igitur videamus hoc quod est aer quandoque fieri aquam, oportet dicere quod aliquid existens sub forma aeris, quandoque sit sub forma aquae: et sic illud est aliquid praeter formam aquae et praeter formam aeris,

Aquinas's view, prime matter has no actual properties of itself and only exists insofar as it composes a complete material substance.[12] In addition to prime matter, Aquinas also acknowledges another notion of matter called "proper matter" (*materia propria*). For each substantial kind of material substance, there is a determinate type of "proper matter" out of which the substance must be made in order to be the kind of thing that it is. For example, regarding the human being's proper matter, Aquinas writes: "Since indeed the proper matter of a human is a body mixed, constituted and organized in a certain way, it is absolutely necessary for man to have in himself certain elements, humors and principal organs."[13] A human being cannot be made out of copper or stone. Rather, human beings must be made of certain organic materials and they must have certain organs. These organs and materials are that through which the human being is able to receive the higher perfection of rationality. Proper matter is not devoid of actual qualities as prime matter is. Rather, proper matter is matter which is actualized by both a substantial form and accidental ones.[14] The actual qualities of proper matter make it suitable matter for the substance's higher perfections. The central question of interest for our purposes is whether Aquinas thought that prime matter or proper matter is that by which substances have the passive potential to undergo action.

Aquinas's perspective on this question is revealed in a passage from his *Metaphysics* commentary. He writes:

> [T]he patient undergoes something on account of some principle existing in it and matter is of this kind. Passive potentiality is nothing other than the principle for undergoing through another. For example, to be burned is an undergoing, and the material principle on account of which something is

---

sicut lignum est aliquid praeter formam scamni et praeter formam lecti. Quod igitur sic se habet ad ipsas substantias naturales, sicut se habet aes ad statuam et lignum ad lectum, et quodlibet materiale et informe ad formam, hoc dicimus esse materiam primam.

[12] *In I Phys.* lec. 14 (ed. Leon., vol. 2, 50): "materia, quae est ens in potentia, est id ex quo fit aliquid per se: haec est enim quae intrat substantiam rei factae." *In I Phys.* lec. 15, n. 139: "Sed primum quod subiicitur in generatione est materia: hoc enim dicimus materiam, primum subiectum ex quo aliquid fit per se et non secundum accidens, et inest rei iam factae …" See also *In XII Meta.* lec. 2.

[13] *ScG* II c. 30 (ed. Marietti, 142, n. 1074): "Quia enim materia propria hominis est corpus commixtum et complexionatum et organizatum, necessarium est absolute hominem quodlibet elementorum et humorum et organorum principalium in se habere." For literature see Antonia Fitzpatrick, *Thomas Aquinas on Bodily Identity* (Oxford: Oxford University Press, 2017), 29–30.

[14] Aquinas maintained that each material substance had just one substantial form. The one substantial form was responsible for actualizing both the lower material qualities of the substances, as well as its higher qualities. For example, through the same substantial form, a human is both a fleshy, organic body and rational. See Wippel, *Metaphysical Thought of Thomas Aquinas*, 237–51.

apt to be burned is the oily or the fatty. Hence the very potentiality in the combustible thing is as it were passive. Similarly, that which yields itself to touching so that it receives a certain impression, just as wax or something of this kind, insofar as it is of such a kind it is malleable.[15]

In the beginning of the passage, Aquinas states that substances undergo action in virtue of their matter or material principle. He then gives several examples to illustrate this point. He says that a substance is combustible on account of being oily or fatty and substances are impressionable on account of having a certain consistency which yields to touch. These examples make clear that the material element through which substances undergo action is not prime matter, which is devoid of all quality, but rather matter which is under certain forms. Oily or fatty material is matter actualized by certain forms. The specific qualities of oily or fatty matter are that which enables a substance to undergo a determinate type of action, such as burning.

Aquinas at times emphasizes the role of form in conferring the ability to undergo action. According to Aquinas, in order for a substance to undergo an action it must have a disposition for undergoing it. He writes: "It is necessary that that which is able to undergo something have within itself some disposition which is the cause and principle of such an undergoing and that principle is called passive potentiality."[16] "Disposition" is a technical term in Aquinas's thought. A disposition is an order which a subject has through one of its qualities toward something else. Aquinas writes: "[D]isposition implies a certain order, as was said. Therefore, someone is not said to be disposed through a quality except with reference to something else."[17] Aquinas identifies various types of dispositions which a substance can have toward something else. One type of disposition is an order of matter toward the reception of a certain form. He writes:

---

[15] *In IX Meta.* lec. 1 (ed. Marietti, 425–26, n. 1782):

> patiens patitur propter aliquod principium in ipso existens, et huiusmodi est materia. Potentia autem passiva nihil aliud est quam principium patiendi ab alio. Sicut comburi quoddam pati est; et principium materiale propter quod aliquid est aptum combustioni, est pingue vel crassum. Unde ipsa potentia est in combustibili quasi passiva. Et similiter illud quod sic cedit tangenti ut impressionem quamdam recipiat, sicut cera vel aliquid huius-modi, inquantum tale est frangibile.

[16] *In V Meta.* lec. 14 (ed. Marietti, 257, n. 963): "Oportet autem illud, quod est possibile ad aliquid patiendum, habere in se quamdam dispositionem, quae sit causa et principium talis passionis; et illud principium vocatur potentia passiva."

[17] *ST* I-II q. 49, a. 2, ad 1 (ed. Leon., vol. 6, 311): "dispositio ordinem quendam importat, ut dictum est. Unde non dicitur aliquis disponi per qualitatem, nisi in ordine ad aliquid." For literature see Vivian Boland, "Aquinas and Simplicius on Dispositions," *New Blackfriars* 82 (2001): 467–78.

"*One way* is how matter is disposed to the reception of form, just as heat is a disposition for the form of fire."[18] Heat is considered a disposition for fire since it is by first becoming hot that other elements are made suitable to undergo transformation into fire.

We saw above that Aquinas claimed that substances do not receive anything in virtue of what is formal in them, but rather only through that which is material.[19] While it is indeed the case that only that which is material can receive or be actualized by form, substances must nevertheless be disposed by form in order to receive further forms through their matter.[20] Since forms are required to dispose matter to receive further forms, Aquinas at times refers to certain qualitative forms as "potentialities." For instance, he writes: "dryness is a potentiality in timbers since according to this they are combustible."[21] This description of a formal quality as a passive potentiality is consistent with Aquinas's earlier claims that matter is that by which substances undergo action since forms are sources of potentiality insofar as they dispose matter for the reception of form. While matter is that through which substances have a capacity to be acted upon in general, it is through form that substances have potentialities for undergoing determinate types of action. This is because qualitative forms dispose a substance toward the reception of determinate types of forms. Thus, both the material and the formal elements of a material substance give rise to its potentialities to undergo actions, namely its passive powers.

At this point, a reader may be wondering how Aquinas's view that forms are sources of passive potentiality fits with his conception of form as active potentiality. In Chapter 3, we saw that Aquinas thinks that form as such is active.[22] Forms by their nature are principles of actuality and goodness, and thus they enable and incline their bearers to communicate a form of the same species to another.[23] We saw, however that not all forms are active powers for transforming matter. Aquinas thinks that the immediate

---

[18] *De virt.* q. 1, a. 1 ad 9 (ed. Odetto, 710): "*Uno modo*, per quam materia disponitur ad formae receptionem, sicut calor est dispositio ad formam ignis."

[19] See fn. 8.

[20] For a text in which Aquinas explicitly claims that accidents are received in virtue of other accidents, see *ST* I q. 77, a. 7 ad 2 (ed. Leon., vol. 5, 247–48): "accidens per se non potest esse subiectum accidentis; sed unum accidens per prius recipitur in substantia quam aliud, sicut quantitas quam qualitas. Et hoc modo unum accidens dicitur esse subiectum alterius, ut superficies coloris, inquantum substantia uno accidente mediante recipit aliud."

[21] *Q.D. de anima* q. 12 (ed. Leon., vol. 24/1, 108): "siccum est potentia in lignis, quia secundum hoc sunt combustibilia."

[22] See Section 3.3.   [23] See Section 3.4.

active powers which affect all change to material substances are the four
elemental qualities.[24] Thus, a reader might wonder whether the forms that
give rise to passive powers are specifically different forms from the elemental qualities that are active powers for changing matter. Or, does Aquinas
think that one the same qualitative form can both be an active power for
changing matter and a disposition through which its bearer has a passive
power to undergo an action? There are texts which suggest that two of the
elemental qualities are active powers, while the other two are passive forms
which dispose for undergoing action. For example, Aquinas writes:
"Nevertheless hot and cold, which are active qualities, are prior to wet
and dry, which are passive qualities . . ."[25] This text suggests that the forms
which are active upon matter are distinct from those which are passive
powers. Yet, there are other texts in which Aquinas claims that one of the
so-called "passive" elemental qualities, namely dryness, is the active power
by which a change is affected. For instance, he writes: "[W]here there are
diverse forms, there are diverse actions, just as a fire which dries and heats
through heat and dryness . . ."[26] So far as I know, Aquinas never explicitly
discusses how to reconcile the claim that wet and dry are passive with his
assertions that they are qualities by which changes are affected. Later
figures were interested in this issue. In commenting on it, Suárez claims
that the reason Aristotle referred to wet and dry as "passive" was because
they are less active than hot and cold. Though they differ in the degree to
which they are active, all four elemental qualities are active.[27] Aquinas
likewise thinks that some elemental qualities are more active than others,
so this may also be a reasonable way to interpret his assertions about the
passivity of wet and dry.[28] It is likely that he thought that the very same
elemental forms were both active powers for affecting changes and dispositions which prepared a substance for receiving further form. For example,
the form of heat is both that which enables a hot substance to heat another
and that which disposes the hot substance to undergoing burning. It seems

[24] See Section 2.1.
[25] *In I Phys.* lec. 10 (ed. Leon., vol. 2, 35): "Tamen calidum et frigidum, quae sunt qualitates activae,
sunt priora humido et sicco, quae sunt qualitates passivae . . ." See also *In II De caelo* lec. 10. For
another text in which Aristotle claims that hot and cold are active, while wet and dry are passive, see
De generatione et corruptione, Bk II, ch. 2 (at 329b24).
[26] *In III Sent.* d. 18, q. 1, a. 1 (ed. Mandonnet-Moos, vol. 3, 556): "ubi sunt diversae formae, sunt
etiam diversae actiones, sicut ignis qui desiccat et calefacit per caliditatem et siccitatem . . ."
[27] See Des Chene, *Physiologia*, 47–48 on Suárez's views and later scholastic debates about whether the
same powers were both active and passive.
[28] For a text in which he claims that heat is the most active quality, see *In De sensu* lec. 10. Pasnau
claims it became common place to treat all four qualities as active. See his "Scholastic Qualities,
Primary and Secondary," 46.

that whether a form's active or passive role is manifested is relative to the other substance with which the bearer is in contact. For example, when dry cotton is in contact with fire, the dryness of the cotton disposes it to undergo burning. By contrast, when dry cotton is in contact with wet grass, the dryness of the cotton functions as an active power, which dries the grass. This example illustrates how the same specific type of form could function as both an active and a passive power in different changes when its bearer is in contact with qualitatively different substances. Though forms are by their nature active, it is not the case that every form will always function in an active way in every change. This is because agents require a suitably disposed patient to communicate their forms. There are certain relationships between certain types of qualities. The same quality can be active in reference to one quality while passive in reference to a different quality.

5.2   The Diversification of Passive Potentialities

In the previous section, we examined Aquinas's views about the constituents of material substances through which they undergo one another's actions. In this section, we will examine Aquinas's views on how passive powers are identified and distinguished from one another. In the last chapter we saw that Aquinas maintains that potentialities are identified and diversified by their corresponding actualities.[29] We saw, for example, that the active potentiality to heat is distinguished from the active potentiality to cool in virtue of the different actions which arise from them, namely heating vs. cooling. Aquinas thinks that passive potentialities are likewise dependent on their corresponding actualities for their identification and individuation. However, the actualities that correspond to passive potentialities differ from the actualities that correspond to active potentialities. No actions arise from passive potentialities. Rather, the actuality that corresponds to a passive potentiality is the actual undergoing of an action. For example, the passive potentiality to be heated is ordered toward the actuality of being heated. We saw that the actualities that correspond to active potentialities are distinguished in virtue of their objects, which are their end points. For instance, heating is a different action from cooling since heating results in heat and cooling results in coolness. Aquinas claims that the actualities that corresponding to passive potentialities are also

[29] See Section 3.2.

distinguished from one another by their objects.[30] Yet, the object of a passive actuality differs from the object of an active one. According to Aquinas, the object of a passive actuality is the active power that initiates its act.[31] This is to say that an undergoing is an undergoing of a particular kind in virtue of arising from a particular kind of active power. For example, an act of being heated is a different undergoing from the act of being cooled since being heated arises from an active power to heat and being cooled arises from an active power to cool. Since passive potentialities are differentiated by their corresponding actualities, which are in turn differentiated by the active powers from which they arise, it follows that passive potentialities ultimately depend on active powers for their identification and diversification. There are just as many types of passive potentialities as there are active ones. Aquinas writes: "every passive potentiality corresponds to some active potentiality in nature, otherwise a passive potentiality would be in vain, since it is not able to be reduced to act except through an active potentiality."[32] It would be senseless for there to be a passive potentiality to which there corresponds no active potentiality, because such a potentiality would never be able to be actualized.

In Aquinas's commentary on Aristotle's *Metaphysics* he follows Aristotle in identifying active and passive potentialities as relatives.[33] As Aquinas puts it "relatives *require each other to exist*" and "one relative is posited in the definition of the other ... one relative is specified by the other."[34] Consider the example of a father and a son. Without a father, one cannot be a son. The reverse also holds true. Without a son one cannot be a father. Being a father and being a son are mutually interdependent. An active potentiality is a potentiality to act on a patient which has the appropriate

<hr/>

[30] See for instance *ST* I q. 77, a. 3 (ed. Leon., vol. 5, 241): "ratio potentiae diversificetur, ut diversificatur ratio actus. Ratio autem actus diversificatur secundum diversam rationem obiecti. Omnis enim actio vel est potentiae activae, vel passivae." For a discussion of Aquinas's views on how objects are prior to acts, see T. K. Johansen, *The Powers of Aristotle's Soul* (Oxford: Oxford University Press, 2012), 97–100.

[31] *ST* I q. 77, a. 3 (ed. Leon., vol. 5, 241): "Obiectum autem comparatur ad actum potentiae passivae, sicut principium et causa movens, color enim inquantum movet visum, est principium visionis."

[32] *ScG* III, c. 45 (ed. Marietti, 58, n. 2222): "omni enim potentiae passivae respondet potentia activa in natura; alias potentia passiva esset frustra, cum non possit reduci in actum nisi per activam." See also *In II Sent.* d. 12, q. 1, a. 1 and *In III Sent.* d. 2, q. 1, a. 1, qc 1.

[33] *In V Meta.* lec. 17 (ed. Marietti, 266, n. 1002): "*Secundus* modus est prout aliqua dicuntur ad aliquid secundum actionem et passionem, vel potentiam activam et passivam; sicut calefactivum ad calefactibile, quod pertinet ad actiones naturales, et sectivum ad sectibile, quod pertinet ad actiones artificiales, et universaliter omne activum ad passivum."

[34] *ScG* II c. 12 (ed. Marietti, 121, n. 913): "relativa sint *quae secundum esse ad aliud quodammodo se habent* ..." and *ST* III q. 35, a. 5 ob. 3 (ed. Leon., vol. 11, 356): "unum relativum ponitur in definitione alterius, ... unum relativorum specificatur ex alio ..."

passive potentiality. Similarly, a passive potentiality is a potentiality to be acted upon by an agent with an appropriate active potentiality. Aquinas claims that, in a sense, correlative active and passive potentialities, such as the potentiality to heat and be heated, comprise just a single potentiality. He writes: "[I]n a certain way the potentialities for acting and for being acted upon are one potentiality . . . They are one potentiality insofar as the order of one to the other is considered; for one is said with respect to the other."[35] For instance, since the potentiality to heat another can only be actualized if there is something capable of being heated and vice versa, it seems that the potentialities for heating and being heated comprise just a single potentiality for the act of heating.

It should be noted that although Aquinas thinks that passive potentialities are diversified in accord with the active powers which actualize them, he nevertheless maintains that not just any difference in the active power which moves a passive potentiality entails a distinct passive potentiality.[36] Differences which are accidental to the nature of the active potentiality do not entail a distinction of passive potentialities.[37] For example, water might be heated by an electric stove or by an open flame, but this does not entail that the water has two different passive potentialities: one to be heated by a stove and another to be heated by a flame. Both the stove and the flame heat through the same active quality, namely heat. It is accidental to the nature of heat whether it belongs to a stove or flame. The nature of the stove's power to heat and the flame's power to heat are the same. Thus, only one passive potentiality is required for a patient to undergo these acts of heating even if they are produced by different types of agents which possess a power to heat.

One final point to note before moving on to the next section is the relationship between Aquinas's views about the individuation of passive potentialities and his views which we saw in the last section about the constituents of material substances through which these potentialities arise. We saw that Aquinas held that substances possess passive potentialities in virtue of their matter and the qualitative forms which dispose it. Yet, he does not think that passive potentialities are identified and distinguished by the constituents that give rise to them. One and the same qualitative form can be a source of two different types of passive potentiality.

---

[35] *In IX Meta.* lec. 1 (ed. Marietti, 425, n. 1781): "quod potentia faciendi et patiendi est quodammodo una potentia . . . Una quidem est, si consideretur ordo unius ad aliam; una enim dicitur per respectum ad alteram."
[36] See *ST* I q. 77, a. 3 (ed. Leon., vol. 5, 241–42).   [37] Ibid.

For example, through being dry, a substance is both combustible and heatable. These potentialities differ from each other, but the form in virtue of which the substance has the potentialities is the same. Furthermore, Aquinas claims that qualitative forms of different species can give rise to passive potentialities which are of the same kind. For example, in various passages he discusses the disposition in virtue of which a substance can be burned. Sometimes he identifies this disposition as dryness.[38] Yet, other times he identifies it as the "oily" or the "fatty."[39] Though these qualities, "oiliness" and "fattiness," differ from each other according to their nature, they nevertheless give rise to the same passive potentiality, namely the potentiality to be burned.

5.3   Obediential Potentiality for Undergoing God's Actions

In addition to passive potentialities for undergoing the actions of other created substances, Aquinas also ascribed to creatures a potentiality to undergo God's actions. As we saw above, Aquinas thinks that there is a passive potentiality which corresponds to every active power. Since God's active power is of a different nature from any type of created power, creatures must have a different passive potentiality for undergoing God's active power. "Obediential potentiality" is what Aquinas, and others in his time, call the passive potentiality in creatures, which corresponds to God's unlimited active power. God can not only bring about any type of change which a created active power can, but he can also effect changes in creatures which surpass the capability of any creature. For example, Aquinas thinks that God can transform any creature into any other type of creature. He gives the example of a piece of wood which can be transformed into a calf by God's power.[40] Since God is able to bring about actualities in creatures which cannot be brought about by natural active powers, creatures must have a different potentiality for the actualities which God can cause. Aquinas writes the following:

> [P]assive potentiality is judged to be twofold, one which is possessed in
> comparison to a natural agent and another which is possessed in

---

[38] See, for instance, the text in fn. 21.   [39] See, for instance, the text in fn. 15.
[40] *In III Sent.*, d. 2, q. 1, a. 1, q. 3 (ed. Mandonnet-Moos, vol. 3, 54): "in creatura *solam potentiam obedientiae*, secundum quam de creatura potest fieri quidquid Deus vult, sicut de ligno potest fieri vitulus, Deo operante. Haec autem potentia obedientiae correspondet divinae potentiae, secundum quod dicitur, quod ex creatura potest fieri quod ex ea Deus facere potest." Nevertheless, Aquinas thought that God could not make that which was impossible in itself. See for instance *ST* I q. 25, a. 3.

comparison to the first agent, which is able to reduce any creature to a higher act than can be reduced by a natural agent, and this has come to be called obediential potentiality in creatures.[41]

Consider Aquinas's example of the wood which God is able to transform into a calf. Considered naturally, wood does not have a passive potentiality to become a calf. Wood, by its nature, does not have the dispositions required to receive the substantial form of calf. Yet, a calf is something that God can transform the wood into. Thus, Aquinas thinks that we must posit some other passive potentiality in creatures which differs from all of the natural passive potentialities that it has in relation to the active powers of created agents. This further potentiality is not a potentiality for some specific actuality. Rather, it is a potentiality to be actualized in any way that God causes through his power.

A question one might have is: What is the intrinsic principle in virtue of which creatures have obediential potentiality? We saw that natural passive potentialities arise in creatures in virtue of their matter and the qualitative forms that dispose it. For instance, wood undergoes burning in virtue of its dryness. By contrast, in the case of divine action on creatures there is no specific form in the patient in virtue of which it is disposed to undergo God's action. God is unique as an agent insofar as his action does not require matter to act upon.[42] He is able to cause actualities in creatures even when they are not naturally disposed to receive those actualities because he is able to produce both form and the matter which it actualizes.[43] No intrinsic principle is required in the creature for God to induce any actuality in it. In response to the question of whether God is prohibited from producing an effect when there is a lack of suitable matter, Aquinas writes the following:

> [H]e is the cause of matter which cannot be caused except through creation. He does not require matter for acting since with nothing pre-existing he produces a thing in existence. So, on account of a defect of matter his action is not able to be impeded from the production of an effect.[44]

---

[41] *ST* III q. 11, a. 1 (ed. Leon., vol. 11, 157): "consideratur duplex potentia passiva, una quidem per comparationem ad agens naturale; alia vero per comparationem ad agens primum, qui potest quamlibet creaturam reducere in actum aliquem altiorem, in quem non reducitur per agens naturale; et haec consuevit vocari potentia obedientiae in creatura." See also *De virt.* q. 1, a.10 ad 13.

[42] See for instance *ScG* II c. 16–17.   [43] See for instance *ST* I q. 44, a. 2.

[44] *ScG* II c. 22 (ed. Marietti, 134, n. 986): "ipse sit causa materiae, quae non possibilis est causari nisi per creationem. Ipse etiam in agendo non requirit materiam: cum, nullo praeexistente, rem in esse producat. Et sic propter materiae defectum eius actio impediri non potest ab effectus productione."

Since God, unlike creatures, does not require matter that is suitably disposed to act upon, there is no intrinsic disposition in creatures which gives rise to their obediential potentiality. For instance, there is no form in the wood through which it has the passive potentiality to become whatever God wills. Creatures are susceptible to become whatever God wills solely in virtue of God's omnipotence and the creature's dependence on God for its being.

5.4 Are Passive Potentialities for Undergoing Action the Same as Potentialities for Existence?

The topic of this final section is the question of how passive potentialities relate to another type of potentiality that Aquinas attributes to material substances, namely potentialities for being a certain way. In the context of discussing the metaphysics of change, Aquinas claims that for every determinate way in which a substance can exist in actuality, there is some corresponding potentiality. For instance, "being just" and "being white" and "being a human" are all ways of existing in actuality. Aquinas thinks that corresponding to each of these there is something which is being "potentially white" or "potentially just" or "potentially a man."[45] These potentialities are actualized by form. Aquinas never addresses how these potentialities relate to the passive potentialities for undergoing an action. Is a substance's potentiality for being a certain way the same as or different from the substance's passive potentiality to undergo an action which terminates in that way of being? For example, is water's potentiality to be hot the same as its passive potentiality to be heated? Contemporary scholars have debated quite extensively about Aristotle's views on this topic.[46] Aquinas's views on this issue are no less difficult to interpret.[47] In what follows, I will discuss some of the relevant considerations in favor of identifying vs. distinguishing passive potentialities for undergoing action

---

[45] *De prin. nat.* c. 1 (ed. Leon., vol. 43, 39): "Ad utrumque esse est aliquid in potentia. Aliquid enim est in potentia ut sit homo, ut sperma et sanguis menstruus; aliquid est in potentia ut sit album, ut homo. Tam illud quod est in potentia ad esse substantiale, quam illud quod est in potentia ad esse accidentale, potest dici materia, sicut sperma hominis, et homo albedinis."

[46] For a summary of some of the positions see Robert Heinaman, "Is Aristotle's Definition of Change Circular?" *Apeiron* 27:1 (1994): 25–37.

[47] The only discussion of Aquinas's views which I am aware of is Can Laurens Löwe, "Mind over Matter: Aquinas's Transformation of Aristotle's Definition of Change," *Archives d'histoire doctrinale et littéraire du Moyen Âge* 82:1 (2015): 45–68. Löwe argues (pp. 49–57) that Aquinas distinguished the potentiality to be a certain way from the potentiality for the change which terminates in that way of being. In this section, I argue that according to Aquinas's principles these potentialities are one in reality and only differ according to concept.

with potentialities for being. I will argue that from Aquinas's principles it follows that these potentialities are the same in reality, though they may differ according to concept.

There are several texts in Aquinas's works which suggest that he regarded a substance's passive potentiality to undergo an action as the same as the substance's potentiality to take on the form that is the end point of the action. In a *De potentia* passage in which he discusses the twofold division of actuality into form (first act) and operation (second act), he goes on to state that potentiality is similarly divided in a twofold manner. He writes:

> Hence potentiality is similarly twofold: *one is active* potentiality, which corresponds to the act which is operation, and it appears that the name 'potentiality' was first attributed to this one. *The other* is passive potentiality, which corresponds to first act, which is form ...[48]

It is important to note what Aquinas does not say in the passage. He does *not* divide passive potentiality further into a potentiality for existing according to a form and a potentiality for undergoing the action that terminates in that form. He simply divides potentiality into active and passive potentiality. Aquinas states that the act that corresponds to passive potentiality is first act or form. He does not differentiate two separate passive potentialities: one that is actualized by a form (i.e. first act) and another that is actualized by the undergoing of an action (i.e. second act). He only refers to a single type of passive potentiality that is actualized by form.

In another passage in his *Summa Theologiae*, Aquinas likewise contrasts the active potentiality for acting with the potentiality for being. He writes: "But the potentiality for being is possessed on account of matter, which is a being in potentiality. However, the potentiality for acting is possessed on account of form, which is a principle of acting, since each one acts insofar as it is in act."[49] We saw above that Aquinas claimed that matter is the principle in virtue of which material substances undergo action, and here he claims that matter is that through which substances have potentiality for being. So, it seems that perhaps there is just a single type of passive

---

[48] *De pot.* q. 1, a. 1 (ed. Pession, 9): "Unde et similiter duplex est potentia: *una activa* cui respondet actus, qui est operatio; et huic primo nomen potentiae videtur fuisse attributum: *alia* est potentia passiva, cui respondet actus primus, qui est forma ..."

[49] *ST* I-II q. 55, a. 2 (ed. Leon., vol. 6, 351): "Sed potentia ad esse se tenet ex parte materiae, quae est ens in potentia, potentia autem ad agere se tenet ex parte formae, quae est principium agendi, eo quod unumquodque agit inquantum est actu."

potentiality in virtue of which substances receive form *and* in virtue of which they undergo action. This fits with Aquinas's conception of action as the communication of a form. If undergoing an action is nothing other than receiving a form, it seems that no further potentiality is required to undergo action beyond the potentiality to have a form.

However, there are some other texts which support a conflicting per-spective. For instance, in Aquinas's discussion of motion in his commen-tary on Aristotle's *Physics*, he states that a changeable substance which is not yet actually undergoing change is in potentiality to two acts. He writes:

> For it must be considered that before something is moved it is in potenti-ality to two acts, namely a perfect act, which is the term of motion, and an imperfect act, which is the motion. For example, water before it begins to be heated is in potentiality to heating and to being hot. While it is being heated, it is reduced to the imperfect act, which is motion; however, it is not yet in perfect act, which is the end of motion, but with respect to this it remains in potentiality.[50]

This passage seems to imply that the potentiality for undergoing the action of a mover is different from the potentiality for being in the end state of the motion. Aquinas states that while a substance is being heated, its poten-tiality to undergo heating is actualized, and yet it seems to have some other unactualized potentiality for the final result of the heating (i.e. being hot to a certain degree). Conversely, even after the source of heating has ceased in its action of heating, the water will still *be* hot – yet it will no longer actually be undergoing heating. Since undergoing heating in actuality differs from being hot in actuality it may seem that there must be two different potentialities, one for being hot and one for undergoing heating. As we saw above, Aquinas maintains that potentialities are diversified in accord with their actualities.[51] The passive potentiality to undergo cooling, for example, differs from the passive potentiality to undergo heating since heating and cooling are different types of actuality. It would seem that if a substance is in potentiality to two actualities, as the passage above claims, and potentialities are individuated by their actualities, then the substance

---

[50] *In III Phys.* lec. 2 (ed. Leon., vol. 2, 106):

> Considerandum est enim quod antequam aliquid moveatur, est in potentia ad duos actus, scilicet ad actum perfectum, qui est terminus motus, et ad actum imperfectum, qui est motus: sicut aqua antequam incipiat calefieri est in potentia ad calefieri et ad calidum esse; cum autem calefit, reducitur in actum imperfectum, qui est motus; nondum autem in actum perfectum, qui est terminus motus, sed adhuc respectu ipsius remanet in potentia.

[51] See Section 5.2.

must have two potentialities. Further on in his *Physics* commentary Aquinas similarly discusses the case of materials which are in potentiality to being built into a house. He describes the actuality of materials insofar as they are "buildable" (i.e. in potentiality to being built) as the very motion of building. He explicitly denies that the act of the materials "as buildable" is the end state of the house. Rather it is the very process of building.[52] Since the act of building and the actual house are two different actualities it would likewise seem that there are two passive potentialities: one for being a house and one for undergoing building. Again, potentialities are diversified in terms of their acts.

One thing to keep in mind with regard to this consideration about the "two actualities" is that Aquinas maintains that only a certain sort of difference between two actualities is sufficient to diversify the corresponding potentialities. In order for different actualities to entail different potentialities, the actualities must differ according to *species*.[53] However, the actuality which a substance has when it is undergoing an action and the actuality which it has when it exists according to the end-state of that action are of the same species. For example, when a substance is undergoing heating and when it exists as hot, it is actualized by the same form of heat. In several texts, Aquinas explicitly claims that the imperfect actuality which a substance has when it is in motion, for instance when it is being heated, is of the same species as the actuality it has at the end of the motion.[54] The difference in the actuality which the substance has when it is being heated vs. existing as hot is not a difference of species. Rather it is a difference in how perfectly the substance is actualized. A substance that is undergoing a motion is imperfectly actualized by the relevant form and it has an order toward being more perfectly actualized by that form at each

---

[52] *In III Phys.* lec. 3 (ed. Leon., vol. 2, 107–08):

> Hoc autem est vel domus vel aedificatio. Sed domus non est actus aedificabilis inquantum est aedificabile, quia aedificabile inquantum huiusmodi reducitur in actum cum aedificatur; cum autem iam domus est, non aedificatur. Relinquitur igitur quod aedificatio sit actus aedificabilis inquantum huiusmodi. Aedificatio autem est quidam motus: motus igitur est actus existentis in potentia inquantum huiusmodi. Et eadem ratio est de aliis motibus.

[53] See for instance *ST* I q. 77, a. 3 (ed. Leon., vol. 5, 241–42).

[54] See, for instance, *In V Phys.* lec. 3 (ed. Leon., vol. 2, 235):

> Qualiter autem motus sit in istis generibus, et qualiter pertineat motus ad praedicamentum actionis et passionis, in tertio dictum est. Unde nunc breviter dicere sufficiat, quod quilibet motus est in eodem genere cum suo termino, non quidem ita quod motus qui est ad qualitatem sit species qualitatis, sed per reductionem. Sicut enim potentia reducitur ad genus actus, propter hoc quod omne genus dividitur per potentiam et actum: ita oportet quod motus, qui est actus imperfectus, reducatur ad genus actus perfecti.

successive instant of the motion.[55] Motion, for Aquinas, involves a special way of being actualized by a form, rather than a different type of form.[56] A substance in motion is actualized in such a way that it *remains in potentiality*.[57] Since the form that is received when a substance undergoes a motion is the same as the form through which it has a way of being in actuality, it seems that a patient should not require a distinct passive potentiality to undergo an action in addition to its passive potentiality to exist according to the relevant form. For instance, since water is actualized by the same form of heat both when it exists as hot and when it is being heated, water does not require two distinct potentialities, one for being hot and another for being heated. Being heated, after all, is just a certain way of being hot, namely being hot while retaining a potentiality toward being continuously hotter.

Though I have argued that according to Aquinas's principles potentialities for being and undergoing action are the same in reality, nevertheless such potentialities differ conceptually. For example, though the potentialities for being hot and undergoing heating are the same in reality, our notion of a potentiality to be hot differs from our notion of a potentiality to be heated. To understand what a potentiality for being hot is, we only need to understand what hotness is. However, to understand a potentiality for being heated, the notion of an active power which heats is also required. Aquinas claims that active and passive potentialities are relatives, which is to say that they can only be specified and defined in relation to each other.[58] The potentiality for being heated is a potentiality for undergoing the action of an active power to heat. The concept of every passive potentiality includes reference to the power which actualizes it. By contrast, the concept of a potentiality for being only includes reference to the

[55] *In III Phys.* lec. 2 (ed. Leon., vol. 2, 105):

> Cum enim aqua est solum in potentia calida, nondum movetur: cum vero est iam calefacta, terminatus est motus calefactionis: cum vero iam participat aliquid de calore sed imperfecte, tunc movetur ad calorem; nam quod calefit, paulatim participat calorem magis ac magis. Ipse igitur actus imperfectus caloris in calefactibili existens, est motus: non quidem secundum id quod actu tantum est, sed secundum quod iam in actu existens habet ordinem in ulteriorem actum; quia si tolleretur ordo ad ulteriorem actum, ipse actus quantumcumque imperfectus, esset terminus motus et non motus, sicut accidit cum aliquid semiplene calefit. Ordo autem ad ulteriorem actum competit existenti in potentia ad ipsum.

[56] On what motion is in external reality, see his *In III Phys.* lec. 5, n. 17 (ed. Leon., vol. 2, 115).
[57] *In III Phys.* lec. 3 (ed. Leon., vol. 2, 108): "motus igitur est actus existentis in potentia inquantum huiusmodi."
[58] *In V Meta.* lec. 17 (ed. Marietti, 266, n. 1002). On what relatives are, see *ST* III q. 35, a. 5 ob. 3 (ed. Leon., vol. 11, 356): "unum relativum ponitur in definitione alterius, ex quo patet, quod unum relativorum specificatur ex alio."

form which is its act. For instance, the potentiality to be hot is defined as a potentiality for receiving the form of heat, while the potentiality to undergo heating is defined as potentiality to receive the form of heat through an agent's active power to heat. In reality, however, the potentiality for undergoing heating and being hot are one and the same potentiality.

5.5 Conclusion

In this chapter we have seen Aquinas's views on material substances' passive potentialities. In his view, material substances have the passive potentiality to receive form in virtue of their matter as well as the forms which dispose it toward the reception of further forms. However, passive potentialities are not identified and diversified through the inherent forms from which they arise. Rather, passive potentialities are identified and diversified through their corresponding actualities. The actualities of passive potentialities are in turn diversified by the active powers from which they arise. Thus, there is an active power which corresponds to each passive potentiality.

Aquinas's view that passive potentiality arises from a substance's material principles, while active potentialities are aligned with form, highlights that it is the hylomorphic composition of material substances that enables them to causally interact. Through being composed of matter and form, material substances have both active and receptive potentiality. Though active potentialities and passive potentialities belong to diverse substances, they fit together on account of the complementarity of matter and form. Form is that which perfects, and matter is that which can be perfected by form. Thus, it is on account of their hylomorphic structure that material substances have two corresponding types of potentialities, namely active and passive, both of which are essential for causal interactions.

CHAPTER 6

Action and Passion

Aquinas conceptualizes causal powers through the lens of the Aristotelian distinction between potentiality and actuality.[1] He regards both the active and passive causal features of substances as potentialities. A potentiality is a reality which is in some respect incomplete, imperfect or unrealized; and for every potentiality, there is a corresponding actuality, which relates to it as its realization and fulfillment.[2] In this chapter, we will consider Aquinas's views regarding the actualities which correspond to the active and passive potentialities of material substances. Aquinas follows Aristotle in using the term "action" to refer to the actuality of an active potentiality and the term "passion" to refer to the actuality of a passive potentiality.[3] A main goal of this chapter is to clarify Aquinas's understanding of what actions and passions are ontologically. What sort of reality is the actuality of an active potentiality? Is it the same as or distinct from the actuality of the corresponding passive potentiality? For example, when fire burns a log, what sort of reality is the actuality of fire's active potentiality to burn? Is the actuality of the fire's active potentiality to burn the same as or distinct from the actuality of the log's potentiality to be burned? Furthermore, how does the actuality that corresponds to active and passive potentialities relate to the motion which the agent causes and the patient undergoes? For instance, when fire burns a log, is fire's action something distinct from the motion of burning which the fire causes? Is the log's passion different from the motion of burning which it undergoes? In regard to these questions, Aquinas maintains that actions and passions are motions. Furthermore, he defends the Aristotelian thesis that correlative actions and passions are one and the same motion. For example, when fire burns

---

[1] See Section 3.1. Several parts of this chapter appeared earlier in "Aquinas's Ontology of Transeunt Causal Activity," *Vivarium* 56 (2018): 47–82. I am grateful to Brill Publishing for permission to reprint.

[2] For a primary text, see *In IX Meta.* lec. 5.   [3] *In III Phys.* lec. 5.

a log, fire's action of burning and the log's passion of being burned are the same as the motion of burning which the fire causes in the log. The chapter will examine some of the key conceptual and interpretive issues surrounding the "action-passion sameness" thesis.

6.1 Motion as Incomplete Actuality and the Actuality of the Patient's Passive Potentiality

In order to understand Aquinas's views on the actualities of active and passive powers, we need to begin with his conception of motion. Motion is that which arises through an agent's active power. Accordingly, every efficient causal interaction between material substances involves at least these entities: (1) an agent with an (2) active power, (3) a patient with a (4) passive power, and (5) a motion which the agent causes in the patient. One of the central questions of this chapter is whether, in addition to these five entities, there is a sixth entity which is the agent's action and perhaps even a seventh entity which is the patient's passion. In his most extensive discussion of the nature of the acts of active and passive potentialities, Aquinas argues that it follows from the very definition of motion that motion is the actuality which corresponds to the patient's passive potentiality.[4] Put otherwise, the motion which the agent causes is itself the passion which the patient undergoes. In this sub-section, we will examine Aquinas's definition of motion and how he reasons from his definition of motion to the conclusion that motion is itself the actuality of the patient's passive potentiality. Next (in Section 6.2), we will turn to Aquinas's intriguing argument for the thesis that the same motion which is the actuality of the patient's passive potentiality is also the actuality of the agent's active potentiality.

Though motion is a very ordinary phenomenon and one which is easy for our senses to grasp, it is quite difficult to define. Following Aristotle, Aquinas accepts that the best way to understand motion is in terms of potentiality and actuality.[5] Yet, he realizes that motion cannot be defined as a "going" (*exitus*) from potentiality to actuality because a "going" would

---

[4] *In III Phys.* lec. 1–5. Aquinas also discusses this issue in *In XI Meta.*, lec. 9. This discussion is shorter and the main arguments overlap substantially with the *Physics* commentary discussion.

[5] For discussions of Aquinas's views on motion, see Brock, *Action and Conduct*, 76–79; and Rudi Te velde, *Aquinas on God* (London: Routledge, 2006), 55–60; Cecilia Trifolgi, "Thomas Wylton on Motion," *Archiv für Geschichte der Philosophie*, 77:2 (1995): 135–54; and MacDonald, "Aquinas's Parasitic Cosmological Argument."

itself be a motion.[6] Thus, it would be circular to define motion in this way. Aquinas takes this point from Avicenna.[7] Since motion cannot be defined as the process of going from potentiality to actuality, Aquinas maintains that it should be conceptualized as a certain type of actuality, namely an incomplete actuality. According to him, motion is the actuality of a thing that is in potentiality to further actuality. Aquinas uses the motion of heating as an example to illustrate this definition. The heat in an object while it is being heated is both the realization and fulfillment of a prior potentiality for heat and it is also incomplete or unrealized with respect to the greater heat the object is in the process of acquiring.[8] Thus, the heat is an actuality which is part-way between potentiality and actuality. It has both (i) the order of potentiality to further actuality and (ii) the order of actuality to a prior potentiality. For instance, the motion of heating is that very heat in an object which is both in actuality with respect to a prior state and in potentiality with respect to a greater posterior state.

It should be noted that in Aquinas's view, an actuality is only considered to be an incomplete actuality, namely a motion, in reference to a particular end state. No actuality is of itself a motion.[9] For example, suppose my coffee is 80 degrees Fahrenheit and it could potentially be hotter. The fact that my coffee could potentially be hotter, and thus is imperfectly hot, does not suffice for my coffee to be undergoing motion. The incomplete actuality which a substance has must also have the order of potentiality to the substance's immediately posterior state and the order of actuality to the substance's immediately prior state. For example, my coffee's degree of heat must be the actualization of its immediately prior state of heat and a potentiality for a greater degree of heat, which will be actualized at an immediately posterior interval. Put otherwise, my coffee must be getting successively hotter for its present incomplete degree of heat to

---

[6] *In III Phys.* lec. 2 (ed. Leon., vol. 2, 105).

[7] See Avicenna, *Liber Primus Naturalium: Tractatus Secundus de Motu et de Consimilibus* (ed. Van Riet, 149): "[F]acile est dicere quod motus est exitus de potentia ad effectum in tempore, continue et subito. Sed in omnibus istis descriptionibus est declaratio circularis implicita." On how Averroes and Avicenna influenced scholastic discussions of motion see Steven Baldner, "Albertus Magnus and the Categorization of Motion," *The Thomist* 70 (2006): 203–35.

[8] *In III Phys.* lec. 2 (ed. Leon., vol. 2, 105).

[9] *In III Phys.* lec. 2 (ed. Leon., vol. 2, 105):

> Sic igitur actus imperfectus habet rationem motus, et secundum quod comparatur ad ulteriorem actum ut potentia, et secundum quod comparatur ad aliquid imperfectius ut actus. Unde neque est potentia existens in potentia, neque est actus existens in actu, sed est actus existentis in potentia: ut per id quod dicitur actus, designetur ordo eius ad anteriorem potentiam, et per id quod dicitur in potentia existentis, designetur ordo eius ad ulteriorem actum.

count as motion. Thus, whether an incomplete actualization counts as motion is always relative to a future state. As Aquinas understands it, reference to prior and posterior states of a substance is built into the very nature of what motion is. Thus, every object that undergoes a change requires a first, last and at least one intermediate state. Aquinas rejects the possibility of instantaneous motions.[10] Objects in motion are seamlessly transitioning between states of less perfect actuality to more perfect actuality. The motion itself is the very actuality (e.g. the form of heat) considered together with its order to the prior and posterior states of potentiality and actuality. As Aquinas writes: "motion therefore is the actuality of a thing existing in potentiality insofar as it is in potentiality."[11] What is characteristic of the actuality which is motion is that it belongs to a substance in virtue of its being in potentiality to a greater actuality.

This point about the very nature of motion is important for understanding Aquinas's views on the actuality which corresponds to a passive potentiality. When Aquinas discusses the definition of motion and concludes that it is a type of actuality (i.e. an incomplete actuality), he observes that according to the metaphysics of potentiality and actuality, every actuality must correspond to a prior potentiality. So, after defining motion in his *Physics* commentary, Aquinas asks to which potentiality motion corresponds.[12] Is motion the actuality of the active potentiality to cause motion or the passive potentiality to be moved? Consider a fire which burns a log. Is the burning which happens in the log the fulfillment and completion of the log's potentiality to be burning or is it the fulfillment and completion of the fire's potentiality to cause burning? Aquinas thinks that reflecting on the very definition of motion can help to answer this question.

Since motion by definition is the actuality of a subject remaining in potentiality, Aquinas reasons that it must necessarily be the actuality of the subject which is moved. During a causal interaction, the subject which is moved (i.e. the patient) is the substance which is in actuality while also retaining potentiality for a greater actuality. For example, during an

---

[10] Aquinas analyzes seemingly instantaneous changes as the end-points of processes. See *ST* I q. 53, a. 3. It is also worth noting that Aquinas views time as an infinitely divisible continuum, rather than a succession of discrete indivisible "nows." On his view, there is no basic interval of time that is not able to be further divided into prior and posterior intervals. So even the fastest possible physical change will be such that it can be divided into prior and posterior intervals.

[11] *In III Phys.* lec. 3 (ed. Leon., vol. 2, 108): "motus igitur est actus existentis in potentia inquantum huiusmodi."

[12] *In III Phys.* lec. 4.

instance of heating the water that is being heated retains the potentiality to be more perfectly hot even while it is actually hot. The agent, by contrast, does not necessarily retain a potentiality for a greater actuality even while it acts. Fire, for example, does not necessarily retain the potentiality to heat more perfectly even while it is heating in actuality.[13] So, given that motion is the actuality of a substance that necessarily remains in potentiality, motion must by definition be the actuality of the patient's passive potentiality. In fact, Aquinas states, following Aristotle, that another way to describe motion is as "the act of mobile being insofar as it is mobile."[14] This is to say that motion can be described as the actuality of a thing which can be moved. It follows from Aquinas's claim that motion is the actuality of the patient's passive potentiality that the motion itself is the very reality which the patient undergoes. The patient's passion is not an entity over and above the motion which the agent causes in it.

But what about the agent's action? Is the actuality of an active power some distinct, causally prior reality, which the agent brings about in order to cause the motion that its patient undergoes? It is to this question that we now turn.

6.2   The Same Motion Is Also the Actuality of the Agent's Active Potentiality

Throughout his works, Aquinas defends the view that the correlative potentialities of natural agents and patients share the same actuality. For example, in his *Summa contra Gentiles* Aquinas writes that "motion is the common act of the mover and the moved."[15] His most extensive defense of this thesis occurs in his commentary on *Physics* III. After Aquinas argues

---

[13] *In III Phys.* lec. 4. For more details of Aquinas's argument that motion must be the actuality which corresponds to the patient's potentiality to be moved, see Gloria Frost, "Aquinas's Ontology of Transeunt Causal Activity," *Vivarium* 56 (2018): 47–82, at 52–53.

[14] *In III Phys.* lec. 4 (ed. Leon., vol. 2, 111, n. 1): "actus mobilis inquantum est mobile ..." This reproduces what Aristotle writes in *Physics* III c. 2 202a7–8.

[15] *ScG* II c. 57 (ed. Marietti, 183, n. 1334): "motus sit communis actus moventis et moti ..." There are also a variety of texts in which Aquinas advances the more general view that the actions of transeunt agents exist in and perfect their patients, rather than agents themselves. See, for instance, *ScG* II, c.1 (ed. Marietti, 114, n. 853): "Est autem duplex rei operatio, ut Philosophus tradit, in IX *Metaphysicae*: una quidem quae in ipso operante manet et est ipsius operantis perfectio, ut sentire, intelligere et velle; alia vero quae in exteriorem rem transit, quae est perfectio facti quod per ipsam constituitur, ut calefacere, secare et aedificare." See also *De ver.* q. 8, a. 6 & q. 14, a. 3. For recent discussions of Aquinas's views on the sameness of action, passion and motion, see Brower, *Aquinas's Ontology of the Material World*, 205–10 and Robert Pasnau, *Metaphysical Themes: 1274–1671* (Oxford: Oxford University Press, 2011), 230–32. Questions about the ontological status of action were widely discussed by later scholastic authors. On Suárez's views on action, see Jake

that motion according to its definition must be the actuality that corresponds to the patient's passive potentiality, he adds that motion "is also in some way the act of the mover."[16] The motion is the actuality of the agent's active potentiality not in virtue of the essence of what motion is in itself, but rather in virtue of its being caused by the agent. The agent's active potentiality is a potentiality for causing motion and insofar as motion is caused through that potentiality, it is the completion and fulfillment of it.

Aquinas finds it logical that the agent's active potentiality and the patient's passive potentiality have the same actuality since what the agent causes through its active potentiality is the same reality as that which the patient undergoes through its passive potentiality. Aquinas writes: "This is why it is necessary that there is one act of both the mover and the moved: that which is from the mover as agent cause and that which is in the moved as patient and recipient is the same reality."[17] In Aquinas's view, agents act immediately on their patients. The mover does not cause one entity, which then gives rise to a second entity, which is its effect in the patient. What immediately arises from the mover is the very motion which the moved substance undergoes.

Aquinas argues, following Aristotle, that absurdities result when it is assumed that an agent's action is a distinct actuality from its patient's passion.[18] Aquinas assumes that the actuality of the agent's active potentiality must be a motion and every motion must occur in a subject. From these assumptions, he reasons that if an agent's action is a distinct actuality from its patient's passion, then its actuality is a motion which happens in either the patient or the agent. First, he shows the absurdity which follows from the view that an agent's action is a motion in the agent itself. He writes:

> If someone should say that action is in the agent and passion is in the
> patient, then since action is a certain motion, as was stated, it follows that
> motion is in the mover . . . [I]t follows then that either every mover is being

Tuttle, "Suárez's Non-Reductive Theory of Efficient Causation," *Oxford Studies in Medieval Philosophy* 4 (2016): 125–58.
[16] *In III Phys.* lec. 4 (ed. Leon., vol. 2, 110): "est etiam quodammodo actus motivi."
[17] *In III Phys.* lec. 4 (ed. Leon., vol. 2, 110): "Quare oportet unum actum esse utriusque, scilicet moventis et moti: idem enim est quod est a movente ut a causa agente, et quod est in moto ut in patiente et recipiente."
[18] *In III Phys.* lec. 5.

moved or something has motion and it is not being moved. Both of these possibilities are unreasonable.[19]

Prior to this passage, Aquinas had already explained earlier in his commentary on the *Physics* why it is unreasonable to think that movers are themselves moved insofar as they act.[20] As we saw in Chapter 3, agents act in virtue of being actualized by a form.[21] Through being actualized by a form an agent is capable of communicating that form to another in action. We have also seen that patient substances undergo motions insofar as they are in potentiality to receiving a form.[22] Since being a mover presupposes that an agent substance is already actualized by the relevant form, movers cannot be conceived of as being moved (i.e. as acquiring form) insofar as they are movers. If a substance is in the requisite state for causing an action, it necessarily lacks the requisite state for undergoing the action. Aquinas considers the possibility that action is a motion in the agent, but somehow the agent is not changed by it. Perhaps this is how we might imagine action like a surge of energy which wells up in an agent and then bursts out into another substance. Aquinas, however, finds it absurd to posit that there is a motion in a substance which is not being moved by that motion. As we have seen, for a substance to have motion in it just is for it to be successively more actual with respect to a given form.

Aquinas next considers the possibility that an agent's action is a distinct motion from the patient's passion and that motion exists in the patient, rather than in the agent.[23] It seems that one might imagine that action is something the agent does to the patient which then gives rise to the passion in it. For example, a flame might trigger an initial reaction in water, which in turn leads to the motion of heating that the patient

[19] *In III Phys.* lec. 5 (ed. Leon., vol. 2, 112): "Si enim aliquis dicat quod actio est in agente et passio in patiente; actio autem est motus quidam, ut dictum est; sequitur quod motus sit in movente ... sequitur vel quod omne movens moveatur, vel quod aliquid habeat motum et non moveatur; quorum utrumque videtur inconveniens."

[20] *In III Phys.* lec. 4 (ed. Leon., vol. 2, 110). It is important to note that Aquinas thought that agents which were material bodies did in fact undergo changes when they acted on material patients. As discussed in Section 2.3 natural agents act of necessity when they are in contact with a suitable patient. Since physical contact has a mutuality to it both bodies in contact touch each other. Thus, often when an a material body acts as an agent on a patient, it is also acted upon by its patient as well. This is to say that many causal interactions between material substances involve two instances of efficient causation. The two substances in the interaction have reversed agent-patient roles in each instance. On this point in the Aristotelian system see John Russell, "Action and Reaction before Newton," *British Journal for the History of Science* 9:1 (1976): 25–38. When Aquinas claims that movers are not moved insofar as they act, he is not claiming that movers are not moved in any respect when they act. Rather his point is that the very action of the mover cannot consist in the mover itself being moved.

[21] See Section 3.3.   [22] See Sections 5.1 and 5.2.   [23] *In III Phys.* lec. 5.

undergoes. Aquinas, however, finds it absurd to posit two numerically distinct changes in a substance which both tend toward the same end result. Consider again the example about the water and the change of heating which is brought about by a preliminary change. We can ask, what is the outcome or goal which this initial change would be leading up to? The answer would have to be the final state of the water's being more perfectly hot. But this is the same goal that the subsequent change leads up to. Thus, there would be no basis to distinguish these two motions as two motions. One would simply be an earlier stage and the other a later stage of the same motion.

Since Aquinas thinks there is no coherent way to understand the causal interaction between agent and patient as involving more than one motion, he follows Aristotle in concluding that the action of the agent must be the same motion as the passion in the patient. The single motion is the very nexus of the causal interaction between the agent and the patient. It is neither a posterior effect of a prior doing by the agent nor is it something which prepares the way for a posterior undergoing of the patient. The motion is at once both the causal activity of the agent and the reception of causal activity on the part of the patient. It is both what the agent does and what the patient undergoes.

While Aquinas thinks that the agent's active potentiality and the patient's passive potentiality share the same actuality, he is careful to explain that this single actuality fulfills each of these two potentialities in a different way. The motion is the actuality of the mover (i.e. the agent) insofar as it is caused by it and it is the actuality of the mobile (i.e. the patient) insofar as it is undergone by it. Aquinas tries to illuminate the concept of a single reality which bears different orders to different terms by providing some analogies. He writes:

> For the proportion of one to two and of two to one is the same according to reality, but they are different according to account (*secundum rationem*); since if we begin the comparison with two and then proceed to one, it is said to be "double"; but if we begin with one and then proceed to two, is said to be "half." Similarly, the same space is traversed by the one ascending and the one descending, but according to the difference of the starting point and the end point, it is called an ascent or a descent. It is similar with the one moving and the mobile. For motion as it is proceeding from the mover into the mobile is the act of the mover; and as it is in the mobile as from the mover is the act of the mobile.[24]

---

[24] *In III Phys.* lec. 4 (ed. Leon., vol. 2, 110):

> Eadem enim distantia est unius ad duo et duorum ad unum secundum rem, sed differunt secundum rationem; quia secundum quod incipimus comparationem a duobus procedendo

In each of the examples, there is one reality which is between two terms. There is one numerical distance between the numbers of one and two; and one physical stretch of land between two points. But two different accounts of that one reality can be given depending on which term one begins with. The stretch of land, for example, is an ascent if one begins at the lower point. Yet, it is a descent if one begins at the higher point. The proportion between two to one is "double" if one starts with two; it is "one-half" if one begins with one.

It is tempting to think that when Aquinas claims that the ascent and the descent and the proportion of "double" and of "one-half" are the same in reality and different only according to account, he is claiming that there is merely a conceptual distinction between these correlatives. On this reading, there is no real difference between an ascent and a descent and 1:2 and 2:1. The difference is merely between two ways in which a mind can conceive of the one reality. I think this reading is mistaken.

For Aquinas, distinctions according to account (*secundum rationem*) are not always merely conceptual distinctions. Aquinas maintains that many of the accounts of things (i.e. *rationes*) grasped by our intellect are also found in reality.[25] Though corresponding ascents and descents are in reality constituted by the same stretch of land, anyone with experience hiking can tell you that there is a difference in reality between whether one begins at the bottom of a stretch of land or the top. It is not a difference between two different entities, but rather it is a difference between two different orders involving one and the same entity. There is a mind-independent difference between the order that the hiker at the bottom has to the stretch of land and the order that the one at the top has to it. The accounts (i.e. *rationes*) "ascent" and "descent" pick out the same entity, but each according to a different one of these two mind-independently distinct orders.

Similarly, the two different accounts which can be given of motion as the "actuality of the mover" and as the "actuality of the mobile"

---

ad unum, dicitur duplum, e contrario vero dicitur dimidium. Et similiter idem est spatium ascendentis et descendentis; sed secundum diversitatem principii et termini, vocatur ascensio vel descensio. Et similiter est in movente, et moto. Nam motus secundum quod procedit a movente in mobile, est actus moventis; secundum autem quod est in mobili a movente, est actus mobilis.

[25] See, for instance, *In I Sent.* d. 2, q. 1, a. 3 (ed, Mandonnet-Moos, vol. 1, 67): "ratio dicitur esse in re, inquantum significatum nominis, cui accidit esse rationem, est in re: et hoc contingit proprie quando conceptio intellectus est similitudo rei." *ScG* II c. 75 (ed. Marietti, 218–19, n. 1550): "Id vero quod intelligitur, est ipsa ratio rerum existentium extra animam … [R]es in suis naturis existentes cognoscantur."

respectively respond to a real, mind-independent difference between the manner in which motion is ordered to the agent and the manner in which it is ordered to the patient. Though the motion is one in reality, it realizes each potentiality in a different way. The motion actualizes the active potentiality of the mover by arising from it causally. The motion actualizes the passive potentiality of the patient by existing in it as a form in matter. Though the accounts "actuality of the mover" (i.e. action) and "actuality of the moved" (i.e. passion) both respond to one and the same entity, namely a motion, there is a basis in reality for distinguishing these two accounts from each other, namely the two different orders which obtain between the motion in the agent and the motion in the patient.

6.3 Responses to Some Difficulties for the "Action-Passion Sameness" Thesis

In his commentary on *Physics* III, Aquinas enumerates and responds to a host of difficulties for the view that the mover and the moved have one actuality. He considers and responds to objections not discussed by Aristotle, which further shows that Aquinas was not merely commenting on Aristotelian views, but also defending this thesis as his own.[26] Here I will discuss a few of the most important objections since they contribute to a greater understanding of the "action-passion sameness" thesis itself.

The first difficulty is what one could call the problem of the separation of actuality from its corresponding potentiality. If the actuality of an agent's potentiality is a motion in its patient, then it follows that the potentiality of one substance is completed and fulfilled in a different substance. But it seems that the actualization of a potentiality ought to be in the same subject in which the potentiality is. It would be absurd to think that Socrates's potentiality to be tan can be realized in Plato or that Aristotle's potentiality for learning English be actualized in Shakespeare. So, how can fire's active potentiality to burn be actualized in the log which it burns? Mustn't the actualization of fire's potentiality to burn be some reality in the fire itself?

---

[26] It has been noted that nearly half of Aquinas's *In III. Phys.* lec. 5 is devoted to objections to the thesis that action and passion are the same motion which were not even raised by Aristotle. See Timothy McDermott, "The Subject of Predicamental Action," *The Thomist* 23 (1960): 189–210, at 190. The two difficulties not found in Aristotle which Aquinas considers at length both have to do with the categories. They are: (1) How can action and passion be distinct categories if they are the same motion? (2) If motion is action and passion, how can there be motion in other categories, such as substance and quality?

In response to this difficulty, Aquinas writes: "[I]t is not unfitting that the act of one be in another because ... it is nevertheless continuously tending from it into the other and without any interruption. The same act of the agent as from it is the very act in the patient as received in it."[27] Aquinas's point in this text is that the agent is not metaphysically separated from the actualization of its active potentiality. There is a causal connection between the two since it is through the agent's active potentiality that the actuality comes to be. Thus, though the actuality of the agent's active potentiality is not a form inhering in it, it nevertheless bears a real dependency on the active potentiality which it completes: it is immediately and continuously arising from it.

Another difficulty for the position that action and passion are the same motion is that there will be only one actuality for two distinct potentialities. The same motion of burning, for instance, will be both the actuality of the log's potentiality to be burned and the fire's potentiality to burn. It seems problematic for two distinct potentialities to have the same actuality because, as we have seen, potentialities are supposed to be individuated by their actualities.[28] Thus it seems that if the potentiality to cause a motion and the potentiality to undergo motion are in fact really distinct potentialities, then their actualities must be really distinct as well.

In response to this worry Aquinas claims that it is not problematic for two potentialities to have the same actuality, so long as that actuality relates to each potentiality in a different way. He writes:

> [N]othing prohibits one act from being the act of two so long as it is not one and the same act according to account (*secundum rationem*), but only according to reality (*secundum rem*) ... The very same act according to reality corresponds to two according to diverse accounts (*rationem*): It is of the agent insofar as it is from it, and it is of the patient insofar as it is in it.[29]

Aquinas claims that it is possible for the same actuality to be the actuality of two different potentialities so long as it is not the actuality of each according to the same way in which an actuality can complete a potentiality.

---

[27] *In III Phys.* lec. 5 (ed. Leon., vol. 2, 113): "[N]on est inconveniens actum unius esse in altero quia ... ab eo tamen in alterum tendens continue et sine aliqua interruptione: unde idem actus est huius, idest agentis, ut a quo; et tamen est in patiente ut receptus in eo."

[28] On the individuation of potentialities, see for instance *ST* I q. 77, a. 3. See also Sections 3.2 and 5.2.

[29] *In III Phys.* lec. 5, n. 10 (ed. Leon., vol. 2, 113): "[N]ihil prohibet unum actum esse duorum, ita quod non sit unus et idem secundum rationem, sed unus secundum rem ... Sic enim idem actus secundum rem est duorum secundum diversam rationem: agentis quidem secundum quod est ab eo, patientis autem secundum quod est in ipso."

In his commentary on Aristotle's *Metaphysics*, Aquinas explains that "actuality" is an analogous term. There are two different ways in which an actuality can be the fulfillment or realization of a potentiality. He writes:

> [T]he *term 'actuality' is said in different ways* . . . [W]e do not predicate actuality of all things in the same way, but in diverse ways. This diversity can be illustrated through diverse proportions. There is one proportion when we say that just as *A* is *in B*, likewise *C* is *in D*. For example, just as vision is in the eye, so is hearing in the ear. This type of proportion involves the comparison of substance, namely of form, to matter. For form is said to be in matter. *There is another proportion* when we say that just as *A* is *ordered to B*, likewise *C* is *ordered to D*. For example, just as vision is ordered to that which is to be seen, so is hearing ordered to that which is to be heard. It is by this kind of proportion that motion is compared to the potentiality to move, or any operation is compared to an operative potentiality.[30]

While every actuality is the fulfillment and realization of a corresponding potentiality, not every actuality fulfills or realizes its corresponding potentiality in the same way. Some actualities, such as forms, are such that they perfect or complete the potentiality in which they inhere. Aquinas explains that the potentiality for vision is the actuality of the eye in this way. Sight is the form of the eye insofar as a material organ is an eye in actuality, rather than merely a potential eye, when it has the potentiality for vision existing in it.[31] Other actualities, however, fulfill or realize their corresponding potentialities by arising from them. Actualities of this other sort do not exist in their corresponding potentialities as a form actualizing matter. The action of seeing, for instance, is not that in virtue of which the potentiality for sight is an actual potentiality for sight. Rather, the action of seeing is an actuality that arises from the potentiality for sight in virtue of its already being perfected as an actual potentiality for sight. Put otherwise, the act of seeing is not what makes an eye an eye. Rather, the act of seeing

---

[30] *In IX Meta.* lec. 5 (ed. Marietti, 437, nn. 1828–29):

> *diversimode dicatur actus* . . . non omnia dicimus similiter esse actu, sed hoc diversimode. Et haec diversitas considerari potest per diversas proportiones. Potest enim *sic* accipi proportio, ut dicamus, quod sicut hoc est in hoc, ita hoc in hoc. Utputa visus sicut est in oculo, ita auditus in aure. Et per hunc modum proportionis accipitur comparatio substantiae, idest formae, ad materiam; nam forma in materia dicitur esse. *Alius modus* proportionis est, ut dicamus quod sicut habet se hoc ad hoc, ita hoc ad hoc; puta sicut se habet visus ad videndum, ita auditus ad audiendum. Et per hunc modum proportionis accipitur comparatio motus ad potentiam motivam, vel cuiuscumque operationis ad potentiam operativam.

[31] See for instance *In II De anima*, lec. 2.

is the manifestation of the eye's being an eye. Potentialities of the second type, such as the power for sight, are not matter for their actualities, as the first type are, but rather they are "ordered to them." Aquinas claims that it is in this way that motion relates to the active potentiality to move. The motion which is its fulfillment does not inhere in the active potentiality to move as a form in matter. Nevertheless the motion is the realization or fulfillment of this active potentiality as an actuality arising from it. Motion is that to which the power to move is ordered.

We can now see how the distinction between two ways in which an actuality can fulfill or realize a potentiality responds to the initial difficulty. Even though potentialities are individuated by actualities, Aquinas thinks that a single actuality can correspond to two potentialities in the case of a correlative agent and patient because the actuality realizes each potentiality in a different way. In the case of the agent, the actuality fulfills its potentiality to cause the actuality. In the case of the patient, the actuality perfects its potentiality as a form inhering in matter. There is no difficulty with one and the same actuality fulfilling one potentiality by being from it, while fulfilling another potentiality by being in it as a form in matter.

According to Aquinas, the two different ways in which an actuality can complete or fulfill a potentiality (i.e. by being in it or by arising from it) is the basis in reality for the difference between action and passion. Aquinas considers the worry that the difference between action and passion will be destroyed if a single actuality is the fulfillment of the agent's and the patient's respective potentiality. For example, if teaching and learning are one and the same motion, which happens in the student, then it seems that teaching and learning would be the same in reality. This implies that anyone who is learning would also be teaching and vice versa. In response to this worry, Aquinas writes:

> [I]t must be said that it does not follow that action and passion are the same, or that teaching or learning are the same, but rather that the motion in which both are is the same. For motion according to one account (*secundum unam rationem*) is action and according to another account (*secundum aliam rationem*) is passion. For it is different according to account (*secundum rationem*) to be the actuality of something as existing in it and to be the actuality of something as from it.[32]

---

[32] *In III Phys.* lec. 5 (ed. Leon., vol. 2, 114): "[D]icendum est, quod non sequitur quod actio et passio sint idem, vel doctio et doctrina, sed quod motus cui inest utrumque eorum, sit idem. Qui quidem motus secundum unam rationem est actio, et secundum aliam rationem est passio. Alterum enim est secundum rationem esse actum huius ut in hoc, et esse actum huius ut ab hoc."

While the actuality which completes and fulfills the agent's and the patient's potentiality is one actuality, there is nevertheless a real (i.e. mind-independent) difference between how this actuality completes and fulfills each potentiality. The actuality arises from the agent's potentiality and when it is considered precisely as something that arises from the agent, the actuality is counted as an action. An action is an actuality arising from a potentiality. The same actuality, however, inheres in the patient's passive potentiality and considered precisely as an actuality existing in the patient, the actuality is counted as a passion. A passion is an actuality which exists in a potentiality. Thus, though teaching and learning are the same process as that which happens in the student, it does not follow that there is no mind-independent difference between teaching and learning. The process is teaching insofar as it is arising from the teacher. The process is learning insofar as it is existing in the student. *Arising from* and *existing in* are two different orders which the process has to the teacher and the student and this is the mind-independent basis for distinguishing the action of teaching from the passion of learning.

In concluding this section, we can summarize the main theses which Aquinas accepts about the actuality which corresponds to correlative active and passive potentialities: (1) a single actuality fulfills and completes both an agent's active potentiality and its patient's passive potentiality; (2) this actuality exists in the patient – the fulfillment of an agent's active potentiality is not an actuality existing in it; (3) there are two different ways in which an actuality can fulfill and complete a potentiality: by *existing in it* or *arising from it*. Active potentiality is fulfilled in the latter way.

6.4   Action and Passion as Distinct Categories of Accident

The remaining sections of the chapter focus on some of the central interpretive difficulties in Aquinas's views on action and passion. As we saw above, Aquinas maintains that action and passion are the same motion. Yet, he also maintains that action and passion are distinct and irreducible categories of being. As Aquinas notes at the beginning of his commentary on *Physics* III and also in his commentary on the *Metaphysics*, being, namely reality, is divided in various ways. First, there is the division of reality into potentialities and actualities. This division does not distinguish between different kinds of beings in terms of what they are (e.g. substances vs. qualities vs. quantities). Rather, as we have seen, the division between potentiality and actuality is a division between what is incomplete or unfulfilled vs. its realization, completion or perfection. Beings of various kinds can be potential or actual. The second division of being is the division of beings into the ten categories. This division divides beings according to what kind of being they are.[33] Following Aristotle, Aquinas identified the following ten categories: substance, quality, quantity, relation, time, place, position, habit (i.e. clothing), action and passion.[34] The latter nine categories are known as the categories of accidents.[35] They divide types of beings which exist in dependence on a substance, as opposed to existing of themselves. What has puzzled readers of Aquinas for centuries are the seemingly incompatible assertions he makes about action and passion with respect to these two schemata.[36] Regarding the actuality–potentiality division, Aquinas claims that correlative actions and passions are *one and the same actuality*, namely a motion in the patient. Yet, with regard to the categories, he claims that action and passion are distinct, irreducible categories of being. For instance, this is to say that the actuality of the active power to burn and the actuality of the passive power to undergo burning are one and the same motion of burning which occurs in the log and that undergoing burning and burning something else are nevertheless two different accidental beings. The goal of this section is explain how these views of Aquinas can be coherently maintained.

To understand Aquinas's views on how action and passion can be the same motion and yet distinct categories of accident, we must begin with

---

[33] *In III Phys.* lec. 1 and *In IX Meta.* lec. 1. In the *Physics* texts, he also mentions a third division, which is a division between types of relations contained under the category of relation.

[34] On Aquinas's derivation of the categories see John F. Wippel, "Thomas Aquinas's Derivation of the Aristotelian Categories (Predicaments)," *Journal of the History of Philosophy* 25:1 (1987): 13–34.

[35] Notice that "motion" does not appear on the list of categories. In Aquinas's view, motion is not one of the ten genera. As we have seen, motion is a type of incomplete act. It is defined in terms of the potentiality–act division. The incomplete act which is motion can be of many different categorical types. Put otherwise, "motion" does not express what kind of being something is, but rather it expresses that the being is in an in-between state with respect to potentiality and act. Substances can be moving with respect to quantities, qualities and places. Thus, there are motions which are of each of these categorical types. See *In XI Meta.* lec. 9 (ed. Marietti, 544, n. 2291): "motus non est aliquod unum praedicamentum distinctum ab aliis praedicamentis; sed sequitur alia praedicamenta." See also *In III Phys.* lec. 1. Aquinas rejects the Avicennian view which identifies motion with the category of passion.

[36] For an overview of the different scholastic and neo-scholastic interpretations of Aquinas's position on action, see Miller, "The Problem of Action in the Commentary of St. Thomas Aquinas on the *Physics* of Aristotle." Miller's article summarizes the interpretations of Thomas de Vio (1469–1534) and Francesco Sylvestri (1474–1528), as well as early twentieth-century Thomists. For an exposition and defense of the interpretation of Johannes Poinsot (1589–1644), see W. Declan Kane, "The Subject of Predicamental Action according to John of St. Thomas," *The Thomist* 22:3 (1959): 66–388. For a critique of Kane's interpretation, see McDermott, "The Subject of Predicamental Action."

his views about what it is that the categories classify in reality. Aquinas claims that the ten categories mark out a division in reality between modes of being or ways of existing. He writes in his *De veritate*:

> There are diverse grades of being according to which we understand the diverse modes of being and through these modes are understood the diverse genera of things. For substance does not add some difference to being which designates some nature superadded to being, but rather the name 'substance' expresses a certain mode of being, namely *per se* being and so it is in the other genera.[37]

A difference of mode of being is a difference in how an entity exists, as opposed to a difference that arises through the addition of a nature.[38] What it means for two beings to exist in different ways from each other can most easily be grasped by the example of a substance and an accident. Substances exist of themselves, whereas accidents exist as modifications of substances.[39] Socrates, for example, is not a being that modifies some more fundamental subject. He exists through himself. By contrast, Socrates's whiteness, courage, height, and fatherhood only exist insofar as they belong to Socrates. The difference between a particular substance and a particular accident is not merely a difference in their nature, as is the difference between a cat and a dog or between brownness and greenness. More fundamentally, a substance and an accident differ with respect to how they exist. One exists of itself, while the other exists as something belonging to another being.

Since all accidents are beings which depend on a subject it might seem that all accidents have the same mode of being, namely existing in dependence on a substance. But in the passage above Aquinas claims that all of the genera marked out by the Aristotelian categories similarly track a division in reality between modes of being. While all accidents depend

---

[37] *De ver.* q. 1, a.1 (ed. Leon., vol. 22/1, 5): "Sunt enim diversi gradus entitatis, secundum quos accipiuntur diversi modi essendi, et iuxta hos modos accipiuntur diversa rerum genera: substantia enim non addit super ens aliquam differentiam quae designet aliquam naturam superadditam enti sed nomine substantiae exprimitur specialis quidam modus essendi, scilicet per se ens, et ita est in aliis generibus."

[38] On Aquinas's understanding of "modes of being" see John Tomarchio's papers "Aquinas's Division of Being according to Modes of Existing," *Review of Metaphysics* 54:3 (2001): 585–613; "Four Indices for the Thomistic Principle *Quod recipitur in aliquo est in eo per modum recipientis*," *Mediaeval Studies* 60:1 (1998): 315–67; "Thomistic Axiomatics in an Age of Computers," *History of Philosophy Quarterly* 16:3 (1999): 249–75.

[39] *In VII Meta.* lec. 1 (ed. Marietti, 317, n. 1254): "modus essendi accidentium non sit ut per se sint, sed solum ut insint ..." *In VII Meta.* lec. 1 (ed. Marietti, 316, n. 1248): "Sed substantia est ens simpliciter et per seipsam: omnia autem alia genera a substantia sunt entia secundum quid et per substantiam: ergo substantia est prima inter alia entia."

upon substance for their existence, accidents can be distinguished according to different genera in virtue of the differences in how they depend upon or are of a substance. Quality, for example, is a different category of accident from quantity because belonging to a substance as a qualitative modification of it is a different way of being of a substance than belonging to a substance as a measure of it. Thus, each of the nine types of accident is said to exist in a different way from every other because each is of or belongs to a substance in a different way. Put otherwise the nine different types of accident mark out different ways in which a dependent entity might modify or depend on a subject.

Aquinas thinks that the point about how different categories of accident are distinguished from each other, namely in terms of modes of being – or as I have glossed it different ways of being of or belonging to substance – is crucial for understanding how action and passion can both be the same motion (i.e. the same actuality), and yet, different accidents from each other. After introducing the worry that the distinction between action and passion as categories will collapse if action and passion are the same motion, he writes in his *Physics* commentary: "[I]t must be understood that being is divided into the ten categories not univocally, as a genus into its species, but rather according to diverse modes of being."[40] Aquinas's point here is that if the division between types of accidents were a division of types of actualities each of which existed in the same way (i.e. each of which belonged to its subject in the same way), then the objection would prevail. There would be no way for action and passion to be the same actuality (i.e. the same motion) and yet different accidents. However, Aquinas emphasizes that this assumption about how the categories are distinguished is mistaken. The fact that the categories of accident are distinguished in virtue of different ways in which a being might be of or belong to a substance makes it possible for two different accidents to consist of the same actuality and yet be different accidents from each other. This is because one and the same actuality can belong to different substances in different ways.

In his *Metaphysics* commentary, Aquinas provides an example to show how the diversification of accidents in terms of modes of being (i.e. ways of

---

[40] *In III Phys.* lec. 5 (ed. Leon., vol. 2, 114): "[S]ciendum est quod ens dividitur in decem praedicamenta non univoce, sicut genus in species, sed secundum diversum modum essendi." See also *In V Meta.* lec. 9 (ed. Marietti, 238, n. 890): "Unde oportet, quod ens contrahatur ad diversa genera secundum diversum modum praedicandi, qui consequitur diversum modum essendi; quia quoties ens dicitur, idest quot modis aliquid praedicatur, toties esse significatur, idest tot modis significatur aliquid esse."

being of or belonging to substances) makes it possible for there to be a sameness between diverse accidents. He writes:

> Therefore, one and the same thing pertains to different categories insofar as it is predicated in diverse ways of diverse things. A place, for example, insofar as it is predicated of the thing which locates, pertains to the category of quantity. Yet insofar as it is predicated denominatively of the thing which is located, it constitutes the category of where.[41]

Since accidents are divided into categories in terms of how an actuality is of or belongs to a subject there can be a sameness with regard to actuality between diverse types of accidents. This is because one and the same actuality A can belong to two different substances in two different ways. In such a case, A will be the same as two types of accidents $a1$ and $a2$. Consider, for example, the place on the table where my coffee cup is now set down. Compared to my coffee cup, that place is its location.[42] Compared to the table, however, that place is a quantity of it. The coffee cup's location is one and the same actuality as a certain quantity of the table's surface. This actuality both completes and fulfills the table's potentiality to be quantified and the cup's potentiality to be located. Yet, the coffee cup's location is a different accident from a portion of the table's quantity. This, as we have seen, is because accidents are distinguished into their types according to different ways of being of or belonging to substances. To be the location of a substance is a different way of being of or belonging to a substance than the way of being of or belonging to a substance that is being a quantity of it.

Aquinas continues on in the passage quoted above from his commentary on the *Metaphysics* to explain how these points apply to action and passion. He writes: "Similarly, motion, insofar as it is predicated of the subject in which it is, constitutes the category of passion. However, insofar as it is predicated of the one from which it is, it constitutes the category of

---

[41] *In XI Meta.* l. 9 (ed. Marietti, 547, n. 2313): "Unde idem, secundum quod diversimode de diversis praedicatur, ad diversa praedicamenta pertinet. Locus enim, secundum quod praedicatur de locante, pertinet ad genus quantitatis. Secundum autem quod praedicatur denominative de locato, constituit praedicamentum ubi." Aquinas speaks of predication in this passage because in his view the different ways in which a predicate can be applied to a subject track the different modes of being in reality, namely the different ways in which a being can belong to a substance. See for instance *In III Phys.* lec. 5 and *In V Meta.* lec. 9, n. 890.

[42] In this example of place and quantity, Aquinas does not use a neutral term to refer to the actuality that belongs to the locating body (as its quantity) and the located body (as its place). He simply refers to it as a "place." Strictly speaking, though, "place" signifies the actuality which is predicated of the located body *together with* the order this body has to it as located by it.

action."[43] In Aquinas's view, motion is a single actuality that is of or belongs to two different substances in two different ways. Motion considered in itself, apart from how it belongs to the agent or the patient, is merely an incomplete actuality. But since the motion is of or belongs to two substances according to two different ways, the motion is the same as two different types of accident. "Sameness" here should not be taken as "identity" in the modern sense. In the modern sense, two entities are identical if they share all of the same properties. In Aquinas's view, motion considered in itself does not share all of the same properties as action and passion. In addition to the properties of the motion, action and passion each include a different order to a particular substance. Motion, of itself, does not include these orders to an agent and patient among its properties. Put otherwise, an accident is not merely an actuality considered in itself. It is an actuality taken together with a particular way of belonging to, being of, or depending on a substance. If one and the same actuality is of two different substances, then there will be two different accidents.

In other texts, Aquinas more explicitly clarifies how it is that action and passion can be different accidents though they are each the same as a single motion. He writes in his *Summa Theologiae*:

> [A]ccording to the Philosopher in *III Physics* this argument holds: whatever are the same as one thing are the same as each other in those things which are the same according to reality and account (*ratione*), just as 'tunic' and 'garment.' It is not the case in those things which differ according to account (*ratione*). Hence he says in the same place that although action is the same motion as passion, nevertheless it does not follow that action and passion are the same as each other, because action implies an order toward that from which there is motion in the mobile, and passion implies something which is from another.[44]

---

[43] *In XI Meta.* l. 9 (ed. Marietti, 547, n. 2313): "Similiter motus, secundum quod praedicatur de subiecto in quo est, constituit praedicamentum passionis. Secundum autem quod praedicatur de eo a quo est, constituit praedicamentum actionis." See also *In III Phys.* lec. 16 (ed. Leon., vol. 2, 115): "Sic igitur patet quod licet motus sit unus, tamen praedicamenta quae sumuntur secundum motum, sunt duo, secundum quod a diversis rebus exterioribus fiunt praedicamentales denominationes. Nam alia res est agens, a qua sicut ab exteriori, sumitur per modum denominationis praedicamentum passionis: et alia res est patiens a qua denominatur agens. Et sic patet solutio primae dubitationis."

[44] *ST* I q. 28, a. 3 ad 1 (ed. Leon., vol. 4, 324):

> [S]ecundum Philosophum in III *Physic.*, argumentum illud tenet, quod quaecumque uni et eidem sunt eadem, sibi invicem sunt eadem, in his quae sunt idem re et ratione, sicut tunica et indumentum: non autem in his quae differunt ratione. Unde ibidem dicit quod, licet actio sit idem motui, similiter et passio, non tamen sequitur quod actio et passio sint idem: quia in actione importatur respectus ut a quo est motus in mobili, in passione vero ut qui est ab alio.

According to this text, one cannot infer that action and passion are the same accident as each other from the fact that they are the same motion because action and passion each imply something more than the motion which they are the same as. "Motion" signifies the very actuality which is caused and received – abstracting from its order to the agent as caused by it and its order to the patient as received by it. By contrast, "action" signifies both a motion and its being from a substance as its origin; and "passion" signifies both the motion and its being of a substance as received by it.[45] As we have seen, accidents are not mere actualities. They are actualities taken together with a particular way of belonging to a substance. Because the accidental name terms "action" and "passion" each signify the motion together with a different order to a different substance, one cannot infer that action and passion are the same accident from the fact that they are the same motion. The action is the motion taken together with one order a substance has to it, while the passion is the motion taken together with another order a substance has to it.

It must be emphasized that the ways in which motion is ordered to the agent and to the patient respectively are real, mind-independent orders in reality. They are not merely different ways of conceiving of the motion in relation to other things. There is a real difference between how the motion is of the agent and how it is of the patient. In Aquinas's view, unlike David Hume's, causal orders are not projections of the mind.[46] In reality, it is the case that motion arises from an agent and is received in a patient. This different way in which the motion is of the agent from how it is of the patient is what the categories of action and passion distinguish. Aquinas writes in his *Summa contra Gentiles*:

> The passage occurs in the context of a discussion of the Trinity. According to Christian belief, there is one God, and yet three divine persons (i.e. the Father, the Son and the Holy Spirit). While each of the three persons is a numerically distinct person from the other, each is the same as the divine essence. Aquinas appeals to the relationship between action, passion and motion as a model for how two entities A and B can be the same as a third C without implying that A and B are the same as each other.

[45] In the following passage Aquinas gives particularly clear account of the meaning of "action": *ST* I q. 41, a. 1 ad 2 (ed. Leon., vol. 4, 421): "Et ideo actio, secundum primam nominis impositionem, importat originem motus . . . ita origo ipsius motus, secundum quod incipit ab alio et terminatur in id quod movetur, vocatur actio. Remoto igitur motu, actio nihil aliud importat quam ordinem originis . . ." Regarding the meaning of "passion," he writes *De ver.* q. 26, a. 1 (ed. Leon., vol. 22.3/1, 747): "Communiter quidem dicitur passio receptio alicuius quocumque modo et hoc sequendo significationem vocabuli, nam passio dicitur a patin graeco, quod est recipere. Proprie vero dicitur passio secundum quod actio et passio in motu consistent, prout scilicet aliquid recipitur in patiente per viam motus."

[46] Aquinas recognizes that we cannot perceive causality with our senses, but nevertheless, he thinks that one can know on the basis of rational argumentation that there must be entities ordered to each other as cause and effect in the reality. See Section 2.4 and for a primary text, *In VI Meta.* lec. 1, n. 1146.

"Although motion is the common act of the mover and the moved, nevertheless it is one operation to cause motion and another to receive motion, and thus there are two categories posited: *to do* and *to suffer*."[47]

Though the actuality (i.e. the motion) involved in action and passion is one and the same, the categories of action and passion nevertheless pick out two really different ways in which motion can belong to a substance in reality, namely as something arising from it and something received by it from another. The mind-independent difference between the order which the agent has to motion and the order which the patient has to it is underscored by Aquinas's repeated claim that "passion is an effect of action."[48] Initially, it seems incoherent to hold that action is the cause of passion, while also maintaining that action and passion are the same motion, since this seems to imply that one and the same motion causes itself.[49] But what must be kept in mind is that action and passion do not signify the motion alone. As we have seen, these terms refer to the motion together with a real, mind-independent way in which it belongs to a substance. When Aquinas claims that passion is an effect of action, what he means is that the motion's being of the agent as something causally arising from it is naturally prior to the motion's being of the patient as something received by it. Actions cannot be temporally prior to passions because what time measures is motion. As we have seen, in Aquinas's view, the agent's causation of motion and the patient's reception of motion are not themselves motions. *Causing* and *receiving* are really different ways in which a substance can be ordered to or have it itself with respect to a single motion.[50] Thus, the priority of action over passion is not temporal priority. It is ontological priority. Passions depend on actions, but actions do not depend on passions. When Aquinas describes action as the cause of passion what he means is this: a motion's belonging to the patient as

---

[47] *ScG* II c. 57 (ed. Marietti, 183, n. 1334): "Licet motus sit communis actus moventis et moti, tamen alia operatio est facere motum et recipere motum: unde et duo praedicamenta ponuntur *facere* et *pati*."

[48] *ST* I q. 44, a. 2 ad 1 (ed. Leon., vol. 4, 458): "passio est effectus actionis." *De ver.* q. 26, a. 2 (ed. Leon., vol. 22.3/1, 752): "passio patientis derivatur ab agente, eo quod passio est effectus actionis." See also *ST* I q. 97, a. 2; *In V Ethic.* lec. 14, n. 7.

[49] In fact, Peter Auriol argued against Aquinas's view that the agent's action is the same as the motion which it causes in the patient because he saw it as implying that the motion causes itself. I discuss this argument and later replies to it in section 3 of my article "What Is an Action? Peter Auriol vs. Thomas Aquinas on the Metaphysics of Causality."

[50] *ST* I q. 45, a.2 ad 2 (ed. Leon., vol. 4, 466): "Sed cum actio et passio convenient in substantia motus, et differant solum secundum habitudines diversas ... oportet quod subtract motu, non remaneat nisi diversae habitudines."

something undergone by it ontologically depends on the motion's being of the agent as something arising from it.

As the texts above make clear, the real difference between how the single motion belongs to the agent and how it belongs to the patient provides the basis for distinguishing action and passion as two distinct accidents. Though there is one motion, there are two accidents because each accident is not merely the motion, but the motion taken together with a certain way in which it belongs to a given substance. Aquinas's discussion of cooperative action further confirms that he thought that action accidents were not reducible to the actuality (i.e. the motion) which they involved. In a case in which two agents together move one patient, there is just one motion. Yet, Aquinas claims here that there are two action accidents. He writes: "one passion corresponds to two actions when neither of the agents is sufficient through itself to complete the action."[51] When two agents cooperate to cause a single motion there are two action accidents because the motion arises from two distinct substances. As we have seen, an accident is an actuality taken together with a certain order it has to a particular substance. Elsewhere he writes:

> It is impossible for there to be one operation of things which are diverse according to being. I say that an operation is one, not on account of that in which the action terminates, but rather on account of how it arises from the agent. For when many people pull a boat they perform one action with respect to the work done, which is one, but nevertheless with respect to the ones pulling there are many actions because there are many impulses (*impulsus*) toward pulling. Since action follows upon form and power, it is necessary that those things which have diverse forms and powers, also have diverse actions.[52]

In this passage, Aquinas makes clear that action accidents are counted not in terms of the number of motions (i.e. actualities) which they involve, but rather in terms of the number of sources from which the motion or actuality arises. It is Aquinas's general view that accidents are distinguished

---

[51] *In III Sent.* d. 8, a. 5, q. un. (ed. Mandonnet-Moos, vol. 3, 293): "una passio respondet duabus actionibus, quando neutrum agens sufficit per se ad actionem complendam ..."
[52] *ScG* II c. 57 (ed. Marietti, 183, n. 1331):

> Impossibile est quod eorum quae sunt diversa secundum esse, sit operatio una. Dico autem operationem unam, non ex parte eius in quod terminatur actio, sed secundum quod egreditur ab agente: multi enim trahentes navim unam actionem faciunt ex parte operati, quod est unum, sed tamen ex parte trahentium sunt multae actiones, quia sunt diversi impulsus ad trahendum, cum enim actio consequatur formam et virtutem, oportet quorum sunt diversae formae et virtutes, esse et actiones diversas.

numerically in virtue of the numerical distinction of the subjects to which they belong.[53] If, for example, one agent quits pulling and the others carry on, there continues to be one motion, but there are fewer accidents in the category of action because that motion is of or belongs to fewer substances as arising from it.[54] This further illustrates that a motion is not of itself an accident in the category of action. Rather, a motion constitutes an accident in the category of action in virtue of its order to the substance from which it arises. When one motion arises from many numerically distinct substances, the motion constitutes many numerically distinct accidents in the category of action.[55]

From this section we can conclude that since Aquinas maintains that accidents are not generically and numerically diversified in accord with the number of actualities which they involve, he did not find any inconsistency in maintaining that the agent's and patient's respective potentialities have one actuality, and yet action and passion are numerically and generically different accidents. Though there is just one actuality (i.e. one motion) involved in correlative actions and passions, that actuality constitutes two specifically distinct types of accident since that actuality actualizes the potentialities of two different substances in two different ways. There is not a one-to-one correspondence between actualities and accidents because the division of accidents takes into account the different ways in which actualities complete the potentialities of substances. An accident is not merely an actuality. It is an actuality taken together with a particular way in which it belongs to a particular substance. As we have seen, a particular action accident is not merely a motion. It is a motion which is of or belongs to a particular substance as arising or originating from it. Since part of what it is to be a particular action accident includes a

---

[53] See for instance, *ST* III q. 77, a.1 (ed. Leon., vol. 12, 193–94): "*accidentia non transeunt de subiecto in subiectum*: ut scilicet idem accidens numero quod primo fuit in uno subiecto, postmodum fiat in alio. Accidens enim numerum accipit a subiecto. Unde non potest esse quod, idem numero manens, sit quandoque in hoc, quandoque in alio subiecto."

[54] In Aquinas's view, for a motion to be the same motion it must be in the same subject, toward the same term, and it must be continuous. See *In V Phys.* lec. 7, n. 706. Thus, the motion in the example stipulated here would only be one motion if the switch in which agents were producing it did not involve any interruption to the motion. So far as I know, Aquinas nowhere claims that being produced by a particular agent is essential to motion's identity.

[55] Furthermore, supposing that the agents who are pulling the boat are doing so through an exercise of their wills, it is possible that the agent's distinct actions have different moral species. One agent's act of pulling might be morally good, while another's pulling is morally evil depending upon the end for which each is pulling. On a related note, Aquinas explicitly claims that in the moral order, action and passion can have different moral classifications. For example, an act of cutting can be morally evil, while its corresponding passion of being cut is not evil. See, for example, *ST* I-II q. 20, a. 6 ad 2; *ST* I-II q. 20, a. 3 ad 1and *ST* I-II q. 18, a.7 ad 1.

particular order to a particular substance it follows that though action and passion consist of the same motion, they are nevertheless two different accidents.

6.5 Action as an Accident in the Agent as Subject

In addition to the puzzle discussed above about how action and passion can be the same motion and yet distinct categorical accidents, Aquinas's texts on action include another interpretive difficulty. This difficulty regards the question of which substance is the subject of the agent's action. As we saw above in Section 6.2, Aquinas argued that an agent's action is the same motion as the patient's passion. This motion exists in the patient. Thus, it would seem that the subject of the agent's action is the patient. However, in multiple texts Aquinas asserts that transeunt actions are accidents in the agent as subject. For example, he writes his early commentary on the *Sentences*: "Action, insofar as it is action . . . is in the agent, [and] this applies to it insofar as it is an accident."[56] In the later *Summa contra Gentiles*, he again writes: "Action which is not the substance of an agent is in it as an accident in a subject: hence action is numbered among the nine categories of accidents."[57] How can it be that the actuality of an agent's potentiality is an actuality inhering in the patient and that an agent's action is an accident in it as subject? Aquinas's interpreters have reached no consensus about how to fit together his varying claims about the subject of an agent's transeunt action.[58] Some have claimed that his views on transeunt action changed over time.[59]

A reader may initially think that passages such as the ones above refer only to immanent actions, namely those which remain in the agent, such as knowing and willing. On this reading, the passages pose no tension for the view that an agent's transeunt action is a motion in its patient because such passages are not even about transeunt action. This would certainly be an easy resolution to the interpretive difficulty. However, it will not work because there are other texts in which Aquinas explicitly claims that actions

---

[56] *In I Sent.* d. 32, q.1, a.1 (ed. Mandonnet-Moos, vol. 1, 743): "Actio enim, secundum quod est actio . . . sit in agente, hoc accidit sibi inquantum est accidens."

[57] *ScG* II c. 9 (ed. Marietti, 120, n. 902): "Actio quae non est substantia agentis, inest ei sicut accidens subiecto: unde et actio unum inter novem praedicamenta accidentis computatur."

[58] For references, see fn. 36 above.

[59] Bernard Lonergan is one especially prominent interpreter who has defended this view. See his *Grace and Freedom: Operative Grace in the Thought of St. Thomas Aquinas*, in *The Collected Works of Bernard Lonergan*, vol. 1, ed. F. Crowe and R. Doran (Toronto: University of Toronto Press, 2013), 254–67.

which pass over into an external patient, namely transeunt actions, are likewise in the agent. Aquinas writes in a different *Sentences* passage:

> [A]s is clear in natural actions such as when fire heats wood, and in artificial actions, as when a builder makes a house from matter, ... the action is received in that which is made through the mode of passion insofar as motion is in the moved thing as its subject. Therefore in such cases one finds action in the acting thing and passion in the thing undergoing change.[60]

This text claims in its last lines that action is in the agent and it makes quite clear by its examples of heating and building that it is referring to transeunt, rather than immanent, actions.

It likewise will not work as an interpretive strategy to suggest that Aquinas's position developed over time. This is because Aquinas asserts that action is *in the agent* and that action is *in the patient* in proximate passages within one and the same work. For example, in *Summa contra Gentiles*, Bk. II, ch. 9 Aquinas claims: "Action which is not the substance of an agent is in it as an accident in a subject."[61] Just seven short chapters later in this same work, he writes:

> Matter is compared to the agent as recipient of the action which is from it: for the act which is of the agent as from it is of the patient as in it. Therefore matter is required by some agent in order that matter might receive its action. For the very action of the agent is received by the patient and it is the act and form of the patient ...[62]

The proximity of these two passages in the *Summa contra Gentiles* shows that Aquinas held within the same time period both (1) that the actualization of an agent's active potentiality is the motion which it causes in the patient and (2) that action is in the agent as its subject. Yet, it is hard to see how these views are not straightforwardly contradictory. How can the agent's action be the same as what the patient undergoes and also be something in the agent?

---

[60] *In I Sent.* d. 40, q. 1, a.1 ad 1 (ed. Mandonnet-Moos, vol. 1, 942): "ut patet in actionibus naturalibus sicut ignis calefacit lignum, et in artificialibus, sicut aedificator facit domum ex materia ... actio est recepta in eo quod fit, per modum passionis, secundum quod motus est in moto ut in subjecto: et ideo in talibus est invenire actionem in re agente, et passionem in re patiente."

[61] See fn. 57 for the Latin.

[62] *ScG* II c. 16 (ed. Marietti, 125, n. 938): "Materia comparatur ad agens sicut recipiens actionem quae ab ipso est: actus enim qui est agentis ut a quo, est patientis ut in quo. Igitur requiritur materia ab aliquo agente ut recipiat actionem ipsius: ipsa enim actio agentis in patiente recepta est actus patientis et forma, aut aliqua inchoatio formae, in ipso."

It is important to note that in some of the passages quoted above Aquinas qualifies the respect in which action is in the agent. In one of the *Sentences* passages above he claims that action insofar as it is an accident is in the agent, and in the *Summa contra Gentiles* text he similarly claims that action is in the agent as an accident in a subject. This qualifier is important because it indicates that when Aquinas asserts that "action is in the agent" he is referring to the categorical division of being, rather than the division between potentiality and actuality which was central to the discussion in *Physics* III. Action considered as an accidental type of being is in the agent while action considered as an actuality of a potentiality is in the patient as subject.[63] While the explicit contradiction in Aquinas's texts can be resolved by referring his claims about the subject of action to either the accident of action or the actuality of the agent's potentiality, it is nevertheless difficult to see how the actuality of the agent's active potentiality could be in the patient, while the accident that is action exists in the agent as subject. Aquinas, like his Aristotelian counterparts, rejected that one accident could be in two distinct subjects, as well as the possibility of the same numerical accident passing from one subject to another. Thus, it seems that what is in the agent as subject cannot be the very motion which exists in the patient.

I believe that the key to understanding how it is that Aquinas can maintain both that the agent's action is an accident in it as subject and that the motion or actuality which constitutes the accident is in the patient is recognizing that not all accidents exist in their subjects as forms actualizing their matter. In Aquinas's view, actualities that are extrinsic to a given substance can nevertheless belong to it as an accident in a subject. For Aquinas, "existing in a subject" is an analogous term. Not all accidents exist in their subjects as forms in matter. An actuality which is not inhering

---

[63] When Aquinas writes about an agent's causal activity it is not always clear whether he is referring to the actuality which completes the agent's potentiality or the categorial accident of action. In Aristotle's Greek, the term used for actuality is *energeia*. The term for action as a categorial accident is *poiesis*. However, Latin translators of Aristotle often rendered both *energeia* and *poiesis* as *actio*. For an example where *energeia* is translated as *actio* (rather than the more frequent *actus*), see *Aristoteles Latinus XXV 3 Metaphysica, lib. I-XIV. Recensio et Translatio Guillelmi de Moerbeka*, 2 vols, ed. Gudrun Vuillemin-Diem (Leiden: Brill, 1995), vol. 2: 190, 1050a35: "Quorum vero non est aliud aliquod opus praeter actionum, in ipsis existit actio, ut uisio in uidente et speculatio in speculante et vita in anima (quare et felicitas; uita namque qualis quedam est)." Aristotle's Greek reads: "ὅσων δὲ μὴ ἔστιν ἄλλο τι ἔργον παρὰ τὴν ἐνέργειαν, ἐν αὐτοῖς ὑπάρχει ἡ ἐνέργεια (οἷον ἡ ὅρασις ἐν τῷ ὁρῶντι καὶ ἡ θεωρία ἐν τῷ θεωροῦντι καὶ ἡ ζωὴ ἐν τῇ ψυχῇ, διὸ καὶ ἡ εὐδαιμονία: ζωὴ γὰρ ποιά τίς ἐστιν)" (Aristotle's *Metaphysics*, ed. W. D. Ross (Oxford: Clarendon Press, 1924), line 1050a34–b1). For discussion of these terminological difficulties, see Lonergan, *Grace and Freedom*, pp. 269–70.

in the matter of a given substance can nevertheless belong to it as its accident. Regarding what it means for an accident to be in a subject, Aquinas writes: "being in (*inesse*) does not mean the being of an accident absolutely, but rather a mode of being which belongs to it from an order to the proximate cause of its being."[64] According to this passage, to exist in a subject does not imply that what exists in the subject is itself a form in the subject as in matter. Rather for an entity to exist in a subject is for it have a mode of being in virtue of an order to that subject. Aquinas explicitly claims that one substance can belong to another substance as its accident. He writes: "Nevertheless something might be an accident with respect to something else even though it is a substance in itself, just as clothes are with respect to a body ..."[65] While no substance can exist in another substance as a form inherent in its matter, nevertheless some substances are accidents of other substances when they are extrinsically ordered to them in the right sort of ways. Aquinas counts clothes as an accident of the wearer because they belong to the wearer in such a way as to actualize its potentiality. It is in virtue of actualizing the wearer's potentiality to be clothed that wool or the cloth is an accident in the category of habit. While the clothes do not depend on the wearer to exist absolutely, they depend on the wearer to exist as clothing. Wool is clothing in virtue of belonging to the wearer in a certain way. Aquinas's remarks on the meaning of what it is to exist in a subject and his willingness to count clothes as an accident of the wearer show that he thinks that it is possible for something which is extrinsic to a substance to belong to it as an accident.[66] This is significant

---

[64] *In IV Sent.* d. 12, q. 1, a.1 ad 1 (ed. Mandonnet-Moos, vol. 4, 499): "quod inesse non dicit esse accidentis absolute, sed magis modum essendi qui sibi competit ex ordine ad causam proximam sui esse." Aristotle similarly writes in his *Categories*: "By 'present in a subject' I do not mean present as parts are present in a whole, but being incapable of existence apart from the said subject." *Categories* 2, ll. 24–26, *The Basic Works of Aristotle*, ed. Richard McKeon (New York: Random House, 1941), 7.

[65] *In II Sent.* d. 26, q. 1, a. 2 (ed. Mandonnet-Moos, vol. 2, 671): "Sed tamen aliquid accidentaliter ad aliud se habet quod tamen in se substantia est, sicut indumentum ad corpus ..." See also *I Sent.* d. 17, q. 1, a. 2.

[66] In discussing locomotion, Aquinas draws a distinction between intrinsic and extrinsic actualities. See for instance, *In III Sent.* d. 22, q. 3, a. 1 ad 1 (ed. Mandonnet-Moos, vol. 3, 679–80): "[M]otus localis, ut dicit Philosophus in VII *Phys.*, non mutat aliquid de eo quod est intra rem, sed solum est secundum id quod est extra. Unde motus localis non ponit exitum de potentia ad actum aliquem intraneum rei, sed ad actum extrinsecum." Even though it is not a form within the substance's matter, Aquinas conceives of this extrinsic act (i.e. a substance's location) as actualizing the substance's potentiality. Cf. *De pot.* q. 5, a. 5 ad 7 (ed. Pession, 144): "Ad septimum dicendum, quod res non dicitur esse imperfecta, quacumque potentia in ipsa non reducta ad actum, sed solum quando per reductionem in actum res suum consequitur complementum. Non enim homo qui est in potentia ut sit in India, imperfectus erit, si ibi non fuerit; sed imperfectus dicitur, si scientia vel virtute careat, qua natus est perfici." For Aquinas's statement that locomotion does not involve any

for our present topic because action turns out to be this type of accident. Though the motion that exists in the patient is extrinsic to the agent insofar as it is not a form inhering in the agent's matter, it nevertheless belongs to the agent as its accident in the category of action.

In the following passage, Aquinas distinguishes between two different types of categorial accidents: those which are defined as inherent and those which are not. Accidents defined as inherent are in their subjects as forms in matter while accidents which are not defined as inherent depend on their subjects as "beings from them." Aquinas holds up action as the paradigm case of the latter sort of accident. He writes:

> Certain categories according to their account signify inherence, such as quantity and quality, and others of this kind. Nothing is denominated in these categories except by an inherent form which is that through which something exists either substantially or accidentally. Certain categories, however, signify according to their account being from another (*ab alio ens*), and not as inhering, just as appears especially in action. For action, insofar as it is action, signifies being from an agent; and that it is in the agent accrues to it insofar as it is an accident. Therefore an accident in the genus of action is denominated by virtue of the fact that it is from that [i.e. the agent], and not by virtue of the fact that it is its [i.e. the agent's] principle. Likewise a subject is said to be an agent by its action; nevertheless, the action is not a principle of the agent, but rather the agent is the principle of the action.[67]

As Aquinas explains here, an accident is of the type "action" in virtue of the subject *from which* it is. It is through its order to the subject which causes it that an accident is an action. Though the motion exists in the patient as a form in matter, it is not an action accident through its order to the patient. It is by virtue of its order to the agent (i.e. its arising from the agent) that it has the mode of being which is action. Though action does not inhere in the agent as a form in its matter, the agent is nevertheless the

---

change in forms which inhere in the subject, see for instance, *In II Sent.* d. 8, q. 1, a. 2 (ed. Mandonnet-Moos, vol. 2, 206): "sed quantum ad motum localem, per quem nulla forma ponitur in re mota . . ."

[67] *In I Sent.* d. 32, q. 1, a. 1(ed. Mandonnet-Moos, vol. 1, 743):

> Quaedam enim genera secundum rationem suam significant ut inhaerens, sicut qualitas et quantitas, et hujusmodi; et in talibus non fit denominatio nisi per formam inhaerentem, quae est secundum aliquod esse vel substantiale vel accidentale. Quaedam autem significant secundum rationem suam, ut ab alio ens, et non ut inhaerens, sicut praecipue patet in actione. Actio enim, secundum quod est actio, significatur ut ab agente; et quod sit in agente, hoc accidit sibi inquantum est accidens. Unde in genere actionis denominatur accidens per id quod ab eo est, et non per id quod principium ejus est; sicut dicitur actione agens; nec tamen actio est principium agentis, sed e converso.

subject to whom the action accident belongs. The agent is the subject on which the accident depends according to the mode of being of or belonging to which is action.

Aquinas makes clear in a passage from his *De potentia* that accidents which are not defined as inherent can cease to be without any intrinsic change in the subject upon which they depend for their existence. He writes:

> [A]ction from the fact that it is action is considered as from the agent; but insofar as it is an accident, it is considered as in the agent. Therefore, nothing prohibits an accident of this kind from ceasing to exist without any change of the subject in which it is. This is because the account of an accident is not completed by its being in its subject, but by its passing over into another ...[68]

An agent's action accident can pass in and out of existence without the agent changing intrinsically because the agent's action depends on it by being from it – not by being in it as a form in matter.[69] As Aquinas explains elsewhere, "That which is attributed to something as proceeding from it into another does not make composition with it, just as action does not make composition with the agent."[70] Earlier in that same passage, Aquinas explicitly contrasts accidents which do not make composition with their subjects with the accidents of quantity and quality. He describes the latter accidents as "remaining in the subject."[71] Accidents which do not remain in or make composition with their subjects can be or not be without their subject changing intrinsically. Thus, Aquinas can consistently maintain, as he argues in his commentary on *Physics* III.3, that agents are not moved in virtue of acting and that their actions exist in them

---

[68] *De pot.* q. 7, a. 9 ad 7 (ed. Pession, 208–09): "[A]ctio ex hoc quod est actio, consideratur ut ab agente; in quantum vero est accidens, consideratur ut in subiecto agente. Et ideo nihil prohibet quod esse desinat huiusmodi accidens sine mutatione eius in quo est, quia sua ratio non perficitur prout est in ipso subiecto, sed prout transit in aliud ..."

[69] Aquinas has real changes in mind here, rather than mere Cambridge (i.e. extrinsic) changes.

[70] Aquinas explicitly claims that actions do not make composition with their subject in *De pot.* q. 7, a. 8 (ed. Pession, 206): "Quod autem attribuitur alicui ut ab eo in aliud procedens non facit compositionem cum eo, sicut nec actio cum agente." There is an earlier *Sentences* passage in which Aquinas claims, in contradiction with this text, that all accidents form a composition with their subjects. *In I Sent.* d. 8, q. 4, a. 3 (ed. Mandonnet-Moos, vol. 1, 224): "Sed in unoquoque novem praedicamentorum duo invenio; scilicet rationem accidentis et rationem propriam illius generis, sicut quantitatis vel qualitatis. Ratio autem accidentis imperfectionem continet: quia esse accidentis est inesse et dependere, et compositionem facere cum subjecto per consequens."

[71] *De pot.* q. 7, a. 8 (ed. Pession, 206): "quantitas et qualitas sunt quaedam accidentia in subiecto remanentia."

as accidents in subjects. As he makes clear, there are some accidents that come and go from their subjects without their subjects being moved.

The upshot of Aquinas's recognition of *extrinsic* accidents is that it elucidates how it is that Aquinas could hold both that the actualization of the agent's active potentiality is in the patient as subject and that action considered as an accident is in the agent as subject. The motion in the patient which actualizes the agent's active power is extrinsic to the agent insofar as it is not a form in it as in matter. The motion is a form in the patient. Yet, the motion nevertheless is an accident of the agent because it depends on the agent as a being arising from it. It is tempting to conceive of the way in which all accidents are in their subjects according to the model of quality since sensible qualities are the accidents which are most apparent to us. To conceive of other accidents as if they were qualities is to think of them as forms which exist in their subjects as in matter. If it is assumed that "being in" a subject means being in it as a form in matter then it would be contradictory for the motion which is moving the patient to belong to the agent as an accident. Yet, in Aquinas's view inhering as a form in matter is just one particular way in which an accident can be in a subject. Existing in or being inherent in another as such is a mode of being which is marked by being of or belonging to a substance. The particular way in which actions depend on or inhere in their subjects (i.e. agents) is by being from them. When Aquinas defines the meaning of the term "action" he says that "action" means that which is "arising from a substance and inhering in it as subject . . ."[72] Arising from just is the special way in which actions inhere in (i.e. depend on) their subjects.

6.6   Conclusion

So, ontologically speaking, what is an agent's action and a patient's passion? One conclusion of this chapter is that this question does not admit of a single, unqualified answer. Actions and passions can be viewed both through the lens of the actuality–potentiality division and through the division of the ten categories. With regard to the actuality–potentiality division, action and passion are both the same incomplete actuality (i.e. a motion) in the patient substance. One actuality corresponds to correlative active and passive powers, yet it fulfills each in a different way. The categories that divide being are distinguished from each other not in terms

---

[72] *In I Peri Herm.* c. 3, lec. 5 (ed. Leon., vol. 1, 24): "egrediens a substantia et inhaerens ei ut subiecto . . ."

of numerically distinct actualities, but rather in terms of the diverse ways in which actualities can be of or belong to a substance. In the division of potentiality and actuality, correlative actions and passions are numerically one actuality. However, in the division of the ten categories, actions and passions are specifically and numerically distinct accidents. The category of action signifies an actuality that is arising from a substance's active power by way of origin. The category of passion signifies an actuality which is being received in a substance through another's agency. Although the actuality (i.e. the motion) involved in action and passion is numerically one, the manner in which this actuality belongs to the agent differs from how it belongs to the patient. In Aquinas's view, this sort of difference is sufficient to differentiate action from passion as distinct accidents (both according to species and number). While correlative actions and passions consist of the same motion, the proportion or order between the agent and the motion and the proportion or order between the patient and the motion are different from each other. In Aquinas's view, the nine categories of accident divide different ways in which actualities can be of or belong to substances. An action, considered as a categorical accident, is a motion that is arising from its subject by way of origin, while a passion is a motion that is being received in its subject from another.

PART II

Complications

CHAPTER 7

Non-Paradigm Cases
Efficient Causes within Networks, Absences
and sine qua non *Causation*

In the first part of this study, we examined the details of Aquinas's views on the most fundamental and proper instances of efficient causation in the natural world, namely an agent's *per se* efficient causation of its proper effects. A standard example of such a case is a fire's causation of heat through its active power to heat. We saw Aquinas's views on the temporal and modal relationship that obtains between a natural agent and its *per se* effects, as well as the various ontological elements involved in these cases. As mentioned earlier, Aquinas acknowledges that there are other instances of efficient causation that do not conform to the model of *per se* efficient causation. He recognizes that there are other ways, besides *per se* efficient causation, in which an effect might depend on a substance's action. In these final two chapters of the study, we turn to Aquinas's views on other non-paradigm instances of natural efficient causation.

Aquinas recognizes that *per se* efficient causes do not operate in isolation from other efficient causes. *Per se* efficient causes often depend on the actions of previously acting efficient causes to give them their powers and to prepare the matter upon which they act. Aquinas thinks that these previously acting efficient causes can rightly be considered efficient causes of the final effect since their action was necessary for the being of the final effect. Put otherwise, efficient causes which operated at prior times are often times part of the efficient causal explanation of how another cause's *per se* effect came to be. This present chapter examines Aquinas's views on two types of efficient cause, namely preparing and advising causes, which contribute to bringing about another efficient cause's effect.

The chapter also considers Aquinas's views on two other potential types of efficient causes, namely absences and *sine qua non* causes. Although absences do not cause existence through the exercise of a power, and thus, are not strictly speaking efficient causes, Aquinas thinks that some absences can provide efficient causal explanations for other absences. The chapter will examine the criteria which an absence must meet in order to explain

another absence according to efficient causation. Lastly, we will see
Aquinas's views on *sine qua non* causes. *Sine qua non* causes are entities
that are necessary for an effect to occur, yet they do not act towards the
effect. This type of cause became very important in later discussions of
causality. However, we will see that Aquinas denies that such causes are
truly efficient causes of effects since they do not act.

7.1   Networks of Efficient Causes: The Division of Types of Efficient Causes

Aquinas recognizes that efficient causes do not operate in isolation from
each other. Both a natural efficient cause itself and its patient are affected
by the actions of other efficient causes. For example, the fire that heats
wood was itself generated by a prior efficient cause and the wood which fire
heats has been previously acted upon by other efficient causes. Each
natural efficient cause and its patient is plugged into a network of other
efficient causes.[1] Accordingly, Aquinas recognizes that the proper effect of
one efficient cause can often be attributed to another efficient cause as well.
In order to capture the different ways in which efficient causes within a
network might contribute to an effect, Aquinas adopts a division of types
of efficient causes. In both his commentaries on the *Physics* and
Metaphysics, he claims that there are four different types of efficient causes:
perfecting, preparing, assisting and advising.[2] In his *Metaphysics* commentary, he explicitly attributes this division of efficient causes to Avicenna.[3]
First, it is important to note that this division is unlike the division
between *per se* and *per accidens* efficient causation, which was discussed
in Chapter 2.[4] The difference between a *per se* and *per accidens* efficient
cause regards how the effect that arises from a cause's action relates to its
own intrinsic active powers and natural inclinations. *Per se* efficient causes
have powers and inclinations for their effects, while *per accidens* causes do

---

[1] "Network" is not one of Aquinas's own terms. By network, I mean a group of efficient causes that
   have been or are in physical contact with one another and thus have been or are able to act upon
   one another.
[2] *In V Meta.* lec. 2, n. 766–69 and *In II Phys.* lec. 5 (ed. Leon., vol. 2, 70, n. 5). This division is not
   mentioned in the *De principiis naturae* discussion of causes. Though Aquinas does not explicitly say
   so, it seems that the division between types of efficient causes should be understood as an analogical
   division, rather than a univocal division. In an analogical division, the term which is being divided is
   applied to one of the classes within the division prior to the others. See *ST* I-II 61, a. 1 ad 1. It seems
   that the perfecting cause is prior to preparing and advising causes since advising and preparing causes
   are defined as causes with respect to their relationship to the perfecting cause's effect.
[3] *In V Meta.* lec. 2, n. 766.   [4] See Section 2.1.

not. The Avicennian taxonomy which we are about to examine regards various ways in which one cause's action might relate to the effects of other efficient causes. In Aquinas's view, effects depend for their existence not only on the agents from which they immediately arise, but also on other efficient causes which have acted on the agent and patient to make them suitably disposed for causal interaction. The division between types of efficient causes captures the different ways in which an effect might depend on the action of an efficient cause. For example, when the sun dries a wet log, and thus prepares it to be burned by fire, the burning that occurs depends on the fire and on the sun, but in different ways. Thus, Aquinas finds it helpful to distinguish between types of efficient causes to capture the differing role each has in the production of a final effect.

The first type of efficient cause that Aquinas discusses is the perfecting cause. It is useful to begin with understanding this type of cause since we will see that the preparing and advising causes are defined in relation to the perfecting cause. Aquinas writes: "The efficient cause which is said to be a perfecting cause is the one which causes the ultimate perfection of a thing ..."[5] He provides two different examples to illustrate this type of cause. His first example of a perfecting cause is the cause which induces the substantial form in natural generation. According to Aristotelian metaphysics, substantial changes in the natural world are preceded by a series of accidental changes. For example, wood is heated and blackened prior to becoming ash. Those prior accidental changes which precede substantial change might be brought about by many different causes. The perfecting cause is the one whose agency brings about the final step of the transformation, which terminates in a new substantial form. Aquinas's second example of a perfecting cause comes from the realm of artifacts. Aquinas considers the building of the house. There are many changes which need to occur for a house to be built. For instance, materials such as wood or stone must be cut and moved to the building site. Finally, the materials must be arranged according to the form of a house. Many agents may be responsible for the preparation of the materials. The perfecting cause, however, is the builder who induces the form of the house in the materials.[6] The builder causes the final perfection (i.e. the arrangement or form) in virtue of which the house is a house. The designation of

---

[5] *In V Meta*. lec. 2 (ed. Marietti, 212, n. 766): "Perficiens autem dicitur causa efficiens, quae ultimam rei perfectionem causat ..."
[6] Ibid.

"perfecting cause" distinguishes his causal role from those who prepared and moved the materials. Aquinas does not mention accidental changes in nature in his examples, but it seems these changes also have perfecting causes. Some accidental changes must be preceded by prior ones. For instance, a wet object must be dried before it can be burned. The designation of "perfecting cause" can be used to differentiate the role of the cause that brings about the final accidental change from the causes that were responsible for the prior accidental changes through which the patient was prepared to receive the accidental form in question.

It is worth noting that every *per se* cause is a perfecting cause of its proper effect. For example, when fire heats, fire is a perfecting cause of heating insofar as it directly induces the form of heat. However, *per accidens* causes can also function as perfecting causes. For example, when fire causes cooling in virtue of opening the pores of a substance by heating it, the fire is the perfecting cause of cooling. It is the agent that induces the perfection of cooling even though it induces coolness in virtue of first inducing heat. No other agent intervenes after the fire's action to induce the coolness and thus, fire is the agent that induces this final perfection.

As already mentioned, Aquinas defines preparing or disposing causes by their relationship to the perfecting cause's effect. Aquinas writes: "The cause disposing anything, however, does not induce the final perfecting form, but rather only prepares the matter for that form ..."[7] Aquinas's example is the one who hews stone or cuts timbers, which are then used by the builder to make the house. The one who prepares the stone and timbers efficiently causes the matter which is in potentiality to take on the form of the house. Since the house requires suitable matter to be actualized, it depends for its being on the one who prepared the timbers and stone. Causes as we have seen are those things upon which something depends for its being. Thus, even though the cause that prepares matter does not induce the final form, it nevertheless is a cause of the final effect's being. Furthermore, it is an efficient cause since it prepares matter by its action. To clarify the respect in which the preparing cause is an efficient cause, Aquinas explains that the preparing cause does not efficiently cause the final effect in actuality, but rather it efficiently causes the potentiality for the final effect.[8] In natural changes, those causes which act on the

---

[7] *In V Meta.* lec. 2 (ed. Marietti, 212, n. 767): "Disponens autem quod non inducit ultimam formam perfectivam, sed tantummodo praeparat materiam ad formam ..." See also *In II Phys.* lec. 5 (ed. Leon., vol. 2, 70, n. 5).

[8] Ibid.

patient to induce the forms through which it is in potentiality to the final effect are considered preparing causes of the final effect.

In other texts, Aquinas sometimes uses different terminology to describe perfecting and disposing causes. Sometimes he refers to the agent which disposes matter for the final effect as an "indirect" cause and the one which induces the final perfection as a "direct" cause.[9] The perfecting cause is a "direct" cause insofar as no other actions intervene between its causal activity and the occurrence of the effect. In the case of the disposing cause, a further action, namely the action of the perfecting cause, must occur to achieve the final effect. In this respect, disposing causes are "indirect" causes. Aquinas also describes indirect causes as causing "occasionally."[10] An indirect cause provides an occasion for the final effect, that is, it causes a patient to have a potentiality for the form of the final effect. Yet, without the further operation of a perfecting cause, the final effect does not occur. Put otherwise, an indirect cause causes by its action that which is necessary, but not sufficient, for the final effect to occur.

A reader might worry that Aquinas has no principle for limiting which agents should count as disposing or indirect causes of a final effect. Some effects presuppose a long chain of events unfolding over many years. Consider the house built out of stone again. The stones themselves came to be through a series of reactions within the earth's core. Should all of the substances that exercised agency in the formation of the stones be considered indirect or disposing causes of the house? There are some criteria implicit in Aquinas's thought which can be applied to distinguish true indirect or disposing causes of an effect from earlier causes that are not truly disposing causes with respect to a particular effect. As we saw above, Aquinas claims that all causes contribute to the being of their effects and efficient causes do so by their actions. Regarding disposing causes, Aquinas claimed that they contribute to the being of the final effect by causing the potentiality for the final perfection. Elsewhere Aquinas states that a substance is only in potentiality to a specific form when that form can be

---

[9] *ST* I q.114, a. 3 (ed. Leon., vol. 5, 535):

> Respondeo dicendum quod causa alicuius potest dici aliquid dupliciter: uno modo, directe; alio modo, indirecte. Indirecte quidem, sicut cum aliquod agens causans aliquam dispositionem ad aliquem effectum, dicitur esse occasionaliter et indirecte causa illius effectus; sicut si dicatur quod ille qui siccat ligna, est causa combustionis eorum . . . Directe autem dicitur esse aliquid causa alicuius, quod operatur directe ad illud.

[10] Ibid.

actualized in it by a single action of an active power.[11] These criteria allow us to differentiate between prior conditions for an effect which are nevertheless not causes of it and true disposing causes. Disposing causes are those which act toward the production of that which can be immediately transformed (i.e. by a single action) into the final effect. This principle can be illustrated with the house example again. Although the existence of stone is necessary for a house to be built out of stone to exist, the causes of the stone's existence should not be considered indirect or disposing causes of the house. This is because the stone does not have the potentiality to be a house until it is hewn. The one who hews the stone is a disposing or indirect cause of the house because he causes the potentiality for the final form of the house. The causes of the unhewn stone are not disposing causes of the house since the unhewn stone does not have the potentiality to take on the form of the house. Now that we have examined Aquinas's thinking about preparing causes, we can move on to see his views on advisory causes.

There is a similarity between advisory causes and preparing causes. Like preparing causes, advisory causes have another cause's effect attributed to them on account of a prior action that was necessary for that effect. While preparing causes act on the patient so that it has a potentiality for a final effect, advisory causes act with respect to the agent who causes the subsequent effect. Aquinas defines advisory causes with respect principal causes. Principal causes are causes that act for their own end. *Per se* causes are principal causes. As we have seen, through their nature *per se* causes have certain active powers and inclinations toward certain ends. For example, when a fire heats it acts for the end of heating. Heating is its own end since heating is that toward which its intrinsic form of heat inclines it. An advisory cause is the cause which gives the principal cause its form and, therefore, its end. Since a substance's inclination toward an end follows upon its form, to give an agent a form is also to give it an end.[12] In human affairs, an advising cause is the one who proposes a form to the human agent's intellect.[13] For example, an academic advisor might encourage a student to enroll in a course. The student is the one who performs the act of enrollment, but the advisor's act of advising is what gave her the goal for which she acted. In the realm of nature, Aquinas claims that the

[11] *In IX Meta.* lec. 6 (ed. Marietti, 440, n. 1834): "Illud autem possibile, quod unica actione natura vel ars potest in actum sanitatis reducere, est sanum in potentia." See also, *In IX Meta.* lec. 6 (ed. Marietti, 439, n. 1832).
[12] See Section 4.1.   [13] *In II Phys.* lec. 5 (ed. Leon., vol. 2, 70, n. 5).

agent which generates a natural substance is its advising cause.[14] Initially this may seem like an odd comparison since the generator of a natural being seems wholly unlike the person who gives advice to another human being. Aquinas, however, sees a clear parallel in these two cases. The natural generator gives the substance which it generates its substantial form, and by having a certain substantial form, the generated substance has certain active powers and natural inclinations. Thus, by inducing a substance's substantial form, the generator causes the substance it generates to have certain ends and thus, to act in a certain way. Thus, by generating a substance, the generator becomes an advising cause of the generated substance's future actions and effects.[15] The generator's giving of substantial form functions similarly to the human advisor's proposing of forms to the advisee's intellect. In both cases, the one who gives form also specifies the end for which the recipient of the form will act.

It is important to note that there are important differences between preparing and advising causes, on the one hand, and the paradigm type of efficient cause, namely the *per se* cause. As we saw in Chapter 2, *per se* causes are causes in actuality simultaneous with the effect of their causality.[16] By contrast, preparing and advising causes exercise their causal powers in action prior to the existence of the effect which is attributed them by way of preparing or advising efficient causality. The preparing cause must act to induce the form through which there is a potentiality for the final effect prior to the existence of the final effect. Likewise, the advising cause must generate the principal cause prior to the principal cause's causation of its effect. The modal relationship between preparing and advising causes and their effect also differs from the modal relationship which obtains between a *per se* cause and its effect. As we saw, the effects of natural *per se* causes follow from them by conditional necessity. Their effects will occur on the condition that nothing impedes them. The effects of advising and preparing causes, however, do not follow from them even on the condition that they are not impeded. A preparing and advising cause may provide its necessary action and nevertheless the principal or perfecting cause may not cause its effect. Thus, the effects of preparing and advising causes are conditional upon both their own lack of impediment and the activity of further efficient causes.

---

[14] Ibid.
[15] To be clear, the generator of a natural substance is the principal cause of the generated substance itself. It is an advising cause of the generated substance's actions.
[16] See Section 2.2.

While instances of preparing or advising causation do not meet the criteria of *per se* efficient causation, these instances of efficient causation always occur in virtue of a prior instance of *per se* efficient causation. The actions by which preparing causes prepare a patient for a further perfection and by which advising causes impart a form to another agent will themselves be instances of *per se* efficient causation or reducible to a prior instance of *per se* efficient causation. For example, when fire generates another fire and thereby gives it both its heat and inclination toward heating, the first fire will be the advising cause of the second fire's future effects. The first fire has both the power to generate fire by its nature and the inclination to do so and thus, its act of generating the second fire is an instance of *per se* efficient causation. We saw in Chapter 2 that *per accidens* instances of efficient causation happen in virtue of instances of *per se* efficient causation.[17] So, even if a preparing cause prepares the patient by an instance of *per accidens* efficient causation, there will be a prior instance of *per se* efficient causation by which it functions as a preparing cause.

As mentioned above, Aquinas identifies four types of efficient causation. So far, we have only examined three of these types: perfecting, preparing and advising. The fourth type of cause is an assisting cause. This type of cause will be discussed in the next chapter, which treats of efficient causes which act through another's power. We have seen that advising and preparing causes both contribute by their actions something which is necessary for the perfecting cause to achieve its effect. However, the perfecting cause itself operates through its own power when it causes its effect. It does not act through the power of the preparing or advising cause. The preparing and advising causes need not even remain in existence for the perfecting cause to cause the final perfection. It is quite different with assisting causes. The assisting cause relies on another cause's power (i.e. a principal cause's power) to perform the action by which it contributes to the effect. In the next chapter, the details of Aquinas's views on assisting causes, also known as instrumental causes, will be considered along with his views on another type of cause (i.e. a secondary cause) that acts through another's power.

7.2   Absences and Efficient Causation

In the previous section, we examined various ways in which one cause can efficiently cause another cause's effect. In this section, we turn to the

---

[17] See Section 2.1.

question of whether Aquinas allows for absences to function as efficient causes. As we have seen, Aquinas maintains that efficient causes are causes which act by exercising a power. Since absences have no causal powers, they cannot efficiently cause any positive being. Yet, Aquinas nevertheless acknowledges that an absence might provide an efficient causal explanation for the non-being of an effect. Efficient causal explanations are those which identify the efficient causes of an effect. Aquinas thinks that when an effect is absent we can identify in some cases the reason why it was not efficiently caused. In his *Metaphysics* commentary discussion of types of causes, he writes:

> For that which by its presence is the cause of some effect, we blame when it is absent, that is we hold it responsible for the contrary of the effect insofar as we say it is the cause of the contrary. For example, it is apparent that by his presence the captain is the cause of a ship's safety, and we say that his absence is the cause of the ship's ruin.[18]

Aquinas explicitly states that the type of causation in question in the passage above is indeed efficient causation.[19] Aquinas reasons that if the presence of a cause would have brought about an effect according to efficient causation, then the absence of the cause can be identified as the efficient causal reason for why it is absent. The absence does not act or produce an effect because there is no effect to produce. But it does provide an explanation according to the order of efficient causality for why the effect is absent.

In understanding how absences can provide efficient causal explanations of absent effects, it is important to be clear about what exactly they explain. The example above of the absent captain and the ship's ruin involves some ambiguity. That which follows from the captain's absence can be analyzed in two different ways. On the one hand, there is the mere lack of the action of steering which would have ensured the ship's safety. On the other hand, there are all of the positive changes that are involved in its sinking. In Aquinas's view, absent causes do not provide efficient causal explanations of positive effects. The absence of the captain is the efficient causal

---

[18] *In V Meta.* lec. 2 (ed. Marietti, 213, n. 776): "Illud enim, quod per sui praesentiam est causa huius, quando est absens causamur idest accusamus ipsum de contrario, idest dicimus ipsum esse causam contrarii. Sicut patet, quod gubernator per sui praesentiam est causa salutis navis, dicimus eius absentiam esse causam perditionis."

[19] *In V Meta.* lec. 2 (ed. Marietti, 213, n. 776): "Ne autem putetur quod hoc sit referendum ad diversa genera causarum sicut et priora duo, ideo subiungit quod utrumque istorum reducitur ad idem genus causae, scilicet ad causam moventem. Eodem enim modo oppositum est causa oppositi, quo haec est causa huius."

explanation of the mere absence of steering and the absence of safety that would have resulted through it. The lack of the cause is the efficient causal explanation for the lack of the effect. The non-being of the effect depends on the non-being of the cause. However, each of the positive changes involved in the ship's sinking will be attributed to some other present efficient cause. For example, waves and winds efficiently cause the ship to move off course when the captain is absent from steering it. Absences cannot initiate motions in the world. Absences only explain according to efficient causation the absences of certain motions. The absence accounts for why an effect which one would expect is not present.

Aquinas does acknowledge that an absent agent can be considered an indirect cause of a motion which another agent initiates.[20] As we saw above in the discussion of disposing causes, an indirect cause does not itself work toward the final effect. Rather, it brings about the potentiality for the final effect. The absent cause which is responsible for the non-occurrence of its action can be identified as an indirect cause of any motions which require the non-occurrence of its action for their possibility. For example, the absence of the captain is an indirect cause of the motions of the ship, which take it off course since the absence of the captain's steering is required for those motions to occur. If the captain had been present and steering, the ship would not have had the potentiality to undergo the motions off course. The motions which take the ship off course are directly caused by the waves and the wind alone. But the absent captain is nevertheless judged as an indirect cause insofar as his non-action provides the necessary occasion for the movements taking the ship off course.

Aquinas's view that absent efficient causes provide an efficient causal explanation for the absence of their actions and the missing effects which would have followed from them raises the question of how to identify which absent substances can be invoked to explain absent actions and effects. For example, should the first mate on the ship likewise be identified as the efficient causal explanation of the lack of steering and the ship's lack of safely staying on course? Aquinas provides criteria in the following passage for how to determine whether a substance should be considered as the causal explanation of a missing effect which follows from its non-actions. He writes:

> It must be noted that the effect which follows from a lack of action is not always attributed to the agent as cause because it did not act, but only when

[20] *ST* I-II q. 6, a. 3.

the agent can and ought to act. For if the captain was not able to steer the ship or he were not commissioned to steer the ship, the sinking of the ship, which happened on account of the absence of the captain, would not be attributed to him.[21]

According to this passage, in order for an absent agent to be explanatory of a missing effect which follows from its non-action, the agent must (1) be able to cause the action (i.e. it must have an active power for it) and (2) have an obligation to perform the act. For example, the lack of the ship's safely staying on course cannot be attributed to a passenger, even though she did not act, because she has no power for piloting ships. The first mate has a power for steering ships, but the lack of safety cannot be attributed to his non-action, because he was not charged with steering the ship.

One might wonder how these conditions can be applied to natural causes, which unlike human causes lack moral obligations and duties associated with societal roles. In the case of a natural cause, what a cause "ought" to do can be established by its natural inclination toward an effect. Sometimes when a natural cause has a defect within it, it fails in its performance of an action toward which it is naturally inclined. A seed, for example, has a natural inclination toward sprouting and producing a leafy green tree, yet it might fail to sprout because it has a genetic defect. It seems that Aquinas would regard the natural cause which fails to perform the action toward which it is naturally inclined as an indirect causal explanation of what follows from its non-action. The seed's failure to sprout, for instance, might be regarded as an indirect causal explanation of the ground's lack of shade near where it was planted since had it sprouted, there would have been shade from its leaves. By contrast, the failure of a cloud to block the sun would not be an indirect causal explanation of the lack of shade since clouds have no natural inclination toward being positioned in front of the sun. The seed failed to perform an action toward which it is naturally inclined, while the cloud did not, so only the seed can be considered as an indirect causal explanation of what follows from its non-action.

---

[21] *ST* I-II q. 6, a. 3 (ed. Leon., vol. 6, 58): "Sed sciendum quod non semper id quod sequitur ad defectum actionis, reducitur sicut in causam in agens, ex eo quod non agit: sed solum tunc cum potest et debet agere. Si enim gubernator non posset navem dirigere, vel non esset ei commissa gubernatio navis, non imputaretur ei navis submersio, quae per absentiam gubernatoris contingeret." For a contemporary discussion of absences as causes which is inspired by Aquinas's views, see John Haldane, "Identifying Privative Causes," *Analysis* 71:4 (2011): 611–19. Haldane, however, does not employ Aquinas's distinction between direct and indirect causes to specify that it is only in a certain regard that an absence can be a cause of a positive effect.

7.3   Aquinas on *sine qua non* Causation

The topic of this final section of the chapter is Aquinas's views on *sine qua non* causes. As we will see, Aquinas rejects the view that *sine qua non* causation is truly a type of efficient causation. Yet, it is nevertheless worthwhile to include his views on this type of cause since it became so important in later medieval and early modern discussions of causality.[22] Furthermore, Aquinas's reasons for rejection of *sine qua non* causation as a type of efficient causation further highlights the criteria which he thinks a cause must meet to count as an efficient cause.

Aquinas like other medieval authors typically discussed *sine qua non* causation in the context of explaining how it is that sacraments, such as the Eucharist and baptism, were causes of grace. Medieval thinkers believed that God alone could efficiently cause grace in the human soul. Yet, somehow the sacraments played a role in God's causation of grace. A prominent medieval theory about the role of the sacraments in causing grace claimed that the sacraments were *sine qua non* causes of grace. In the following passage from his *De veritate*, Aquinas explains this theory and what a *sine qua non* cause is:

> Some say that they [i.e. the sacraments] are causes of grace, not because they operate through some power put in them for bringing about grace, but rather because in the reception of them grace is given by God, who assists the sacraments, so that they are called causes of grace in the manner of a *sine qua non* cause. They give as an example someone who handing over a lead coin receives a hundred units of money, not because the lead coin is the cause which makes (*causa faciens*) the reception of the hundred units of money, but rather because it has been decreed by him who is able to give that whoever brings such a coin should receive such an amount of money. It has similarly been decreed by God that whoever sincerely receives the sacraments should receive grace, not indeed from the sacraments, but from God Himself.[23]

---

[22] See William Courtenay, "Covenant and Causality in Pierre D'Ailly," *Speculum* 46:1 (1971): 94–119 and his "The King and the Leaden Coin: The Economic Background of 'Sine Qua Non' Causality," *Traditio* 28 (1972): 185–209. For a discussion of *sine qua non* causation in modern authors see Andrea Sangiacomo, "*Sine qua non* Causation: The Legacy of Malebranche's Occasionalism in Kant's *New Elucidation*," *Oxford Studies in Early Modern Philosophy* 9 (2018): 215–48.

[23] *De ver.* q. 27, a. 4 (ed. Leon., vol. 22 3/1, 804):

> Quidam enim dicunt quod sunt causa gratiae non quia aliquid ad gratiam habendam operentur per aliquam virtutem eis inditam, sed quia in eorum susceptione gratia datur a Deo, qui sacramentis assistit, ut sic dicantur causa gratiae per modum causae sine qua non; et ponunt exemplum de hoc quod aliquis deferens denarium plumbeum accipit centum libras, non ideo quia denarius plumbeus sit causa faciens aliquid ad acceptionem centum

As this passage explains, *sine qua non* causes of effects do not exercise a power or act in the production of the effect. Rather, the *sine qua non* cause is a condition upon which another cause has deemed that it will exercise its causal power to produce an effect. For example, according to the theory which Aquinas describes, the reception of sacraments is the condition upon which God decrees that he will efficiently cause grace through his power. *Sine qua non* causality is sometimes called "juridical" causality or "pact" causality because an entity's functioning as such a cause rests on a law or pact established by an agent with intellect and will. For example, the sacraments can only function as *sine qua non* causes of grace if God decrees that he will cause grace upon a person's reception of a sacrament.

Aquinas rejects the view that the sacraments are merely *sine qua non* causes of grace and his reason for this rejection illustrates his views on the status of *sine qua non* causation. Aquinas argues that the sacraments cannot be *sine qua non* causes of grace because then they would not be causes of grace at all. Aquinas thinks that to count as an efficient cause of an effect, a substance must influence the being of that effect by action. *Sine qua non* causes do not meet this criterion. He writes of a *sine qua non* cause: "it is related to the effect as nothing but a sign. The lead coin is nothing other than a sign for the reception of an amount of money . . ."[24] *Sine qua non* causes are signs insofar as they signal that the effect will be produced. Yet, the *sine qua non* cause does not act toward the being of the effect. The lead coin does not exercise a power that brings about the reception of the money. Aquinas likens *sine qua non* causes to the non-productive accidental causes that were discussed in Chapter 2.[25] Just as the white thing does not act by any power it has as a white thing in the production of a house, so too does the *sine qua non* cause fail to act by any power in the

---

librarum, sed quia sic statutum est ab eo qui potest dare, ut quicumque defert talem denarium accipiat tantam pecuniam. Similiter statutum est a Deo ut quicumque accipit sacramentum non fictus, gratiam accipiat, non quidem a sacramentis, sed ab ipso Deo . . .

[24] *De ver.* q. 27, a. 4 (ed. Leon., vol. 22 3/1, 804): "se habeat ad effectum nisi sicut signum: denarius enim plumbeus non est nisi signum acceptionis pecuniae . . ."

[25] See Section 2.1. For a primary text, see *In IV Sent.* d. 1, q. 1, a. 4, qc. 1 (ed. Mandonnet-Moos, vol. 4, 31):

Causa enim sine qua non, si nihil omnino faciat ad inducendum effectum vel disponendo vel meliorando, quantum ad rationem causandi, nihil habebit supra causas per accidens: sicut album est causa domus, si aedificator sit albus; et secundum hoc sacramenta essent causae per accidens tantum sanctificationis. Illa enim ordinatio quam dicunt, sive pactio, nihil dat eis de ratione causae, sed solum de ratione signi; sicut etiam denarius plumbeus est solum signum indicans quis debet accipere.

production of an effect. Just as the white thing is coincidentally conjoined with a builder who causes a house, so too does the *sine qua non* cause coincidentally exist at the moment at which the true efficient cause acts. *Sine qua non* causes are not truly efficient causes for Aquinas since they do not do anything toward the production of an effect. Rather, they merely coincide with a genuine efficient cause.[26]

7.4 Conclusion

In this chapter we have seen Aquinas's views on some non-paradigm instances of efficient causation. In the first section, we saw that he acknowledges that the causes which prepare a patient for receiving a final effect, as well as the cause which imparts to an agent the form through which it has its end and inclination toward its effect, can be considered as efficient causes of the final effect. These causes do not directly cause the final effect by their action. Nevertheless, the existence of the final effect does depend in some way upon the actions of these causes. Without the actions of the preparing and advising causes, the perfecting cause would not be able to cause the final effect. Thus, the former causes can be considered as efficient causes of the final effect, albeit in a different way than the perfecting cause. Efficient causes as such are causes whose effect depends on them through their action. The division between types of efficient causes discussed in this chapter reveals that Aquinas acknowledges that there are different ways in which an efficient cause's action might contribute to the existence of a final effect. *Per se* efficient causation is the most fundamental form of efficient causation and it is operative in every type of efficient causation. It is by causing their *per se* effects that advising or preparing causes function as efficient causes of other effects. It is significant that Aquinas recognizes these different ways of being an efficient cause because this insight allows his theory to capture the fact that efficient causes do not act in isolation and depend upon one another's prior actions to cause their effects.

---

[26] In later discussions, *sine qua non* causes are often called "occasional causes" since they function as occasions for another cause to act. Above we saw that Aquinas describes dispositive or indirect causes as "causing occasionally." Yet, it is important to note that these causes differ from *sine qua non* causes. Though dispositive causes do not exercise their power in producing the final effect, they do nevertheless exercise their power in producing that which has a potentiality for the final effect. Thus, they do not function merely as signs for another cause to act, but rather they truly operate in the production of the effect.

We also saw Aquinas's views on the respect in which absences can provide efficient causal explanations. Aquinas thinks that the absence of an efficient cause which would have caused an effect by its presence can be considered the efficient causal explanation of the effect's absence. Absences do not act, nor produce an effect. Yet, the absence of an efficient cause with a power and inclination toward the production of an effect can be invoked to explain why the effect was not produced. Finally, we saw Aquinas's views on *sine qua non* efficient causation. Aquinas argued that *sine qua non* causes do not count as efficient causes since they do not act toward an effect. To count as a genuine efficient cause of an effect, a cause must influence the being of the effect by its action.

CHAPTER 8

Efficient Causes Which Act through Another Cause's Power

In this final chapter, we will turn to Aquinas's views on another sort of complicated case of efficient causality, namely efficient causes which act through the power of another efficient cause. So far, the study has focused on how efficient causes act through powers which belong to themselves, but we will see that Aquinas thinks that natural efficient causes also can act through the active powers of substances distinct from themselves.

Aquinas recognizes two different ways in which an efficient cause can depend upon another cause's power to operate. First, there are instrumental efficient causes. These causes are employed by another efficient cause to achieve this latter cause's end, just as a saw is employed by a carpenter to make a bench. Instrumental causes do not act toward another cause's end unless they are moved by that cause. For instance, a saw does not act toward making a bench unless it is moved by the carpenter. In this way, the instrument depends on another cause's simultaneous action to act. The chapter discusses Aquinas's basic understanding of instrumental causality. It also discusses examples of instrumental causality which he recognizes in the natural world. It may initially seem that instrumental causality only applies to the human realm since it would appear that cognition is necessary to employ an instrument to reach an end. However, we will see that Aquinas makes use of the notion of instrumental causality to understand how higher-level natural powers, such as the nutritive power, employ the actions of elemental powers, such as heat, to reach their ends.

In addition to instrumental efficient causes, Aquinas recognizes another type of efficient cause which depends upon another cause to exercise its power, namely secondary causes. Secondary causes are like instruments in so far as they cannot act unless another higher cause, called a primary cause, also exercises its power. However, secondary causes differ from instruments in so far as they act for their own ends. The chapter examines Aquinas's views on primary and secondary causality in general, as well as some particular examples of it that he finds in the natural world.

8.1 Instrumental Causes

In the previous chapter, we saw that Aquinas followed Avicenna in distinguishing four different types of efficient cause: perfecting, preparing, assisting and advising.[1] We saw in the last chapter how Aquinas understood perfecting, preparing and advising causes. Perfecting causes cause a final effect, while preparing causes cause the potentiality in the patient for the final effect. Advising causes give other agent causes their inclination toward an end. Both preparing and advising causes cause something which is necessary for another cause to cause its effect, and thus the final effect can also be attributed to the preparing and advising cause. It is important to note that though the actions of advisory and preparing causes truly effect the conditions necessary for another efficient cause to cause its effect, these causes do not exercise their active power in the production of the effect which is attributed to them by advising and preparing causality. Preparing and advising causes exercise their powers at a time prior to the production of the final effect. Unlike a perfecting cause, which might rely on the prior actions of a preparing cause to prepare its patient and an advising cause to give it its end, the assisting cause relies on another cause's power to perform its very action. The goal of this section is to examine Aquinas's views on assisting causes. Aquinas typically refers to such causes as instrumental causes, and I will use these terms interchangably.[2]

According to Aquinas, the defining feature of an assisting cause is that it acts for the end which is specified by another efficient cause, namely a principal cause. This is to say that the end for which an assisting cause acts is not one toward which it has an inclination. None of its own native powers are ordered toward the end for which it acts. In his *Metaphysics* commentary, Aquinas gives an example of a person who assists a king in war.[3] The assistant performs an action to achieve the goal of winning the war. Winning the war, however, is not a goal which the assistant had through himself. He only acts for this goal on account of the king's command. By acting for the king's goal, the assistant functions as an assisting cause and the king as a principal cause since he specifies the goal.

---

[1] See Section 7.1.

[2] It is reasonable to assume that assisting causes and instrumental causes refer to the same type of cause for Aquinas since he contrasts both with a principal cause and he defines both in terms of how they relate to the end toward which they operate. See for instance *In IV Sent.* d. 3, q. 1, a. 1, qc. 1 (ed. Mandonnet-Moos, vol. 4, 112): "in instrumentis ... quasi tota ratio speciei a fine sumitur."

[3] *In V Meta.* lec. 2, n. 769.

Throughout his works he develops a nuanced theory about the powers and operations of causes which work for the ends of other causes.

Aquinas was particularly interested in instrumental causes because he believed that the Christian sacraments were instrumental causes of God's grace.[4] While supernatural cases are what most motivated him to understand how this type of causality worked, he nevertheless thought that examples of instrumental causality permeated nature as well.[5] The core of Aquinas's views on instrumental causality can be summarized in three key theses:

(1) *Dual action thesis*: Instruments have a twofold action, one of which is proper to the instrument according to its own inherent forms and another action which goes beyond that which the instrument's own native powers can achieve.

(2) *Moved mover thesis*: The instrument operates toward this second action (i.e. the one which is beyond its own power) only in so far as it is moved by the principal cause.

(3) *Borrowed power thesis*: Through being moved, the instrument receives a transitory power from the principal cause which enables it to work toward the second action.

In what follows, we will examine each of these theses in more detail.

Regarding the dual-action thesis, Aquinas writes:

> [A]n instrument has two actions, one instrumental, in accordance with which it acts not by its own power but by the principal agent's power; however, it has another proper action, which belongs to it according to its own form; just as it is proper to an axe to cut on account of its sharpness, but to make a bed in so far as it is the instrument of an art. But it does not accomplish the instrumental action unless it exercises its proper action; for it makes a bed by cutting.[6]

---

[4] For Aquinas's rejection of the view that sacraments are *sine qua non* causes of grace see Section 7.3. On Aquinas's views on the sacraments as instrumental causes see Lynch, *The Cleansing of the Heart*.

[5] For literature on Aquinas's views on instrumental causality in general see J. S. Albertson, "Instrumental Causality in St. Thomas," *New Scholasticism* 28 (1954): 409–35 and Jean-Luc Solère, "Scotus versus Aquinas on Instrumental Causality," *Oxford Studies in Medieval Philosophy* 7 (2019): 147–85.

[6] *ST* III q. 62, a. 1, ad 2 (ed. Leon., vol. 12, 20): "instrumentum habet duas actiones: unam instrumentalem, secundum quam operatur non in virtute propria, sed in virtute principalis agentis; aliam autem habet actionem propriam, quae competit sibi secundum propriam formam; sicut securi competit scindere ratione suae acuitatis, facere autem lectum inquantum est instrumentum artis. Non autem perficit actionem instrumentalem nisi exercendo actionem propriam; scindendo enim facit lectum." See also *De ver.* q. 27, a. 4 and ad 2.

Aquinas's example of the axe which is used to make a bed helps to illustrate what he means when he attributes a dual action to an instrumental cause. There is only a single motion which arises from the instrument when it operates. Yet, this single motion achieves two ends: The axe both hews wood and it induces the shape of a bed in the wood. In this regard, the axe can be described as having two actions. Though there is only a single motion which arises from an instrumental cause, the motion has two specific characters in virtue of the two ends it reaches. In the case of the axe, the motion is both an act of cutting and an act of making a bed. Aquinas thinks that one of these actions is achieved through the native powers of the instrument, and the other only with the help of the principal cause. The forms which are proper to the axe, such as its sharpness and weight, are those in virtue of which it cuts and hews.[7] But there is no form native to an axe which is an active power for inducing shapes of particular artifacts, such as beds. The axe only works towards making a bed in so far as it is being used by a person who has the art of carpentry. However, the axe really contributes to the act of bedmaking and it does so in virtue of the action that arises from its native power. Without the use of a tool to split wood, the carpenter cannot make a bed. The act of bedmaking occurs through the act of cutting and splitting wood. In every case of instrumental causality, the second action depends on the first one. As already mentioned, the instrumental cause does not of itself have the power to achieve the second result that comes about through its action. An instrumental or assisting cause, by definition, operates toward an end which goes beyond its own nature. So, how does an instrument work toward an end which goes beyond what its own powers can reach? This brings us to Aquinas's second thesis about instrumental causality, the "moved mover" thesis.

Aquinas thinks that the instrument's activity reaches the second end only in virtue of being moved by the principal cause. The axe, for example, makes a bed only in so far as it is moved by the carpenter. Aquinas does not think that every instrumental cause is moved by its corresponding principal cause through a corporeal motion just as artificial tools are moved by craftsmen.[8] The king, for example, moves his servant by giving him a

---

[7] Scotus critiques this part of Aquinas's view because he thinks that forms such as "sharpness" and "hardness" cannot be not active with respect to changing matter. In Scotus's view, artificial instruments are purely passive. See Solère, "Scotus versus Aquinas on Instrumental Causality," 167–84.

[8] *ST* III q. 18, a. 1, ad 2 (ed. Leon., vol. 11, 231): "proprium est instrumenti quod moveatur a principali agente: diversimode tamen, secundum proprietatem naturae ipsius. Nam instrumentum inanimatum, sicut securis aut serra, movetur ab artifice per motum solum corporalem. Instrumentum

command. In every case of instrumental causality, however, the principal
cause causes a motion in the instrumental cause.[9] In Aquinas's view, the
motion which the principal causes in the instrument is what enables it to
work toward the end which surpasses its native power. He writes:

> [A]n instrument achieves an instrumental action in so far as it is moved by
> the principal agent and through that motion it participates in some way in
> the power of the principal agent, but not in such a way that the power
> is in the instrument according to perfected being, since motion is an
> imperfect act.[10]

Consider again a carpenter who uses an axe to make a bed. Aquinas thinks
that the carpenter, by moving the axe according to a certain pattern of
locomotion, gives the saw a power to induce that same pattern in the wood
which is to be carved into a bed. By moving the instrument, the principal
transfers a power to it. This brings us to the third thesis, the "borrowed
power" thesis. Aquinas writes: "[S]omething is constituted a principal
agent from the fact that it has some form which it is able to transfer to
another ..."[11] He reiterates in several passages that the instrument does not
have the power of the principal cause in it in the same way that the power
is in the principal cause itself. The instrument only has the power which it
receives from the principal as long as it is being moved by the principal.[12]
Even while the instrument is being used by the principal, the power which
the instrument gains from the principal has a fleeting, transitory, and
imperfect mode of existence in the instrument. The power is not a stable
quality of the instrument, rooted in one of its own forms.[13] Rather, the
power is a motion caused in the instrument by the principal. Nevertheless,
this borrowed power is indeed a power through which the instrument
operates. Referring to the instrument's achievement of the second, higher

vero animatum anima sensibili movetur per appetitum sensitivum, sicut equus a sessore.
Instrumentum vero animatum anima rationali movetur per voluntatem eius, sicut per imperium
domini movetur servus ad aliquid agendum ..."
[9] For discussion of Aquinas's views on motion see Section 6.1.
[10] *De ver.* q. 26 a. 1 ad 8 (ed. Leon., vol. 23 3/1, 750): "instrumentum agit actionem instrumentalem,
in quantum est motum ab agente principali, per quem motum participat aliqualiter virtutem agentis
principalis, non ita quod virtus illa sit in instrumento secundum esse perfectum, quia motus est
actus imperfectus; ..."
[11] *In IV Sent.* d. 19 q. 1, a. 2, qc. 1 (ed. Mandonnet-Moos, vol. 4, 978): "ideo ex hoc aliquid
constituitur principale agens, quod habet aliquam formam, quam in alterum transfundere
potest ..."
[12] *In IV Sent.* d. 1, q. 1, a. 4, qc. 3 (ed. Mandonnet-Moos, vol. 4, 36): "quod instrumentum praedicto
modo virtutem non recipit nisi secundum quod principali agenti continuatur, ut virtus ejus
quodammodo in instrumentum transfundatur."
[13] See for instance *De ver.* q. 27, a. 4 ad 7 and *In IV Sent.* d. 1, q. 1, a. 4, qc. 2.

action, Aquinas writes: "the instrument acts not according to its own form, but according to the power of that by which it is moved."[14] The axe does indeed work toward the action of making the bed. However, it does not do so solely through its own native power, but rather through the power it gains by being moved by the carpenter. Aquinas sees the instrument as a causal intermediary between the principal and its action. The instrument takes on the principal's power and the principal operates through it.

It is important to emphasize, however, that the instrument is not merely a passive medium through which the principal cause's power flows. The instrument, as we have seen, contributes to the action which the principal accomplishes through it with its own native powers. For example, the act of bed making happens in virtue of cutting. Cutting is an action done through the instrument's own native powers. A principal cause chooses a particular sort of instrument, such as a saw as opposed to a hammer or heat as opposed to wetness, because that instrument's own particular powers are suitable for performing the action in virtue of which the principal's action is carried out.[15]

While Aquinas maintains that the instrument has a twofold action and genuinely does work towards the operation which goes beyond its native power, he also acknowledges that the instrument relates to that action in a different way from the principal cause. He writes: "[A]n instrument is compared to the action more as that by which it is done than that which does it, for it is the principal agent that acts by means of the instrument ..."[16] The saw is not the agent that performs the act of bed making. Rather, it is that by which the carpenter makes a bed. Furthermore, Aquinas acknowledges that the final effect resembles the principal cause more than the instrument.[17] The principal cause has through itself the form that is communicated to the effect. The instrument

---

[14] *ST* III q. 64, a. 5 (ed. Leon., vol. 12, 46): "instrumentum non agit secundum propriam formam, sed secundum virtutem eius a quo movetur ..." Aquinas maintains that when a principal agent uses multiple different instruments at once, the principal's power is partially in all of these instruments. *In IV Sent.* d. 8, q. 2, a. 3 ad 9 (ed. Mandonnet-Moos, vol. 4, 347): "aliquod opus perficitur pluribus instrumentis, virtus instrumentalis non est complete in uno, sed incomplete in utroque, sicut manu et penna scribitur."

[15] See *ScG* II c. 21 (ed. Marietti, 130, n. 974): "Instrumentum adhibetur propter convenientiam eius cum causato, ut sit medium inter causam primam et causatum et attingat utrumque, et sic influentia primi perveniat ad causatum per instrumentum."

[16] *De ver.* q. 27, a. 4 ad 8 (ed. Leon., vol. 22 3/1, 806): "instrumentum comparatur ad actionem magis ut quo agitur, quam ut quod agit: principalis enim agentis est ut agat instrumentum ..."

[17] *In IV Sent.* d. 19, q. 1, a. 2, qc. 1 (ed. Mandonnet-Moos, vol. 4, 978): "agens per se et agens instrumentale in hoc differunt quod agens instrumentale non inducit in effectu similitudinem suam, sed similitudinem principalis agentis. Principale autem agens inducit similitudinem suam."

is a means used to communicate the principal's form. So, it is fitting that the final effect is a likeness of the principal cause.

Before moving on to see how instrumental causality is operative in nature, it worth briefly mentioning a distinction that Aquinas draws between two different types of instruments. In the previous chapter, we saw that Aquinas thought that efficient causes could be distinguished into perfecting and preparing causes based on whether the efficient cause causes the final effect in actuality or whether the efficient cause causes a potentiality for the final effect.[18] Aquinas thought different types of instruments could similarly be distinguished based on whether the effect toward which the instrument works is a final perfecting effect or merely a disposition for a final perfection which the principal cause causes on its own.[19] As we have seen, Aquinas thinks that the defining character of an instrument is that it works toward an effect which goes beyond its own native powers. Aquinas recognized that an instrument could be used by a principal to work toward either a disposing effect or a final effect. For example, a sculptor might use a tool to smooth clay so that it is disposed for her to mold it with her own hands or the sculptor might use the tool to shape the clay into a statue. In the first case, the tool does not work towards the final perfection of the form of the statue and thus it is a disposing instrument. In the latter case, the tool is a perfecting instrument since it works toward the final form. In both cases, however, the tool operates toward the end which is specified by the principal cause, namely the sculptor.

In this section, we have seen Aquinas's basic commitments about instrumental causality. As the reader has likely noticed, the examples of principal and instrumental causes which we have seen throughout this section are examples drawn from human agency. Thus, the question arises of whether and how instrumental causality is relevant to the operations of non-cognitive natural beings. It is to this question that we now turn.

8.2   Instrumental Causality in Nature

As we saw in Chapter 6, natural causes do not understand the ends toward which they tend. Thus, it would seem that it is impossible for a natural cause to employ another cause as its instrument to reach its end. Aquinas,

---

[18] See Section 7.1.

[19] See, for instance, *In IV Sent.* d. 1, q. 1, a. 4, sol. 1. Lynch argues that Aquinas changed his mind over time with respect to whether sacraments were dispositive or perfecting instruments with respect to God's final effect of grace. See his *The Cleansing of the Heart*, especially 67–153.

however, thinks that instances of instrumental causality occur in nature even though natural causes lack knowledge of their own ends. One example of instrumental causality in nature which we have already seen is the case of the male who generates a child by semen.[20] Aquinas believes that the male substantial form is an active power for generating another human being. When the male body produces semen, this generative power is transferred from the male body to the semen. The male body acts upon the semen to give it this power without knowledge or choice unlike the carpenter who freely and knowingly moves the saw to make the bed. Rather, the male body's transfer of the generative power to the semen is an action which occurs naturally in the male body. Through the mutual interactions between the parts of the healthy male body, semen is produced and it receives from the male his power to generate offspring. Once the semen has this power in it, it acts toward the end toward which this power inclines. Just as the saw has its own native power to cut, the semen has its own native power to heat. The male's power to generate is exercised through the semen's heat. There is a twofold action which follows from the semen, the action of heating and the action of generating a child, which is properly the male parent's action.

In addition to reproduction, which happens by way of semen, Aquinas acknowledges other cases of instrumental causality in nature. As we saw earlier in the study, Aquinas thinks that all material changes are immediately caused through the elemental powers. Thus, he believes that every higher power of living of an organism which transmutes matter does so by acting through the elemental powers as instruments. For example, when a living body changes its own quantity through growth, Aquinas thinks that the living body uses its heat as an instrument to achieve the end of growth. Similarly, when a body nourishes itself with food, it likewise uses its heat as an instrument. In these cases, Aquinas thinks that there are two powers involved, namely the power for growth or nutrition, and the power of heat. The former power operates through the latter power as its instrument.

Other thinkers, such as the ancient philosopher Empedocles, maintained that vital operations could be accounted for solely through the elemental powers. Aquinas, by contrast, thinks that vital operations must also be attributed to higher powers, which make use of the elements as their instruments. Regarding growth, Aquinas reasons that there are

---

[20] See Section 2.5. For a primary text, see *De pot.* q. 3, a. 11 ad 5. The semen is an example of a separate, as opposed to a conjoined, instrument. Separate instruments retain the power of the principal agent even when they are no longer in contact with it.

regularities and limits observed in the growth of an organism that cannot be accounted for by the power of heat alone. The power of heat is ordered solely to the end of heating. Given that the power of heat is inclined only toward heating, it cannot account for why its bearer's acts of heating are limited in a such a way as to achieve a further goal. A fire, for instance, will continue to burn things endlessly as long as it has fuel.[21] In animal growth, however, we observe that when an animal reaches its mature size, it no longer assimilates more food into its body than is necessary to replenish what has been lost. Growth ceases when an animal reaches a determinate size proper to its species. Aquinas supposes that if the animal's power of heat were the sole power responsible for nutrition and growth, the animal would not cease to grow. The power of heat is of itself indifferent to the final size produced through it in the animal's body. Heat if acting solely through itself will continue to heat without regard to the size of an animal's body. Yet, in the growth of animals we observe that animals of the same kind reach similar mature sizes. Aquinas takes this as evidence that heat is not the principal or primary active power through which the animal nourishes itself. Aquinas reasons that there must be a higher active power of the animal body that uses heat as its instrument to account for the limits observed in growth. He writes: "That which is the principal of any action is that which imposes the end and order upon that which is done. . . . For the instruments are indifferent as to whether they are used to produce this form or quantity or another one."[22] This is to say that there is some other form which is communicating its likeness through the communication of heat. It is this form that is specifying the limitations on heating. Heating heats in a certain way not through itself, but because of this other form. In Aquinas's view, the food that nourishes the body is not merely made hot. It is also made to be of the same kind as the animal body itself. Aquinas writes in the *Summa theologiae*: "However, that which is in potency to the whole [body], is that which is generated from food before it

---

[21] *In II De anima* lec. 8 (ed. Leon., vol. 45/1, 101):

> Manifestum est autem, quod in omnibus quae sunt secundum naturam, est certus *terminus*, et determinata *ratio magnitudinis et augmenti* . . . Illud igitur quod est causa determinationis magnitudinis et augmenti est principalis causa augmenti. Hoc autem non est ignis. Manifestum est enim, quod ignis augmentum non est usque ad determinatam quantitatem, sed in infinitum extenditur, si in infinitum materia combustibilis inveniatur. Manifestum est igitur, quod ignis non est principale agens in augmento et alimento, *set magis anima*.

[22] *In II De anima* lec. 8 (ed. Leon. 45/1, 101): "Illud est principale in qualibet actione a quo imponitur terminus et ratio ei quod fit . . . Nam instrumenta se habent differenter ut cooperentur ad hanc formam vel quantitatem, vel aliam."

is converted into the substance of the members [of the body]."²³ In nutrition and growth, food is eventually transformed into the very body of the animal. Of itself, the power of heat can only make a material substance hot. The power of heat cannot transform matter to be human or bovine or feline unless it operates through a higher power.²⁴

It should be noted that while there is a similarity between the relationship between a principal and instrumental cause and between a principal and instrumental power, there are also some crucial differences. In both cases, that which is principal specifies the end of that which is instrumental. Yet, the manner in which the principal takes the instrument up into its activity differs. Principal causes, which are complete substances, employ instruments by moving them. The craftsman, for example, pulls the saw back and forth over a board. Powers, however, are not the sorts of things that can move other substances. Powers are that by which an agent acts, but they are not agents. It is the animal that heats food by means of its power of heat. That same animal is the agent of nutrition by means of its nutritive power. Therefore, it is important that a reader not imagine that the nutritive power is itself some quasi substance that efficiently causes changes in the bodily temperature of the animal.

In Aquinas's view, powers of living bodies have organs through which they operate. This is to say that there is a determinate integral part of the animal body where each active quality which is a power is manifested. When the various material parts of the animal body interact with each other or with other substances, the powers manifested in various organs may be strengthened or weakened. For example, when a hot part comes into contact with something cold, the power of heat is weakened. In Aquinas's view, it is through the proper functioning of the animal body, which involves interactions among parts and with other substances, that the elemental powers are tempered in the way needed to be subordinated

---

²³ *ST* I q. 119, a. 2 (ed. Leon., vol. 5, 576): "Hoc autem quod est in potentia ad totum, est illud quod generatur ex alimento, antequam convertatur in substantiam membrorum." For a recent discussion of Aristotle's and Aquinas's views on nutrition see Ambrose Little, "Are You What You Eat or Something More?," *American Catholic Philosophical Quarterly* 92:1 (2018): 1–20.

²⁴ Strictly speaking, heat can also induce of itself the secondary qualities which follow upon heat. Solère notes in fn. 19 of his article "Scotus versus Aquinas on Instrumental Causality" that Aquinas wavered on the question of whether the elemental qualities are disposing or perfecting instruments. In *ScG* II c. 89 he asserts that heat does not act toward the final effect of flesh in nutrition, but rather it only disposes the matter for it by causing the potentiality for flesh in the digested food. Yet, in later texts he returns to his earlier view that the elemental qualities do extend to the final effect in generation and nutrition.

to the animal's higher powers. Let us look at how this works specifically with nutrition.

Aquinas thinks that flesh is the physical organ through which the nutritive power operates. In his view, the way that flesh transforms the nutritive substance into the animal body is by mixture. Consider a drop of water which is dropped into a glass of wine. After the drop is added, the liquid in the glass increases in volume and yet all of the liquid in the glass is wine. Through being mixed in, the drop of water becomes wine. Aquinas thinks this is a good analogy for how the nutritive power functions. He writes: "That which is generated from food [i.e. the nutritive substance] is joined to the body by nutrition through the mode of mixture, just as water is mixed with wine."[25] When the nutritive substance is added to flesh, it is transformed into flesh just as the water is transformed into the wine. Heat is crucial to this process. It is through being hot that flesh is capable of uniformly mixing with the right sort of substance.

Aquinas thinks that as more nutritive substance is taken into the flesh and transformed into it, the flesh's power to convert nutrition into itself is weakened.[26] Just as wine that has been watered down will have less of a capacity to transform added water into wine, so too does the flesh which has continually incorporated new matter into itself have a weakened ability to convert nutrients into flesh. The weakening of the power is what in turn explains why the animal's growth ceases when it reaches its mature size. Aquinas writes:

> Therefore, the power for converting [the nutritive substance into flesh] is strong in the beginning so that it is able to convert not only that which is needed for restoring what is lost, but also enough for growth. Later it is not able to convert anything more than what suffices to restore what was lost, and growth ceases. Eventually it is not able to even do this, and then size is lost. Finally, the power of this kind totally fails and the animal dies. Similarly, the power of wine to convert added water into wine is weakened little by little through the addition of water, until finally it becomes watery. This is the example that the Philosopher gives in I *Gen.*[27]

---

[25] *ST* I q. 119, a. 1 ad 2 (ed. Leon., vol. 5, 573): "id quod ex alimento generatur, adiungatur corpori nutrito per modum mixtionis, sicut aqua miscetur vino."

[26] *In I Gen. et Cor.* lec. 17 (ed. Leon., vol. 3, 321): "[V]irtus speciei debilitatur, cum sit in materia contrarietati subiecta, per continuam actionem et passionem, et per adiunctionem materiae extraneae, quae non ita perfecte recipit virtutem speciei sicut prius erat."

[27] *ST* I q. 119, a. 1 ad 4 (ed. Leon., vol. 5, 576):

> Et ideo virtus conversiva in principio quidem tam fortis est, ut possit convertere non solum quod sufficit ad restaurationem deperditi, sed etiam ad augmentum. Postea vero non potest convertere nisi quantum sufficit ad restaurationem deperditi, et tunc cessat augmentum.

Just as wine which is increasingly watered down becomes increasingly paler in color and weaker in taste, so too does the flesh which is continually added to by nutrition become less hot and thus less able to mix food in with itself. Thus, it is in virtue of the flesh's communicating its form by mixing, namely making what is not the animal into the animal's body, that heat is weakened. If not for the mixing, the flesh's heat would stay strong.

Aquinas construes the process just described as the nutritive power specifying the limit of the body's heating because were it not for the power of nutrition communicating the animal species to another, namely taking in the nutritive substance by mixture, the flesh's heat would not be reduced. If the animal's flesh were not such that it was capable of being uniformly mixed, and thus increased by the nutritive substance, then the animal body's heat would not be reduced. Moreover, just as there is a limit to how much water can be added to wine before it ceases to be wine, so too is there a limit to how much nutritive substance can be added to flesh. This is specified not by heat and its limits, but rather by the nature of flesh.

8.3 Primary and Secondary Causes

As we saw above, the defining feature of an instrumental cause is that it operates for the end of another cause, namely a principal cause. Instrumental causes are distinguished from principal causes based on whether they act for their own end or an end imposed by another cause. Aquinas recognizes that even efficient causes which act for their own ends can be dependent upon the power of other efficient causes to perform their actions. Consider a fire which burns a log. The fire acts through its own native form of heat and through this form of heat it is inclined toward the end of burning. Thus, when fire burns, it acts as a principal cause for its own end. Nevertheless, Aquinas thought that fire, as well as all other natural causes, depended on other efficient causes in order to exercise their proper actions. Aquinas employs the categories of primary and secondary

> Demum nec hoc potest, et tunc fit diminutio. Deinde, deficiente huiusmodi virtute totaliter, animal moritur. Sicut virtus vini convertentis aquam admixtam, paulatim per admixtionem aquae debilitatur, ut tandem totum fiat aquosum, ut philosophus exemplificat in I de Generat.

See also *In I Gen. et Cor.* lec. 17 (ed. Leon., vol. 3, 322):

> Quando ergo non potest hoc amplius virtus speciei facere, ut scilicet tantum convertat de nutrimento, quod sit in potentia, non solum ad speciem et ad maiorem quantitatem, sed nec etiam ad aequalem, tunc fit deminutio quantitatis, et tamen conservatur species in quantitate minori. Et finaliter etiam species cessat: sicut si aqua magis et magis vino misceatur, fiet vinum aquatum, et finaliter corrumpetur vinum et fiet totaliter aqua.

cause to specify the relationship which obtains between a dependent principal cause and the other efficient causes upon which it depends to operate. In this section, we will first see Aquinas's views about primary and secondary causes in general and then we will move on to see how he thinks these relationships were instantiated in the natural world.

Medieval thinkers used the categories of primary and secondary cause to capture the causal relationship which obtains between a principal cause and another cause upon which it depends to operate. They inherited the distinction between these two types of causes from the neo-Platonic tradition. Their reading of the *Liber de causis*, in particular, shaped their understanding of how such causes cooperate.[28] Medieval thinkers were especially interested in the primary–secondary cause distinction because they saw it as applying to the causal relationship that obtains between divine and created causality. God was seen as the primary cause of created actions and effects, such as the fire's burning. Creatures were seen as secondary causes of their own actions and effects in so far as they depended on God's causality to exercise their own causality.[29] We will see that Aquinas also thought, along with others of his time period, that the primary–secondary cause relationship also obtained between diverse creatures, such as terrestrial material substances and the heavenly bodies.

The primary–secondary cause relationship can be captured in four central theses:

(1) Correlative primary and secondary causes are each of a different nature.
(2) Each cause supplies a different type of power which is required for the production of the effect.
(3) One nature and its power is greater than the other nature and its power. The greater cause's power has a more universal scope than the lesser cause's power.
(4) The less perfect cause depends on the more perfect one to exercise its power in the production of the effect.

Let us examine each of these theses.

---

[28] On the medieval reception of the ides in this work, see Dragos Calma (ed.), *Reading Proclus and the Book of Causes Volume 1: Western Scholarly Networks and Debates* (Leiden: Brill, 2019).

[29] For some medieval positions and debates on primary and secondary causation as it applies to God and creatures, see Zita Toth, "Medieval Problems of Secondary Causation and Divine Concurrence," PhD diss., Fordham University, 2017, ProQuest Dissertations Publishing, 10273316.

Regarding the first thesis, primary and secondary causes relate to their joint effect in a different way from individuals of the same nature which cooperate to produce an effect. When multiple individuals of the same nature cooperate, the effect which they produce only requires a single type of power which all of the cooperating agents possess. The addition of multiple individuals with the same type of power serves only to strengthen that power. Consider, for example, two men who pull a boat. If one of the men were stronger, he could have pulled the boat on his own. By contrast, in the case of primary–secondary causes the causes are each of a different nature. As the second thesis states, each supplies a different type of power for the effect. Both distinct types of power are required to produce the effect. No augmentation of any degree could enable one of the powers to produce the joint effect on its own.[30] It will be clearer why both powers are necessary in the production of the joint effect after we come to understand the third thesis.

According to the third thesis, one of the causes, namely the primary cause, has a higher nature and power than the other cause, namely the secondary cause. In Aquinas's view, the degree of perfection of an active power is manifested by the scope of its effects. He thought that more perfect natures conferred more perfect active powers, which could produce a wider range of effects. Consider for example, the human being's power to generate another human being. This active power can only produce one type of effect, namely a human being. Even though a human can generate several individual effects, namely multiple human children, all of these effects will have the same species. Aquinas thinks that a greater power can produce multiple species of effect. A power to produce living material beings, for example, can produce many species beyond human beings, such as lions, tigers and bears. Thus, such a power would be a greater active power than a power which merely generates another human. Aquinas explains how the scope of an agent's active power depends on the nobility of its nature. He writes the following in his *Physics* commentary:

---

[30] God's causality was held to be an exception. Medieval Christians thought that God was a primary cause which could produce the effect of any secondary cause without the help of that cause. Non-Christian philosophers had denied that even the highest primary cause could alone produce the effects of secondary causes and this view was condemned at Paris in 1277. Medieval Christians debated, however, about whether God could make the particular effects of created causes alone without their cooperation or whether God could only make effects of the same generic type as creatures without their causal cooperation. See Rondo Keele, "Can God Make a Picasso? William Ockham and Walter Chatton on Divine Power and Real Relations," *Journal of the History of Philosophy* 45:3 (2007): 395–411.

It is manifest that any power extends to some effects in so far as they have in common one nature of an object; and the more effects to which a power extends, the more common the nature of its object must be. Since a power is proportioned to its object according to the nature of it, it follows that a superior cause acts according to a more universal and less contracted form. This is seen in the order of things: to the extent that some are superior among beings, they have forms which are less contracted and more dominant over matter, which contracts the power of form.[31]

Aquinas first explains in this passage how it can be that one power is able to produce effects of multiple species. We saw earlier in Chapter 3 that Aquinas thinks that each natural power extends to just one object, namely one final effect, and thus, it may initially seem confusing that he thinks that there are natural powers which can produce effects of multiple species.[32] Here Aquinas explains how it can be that a power extends to only one effect and that it also produces effects of multiple different species. In such cases, the effect of the power is a more common or universal nature that is possessed by different species. For example, a power which is able to produce multiple species of living, material beings produces these different types of being in so far as they each have the common nature of a living, material being. If there were not some common nature possessed by all of the different species of effect, then the power would not be able to produce them. Thus, even the power which can produce effects of different species, only extends to one effect, namely the nature held in common by the species. Aquinas reasons that the more different types of things to which a power extends, the more common or universal the power's effect must be. This is because the effect of the power must be universal enough to encompass all of the diverse types of things to which it extends. For example, a power which can produce both material beings and immaterial ones must produce them in virtue of causing a universal nature that is shared in by both material

---

[31] *In II Phys.* lec. 6 (ed. Leon., vol. 2, 73):

> Manifestum est enim quod quaelibet virtus extenditur ad aliqua secundum quod communicant in una ratione obiecti; et quanto ad plura extenditur, tanto oportet illam rationem esse communiorem: et cum virtus proportionetur obiecto secundum eius rationem, sequitur quod causa superior agat secundum formam magis universalem et minus contractam. Et sic est considerare in ordine rerum: quia quanto aliqua sunt superiora in entibus, tanto habent formas minus contractas, et magis dominantes supra materiam, quae coarctat virtutem formae.

[32] See Section 3.2.

and immaterial beings. This nature is more universal that any nature which is shared in only by material beings.

Aquinas reasons that the more common an active cause's effect, the "more universal and less contracted" is the form by which it acts. We saw in Chapter 3 that Aquinas thinks that the powers by which a substance acts are the very forms by which the substance is itself actualized.[33] Aquinas thinks that causes with powers that extend to more universal objects must act through forms which are less "contracted and more dominant over matter." Aquinas views matter as restricting or particularizing the power of form.[34] The object to which a power extends is narrower in scope to the extent that the power has been limited (i.e. particularized) by matter. A human male, for example, can only produce a human being and not every type of material being because the male's generative power has been limited by the matter in which it inheres.[35] Aquinas claims that the most common effect of all, namely being itself, is caused by the most universal cause, God.[36] God is the most universal cause, and has the most common effect, because God's power is not limited in any way. He is pure actuality, which is not received by any principle of potentiality.[37] In Aquinas's view, the less limited a form is, the greater its subject is in the hierarchy of beings. Thus, in Aquinas's view primary causes are more perfect than secondary ones because their forms are less limited by matter and as we have seen, their powers have more universal effects than the powers of secondary causes.

This background can help us to understand why primary and secondary causes are both necessary for the production of their joint effect and how the secondary cause depends on the primary cause while also acting for its

---

[33] See Section 3.3.

[34] For a text in which Aquinas explicitly claims that matter contracts form, see *ST* I q. 7, a. 7.

[35] In other texts, Aquinas specifies a hierarchy of terrestrial material substances based on the extent to which the operations of each transcend matter. When discussing this other hierarchy he is not concerned with the universality of the object of each type of being's power, but rather with the extent to which each relies on elemental qualities and bodily organs in its act. See for instance *ScG* II c. 68 (ed. Marietti, 203, n. 1454): "Unde forma cuius operatio superexcedit conditionem materiae, et ipsa secundum dignitatem sui esse superexcedit materiam."

[36] See, for instance, *De pot.* q. 3, a. 7 (ed. Pession, 20): "Ipsum enim esse est communissimus effectus primus et intimior omnibus aliis effectibus; et ideo soli Deo competit secundum virtutem propriam talis effectus …" See also *ST* I q. 45, a. 5 (ed. Leon., vol. 4, 469): "Oportet enim universaliores effectus in universaliores et priores causas reducere. Inter omnes autem effectus, universalissimum est ipsum esse. Unde oportet quod sit proprius effectus primae et universalissimae causae, quae est Deus."

[37] *ST* I q. 9, a. 1 (ed. Leon. vol. 4, 90): "esse aliquod primum ens, quod Deum dicimus: et quod huiusmodi primum ens oportet esse purum actum absque permixtione alicuius potentiae, eo quod potentia simpliciter est posterior actu."

own end. It follows, from what we have seen in this section, that primary and secondary causes each operate toward the final effect under a different nature or aspect. For example, the human father generates a human being in so far as it is a human being while other higher created causes produce the new human in so far as it is a living, material being. Ultimately, God causes the new human in so far as it is a being. In order to act toward their proper effects, secondary causes depend on primary causes to exercise their powers toward the effect. For example, the human father lacks the power to produce being as such and material, living beings as such. Thus, he depends on other causes with these active powers to operate in order for him to exercise his power to generate a human being. Though primary causes operate towards their effects through their own native powers and they act for their own ends, there are nevertheless more universal aspects of their effects which they are incapable of producing on their own.[38] Thus, secondary causes depend on the power of higher, more universal causes in order to exercise their own powers in the production of an effect. In his commentary on the *Liber de causis*, Aquinas writes the following about primary and secondary causes:

> Therefore, to be the cause of the effect belongs first to the primary cause and second to the secondary cause. That which is first in all things is greater because the more perfect are naturally prior. Therefore, the primary cause is more a cause of the effect than the secondary cause.[39]

As Aquinas explains here, because the primary cause is more perfect, the primary cause's causality is naturally prior to the secondary cause's causality. To say that the primary cause is naturally prior is to assert that the secondary cause's exercise of causality ontologically depends on the primary cause. Though both causes act at the same time, the secondary cause's exercise of power relies on the primary cause's power. For this reason, Aquinas concludes that the primary cause is more a cause of the

---

[38] Aquinas thinks that secondary causes are active in producing the more universal aspects of their effects as well. With regard to the universal aspects of the effect, secondary causes function as instruments of the primary cause. For example, Aquinas thinks that creatures do produce their effects in so far as they are existing beings, but they do so only as instruments of God since creatures do not have of themselves a power to cause being. On how Aquinas applies both the principal-instrument and the primary-secondary cause relationship to God and creatures, see Brian Shanley, "Divine Causation and Human Freedom in Aquinas," *American Catholic Philosophical Quarterly* 72:1 (1998): 99–122.

[39] *In De causis*, Prop. 1 (ed. Saffrey, 7): "Esse ergo causam effectus inest primo causae primae, secundo autem causae secundae; quod autem est prius in omnibus, est magis, quia perfectiora sunt priora naturaliter. Ergo prima causa est magis causa effectus quam causa secunda."

effect than the secondary cause. The primary cause is a cause of both the effect and the secondary cause's exercise of power toward the effect.

8.4   Heavenly Bodies as Primary, Universal Causes of Elemental Actions

Now that we have seen Aquinas's general views on primary and secondary causation, we can examine how he thought this form of cooperation between efficient causes occurred in the natural world. We have seen that Aquinas attributes active powers to earthly material substances, such as fire, water, and various types of animals. He believes that though earthly material substances do have genuine active powers through which they act, they depend on higher, material substances, namely the heavenly bodies, to exercise their powers. Like other secondary causes, earthly material substances are principal causes. They act according to their proper powers for their own ends. Yet, they depend on the operations of higher causes to act. Aquinas writes: "to heat is proper to fire, supposing that it has any action, but the action of it depends on another ..."[40] When fire acts, it acts through its native power it has to heat and for an end toward which it is inclined as fire. Yet, fire depends on other causes to actually do this action. In his *De Potentia*, Aquinas writes: "*The elements therefore* act in virtue of the celestial bodies ... For fire by its heat transmutes matter through the power of the celestial bodies."[41] He goes on to claim that if the celestial bodies were to cease their motions, "there would not, however, be action by which matter is transmuted and from which generation and corruption follows."[42] Aquinas states that a terrestrial substance's posses-sion of active power and contact with a suitable patient are not sufficient for action to occur.[43] The activity of the heavenly bodies is also required for the powers of terrestrial substances to be manifested in action. Through their activities, the celestial bodies cause heat and light. Aquinas thinks that the heat caused by the heavenly bodies is required for elements to be able

---

[40] *De pot.* q. 5, a. 8 ad 5 (ed. Pession, 152): "ignis est proprium calefacere, supposito quod habeat aliquam actionem; sed eius actio dependet ab alio ..."

[41] *De pot.* q. 5, a. 8 (ed. Pession, 152): "*Elementa ergo* agunt in virtute corporum caelestium ... Nam et ignis suo calore transmutat materiam, ex virtute corporis caelestis" See also *In II de caelo* lec. 4, n. 13: "virtutes inferiorum corporum sunt sicut materiales et instrumentales respectu caelestium virtutum, ita quod non movent nisi motae."

[42] *De pot.* q. 5, a. 8 (ed. Pession, 152): "non autem erit actio per quam transmutatur materia, quam sequitur generatio et corruptio."

[43] See *De pot.* q. 5, a. 8 ad 1, 5, and 6 where Aquinas claims that the activity of prior causes are required in addition to these conditions.

to transmute one another.[44] The light caused by the heavenly bodies is required for terrestrial substances to communicate their likenesses to air and water.[45] It is through this communication of likeness that material bodies are visible to perceivers. Thus, without the light of the heavenly bodies, terrestrial bodies would not be able to act on the senses of perceivers.

Aquinas thinks that the heavenly bodies, like other primary causes, have a more perfect nature and more universal power than the secondary causes which depend upon them. He writes the following about how the form of a heavenly body relates to its matter:

> [I]ts form satisfies the whole potentiality of matter since it is a certain total and universal perfection. This is evident from the fact that its active power is universal and not particular just as the power of inferior bodies whose forms, as if existing as particular, are not able to satisfy the whole potentiality of matter, so that with one form in matter there simultaneously remains the privation of another which is apt to begin to be in it.[46]

As this passage explains, Aquinas thinks that the forms of celestial bodies actualize matter in such a way that no potentiality is left in for taking on another form. The forms of heavenly bodies fully perfect matter. They confer universal perfection, rather than a particular way of being perfect. By contrast, the forms of terrestrial bodies perfect matter in such a way that there is always some potentiality left for acquiring a different form. Even while terrestrial matter is actualized by a substantial form, there is some perfection lacking that another form can actualize. Aquinas thinks that the evidence which shows that the forms of celestial bodies confer universal perfection, rather than some restricted, particular type of perfection, is the universal nature of the heavenly bodies' power. Heavenly bodies are not capable of merely producing one particular species of material substance. Rather, they have a universal power to generate material bodies as such.

---

[44] See for instance *De pot.* q. 5, a. 7 ad 19 (ed. Pession, 151): "Ad decimumnonum dicendum, quod sol est causa caliditatis per motum, ut Philosophus dicit [lib. II *de Caelo*, comment. 56 et 58]: unde cessante motu tollitur corruptionis causa in elementis, quae est per superexcedentiam caloris." See for example Aristotle, *Generation of Animals*, 737a1–4, 14–18.

[45] *De pot.* q. 5, a. 8.

[46] Aquinas writes the following about the forms of the heavenly bodies: *In I De caelo*, lec. 6 (ed. Leon., vol. 3, 24): "sed forma sua replet totam potentialitatem materiae, cum sit quaedam totalis et universalis perfectio. Quod patet ex hoc, quod virtus activa eius est universalis, non particularis sicut virtus inferiorum corporum; quorum formae, tanquam particulares existentes, non possunt replere totam potentialitatem materiae; unde simul cum una forma remanet in materia privatio formae alterius, quae est apta nata inesse." This passage occurs in one of Aquinas's later works. For an overview of the development of Aquinas's thinking on the matter and form of heavenly bodies, see Steven Baldner, "Aquinas on Celestial Matter," *The Thomist* 68:3 (2004): 431–67.

For example, the sun's heat is active in the production of living things in general, while individual male organisms have a power which can only act toward producing a new member of its own species.[47]

Aquinas justifies his view that terrestrial material substances require the cooperating activity of celestial substances with metaphysical reasoning rather than physical theories. In Aquinas view, there is a hierarchy among all existing beings according to the degree to which each is in actuality (as opposed to in potentiality). At the top of this hierarchy is God, who is pure actuality. God has no potentiality to be otherwise and God exists of himself, and not in virtue of a higher cause actualizing a potentiality for his existence. Next are angels. Angels are pure form, but they are not pure actuality. Though angels lack matter and thus are not in potentiality to taking on certain material forms, they nevertheless have a potentiality to exist which God actualizes. They do not exist of themselves. Celestial bodies are beneath the angels because, as material beings, they have both a potentiality to exist and their matter has a potentiality for form. Yet, as we have seen, their form fully actualizes their matter. Unlike the very lowest substances, terrestrial material substances, celestial bodies are not in potentiality to receiving other forms in their matter. Terrestrial material substances are the very lowest substances in the hierarchy since they have the most potentialities. They have a potentiality for existence which another substance must actualize and their matter is in potentiality to form even while it is actualized by a form. As we have seen, Aquinas thinks that substances are active in so far as they are in actuality. Aquinas applies this principle to the hierarchy of substances. The more potentiality a substance has, the less able it is to act. Because they have a lesser ability for action, lower substances require the activities of higher substances in the hierarchy to act.[48] The celestial bodies are not

---

[47] While Aquinas thinks that celestial bodies have a power to produce living things in general, he recognizes that the active powers of the male parent must cooperate with the celestial bodies in order to generate higher species of living beings. The celestial bodies can only cause lower species of living beings on their own. See for example *ScG III* c. 104, n. (ed. Marietti, 158, n. 2794): "Viventia perfecta non solum generantur virtute caelesti, sed etiam ex semine: *homo enim generat hominem et sol*. Quae vero ex sola virtute caelesti sine semine generantur, sunt animalia generata ex putrefactione, quae inter alia ignobiliora sunt." Aquinas's rationale for why the heavenly bodies need the cooperation of a mediating cause to produce higher species is discussed in Brian Carl, "Thomas Aquinas on the Proportionate Causes of Living Species," *Scientia et Fides* 8:2 (2020): 223–48, see especially 238–39.

[48] *De pot.* q. 5, a. 8 (ed. Pession, 151–52):

> Dicendum quod, sicut habetur in libro *de Causis*, quando causa prima retrahit actionem suam a causato, oportet etiam quod causa secunda retrahat actionem suam ab eodem, eo quod causa secunda habet hoc ipsum quod agit, per actionem causae primae, in cuius

themselves independent of higher causes. They are moved by angels to cause their acts.[49] Ultimately, all substances in the hierarchy depend on God to act. Only God can act without the aid of a higher substance.[50] Not only do terrestrial substances require the activity of the celestial bodies, but their actions also presuppose the actions of the higher causes upon which celestial causes also depend. In the case of the human will, however, Aquinas claims that its actions are caused only through God's power rather than by the other higher created causes as well.[51]

It is important to note that, as in other cases of primary and secondary causation, higher causes function as causes of terrestrial substances' effects according to their more universal aspects. The terrestrial cause itself specifies the species of its own effects. For example, God causes fire's action in so far as it is something which exists and the celestial bodies cause it in so far as it is a material action. Fire causes burning in so far as it is burning. Its native powers specify the type of effect that is caused and cause the effect according to its species.

8.5   Conclusion

In this chapter we have seen Aquinas's views on two different ways in which an efficient cause can depend on another efficient cause in the exercise of its power. First, we saw Aquinas's views about instrumental causes. An instrumental cause is an efficient cause that acts for the end of another efficient cause known as a principal cause. We saw that Aquinas thinks that an instrumental cause is moved by a correlative principal cause. By moving the instrument, the principal cause communicates a transitory power to the instrument which enables it to work toward the principal cause's end. The instrument itself has a twofold action, one which is done through its own native power, and another which is done through the power it receives from the principal cause. It would initially seem that only rational beings can employ instruments to reach their ends; however, we saw that Aquinas employs the notion of instrumental causality to

---

virtute agit. Cum autem omne agens agat secundum quod est in actu, oportet secundum hoc accipere ordinem causarum agentium, secundum quod est ordo earum in actualitate . . . *Elementa ergo* agunt in virtute corporum caelestium et corpora caelestia agunt in virtute substantiarum separatarum; unde cessante actione substantiae separatae, oportet quod cesset actio corporis caelestis; et ea cessante oportet quod cesset actio corporis elementaris.

[49] See for instance *ST* I q. 110, a. 1, especially ad 2.   [50] *De pot.* q. 5, a. 8 ad 4.
[51] See, for instance, *ScG* III c. 88. On Aquinas's views on God's causation of creaturely actions, including the human acts of volition, see Frost, "Three Competing Views of God's Causation of Creaturely Actions."

understand how higher-level natural powers, such as the nutritive power, employ elemental powers, such as heat, to reach their ends. For example, the human being exercises its power to nourish itself through the active power of heat, which is located in determinate bodily organs. The power of heat attains the ends both of heating and of replenishing human flesh. Aquinas argues that it is clear that a higher power is operating through heat as its instrument because the bodily heat does not heat without limits, but only to the extent that is beneficial for human growth and nourishment. This shows that heat is not operating for its own end, but rather the end of another.

We next saw Aquinas's views on how secondary efficient causes depend on primary efficient causes. Unlike instruments, secondary causes act for their own end. Yet, secondary causes depend on the cooperation of higher causes because there are more universal aspects of their effects which they are unable to produce on their own. For example, though an animal father has an active power to produce a new member of his species, he can only exercise this power in cooperation with the active powers belonging to other agents, which are needed to produce living material things as such. Aquinas holds that correlative primary and secondary causes must each be of a different nature and each supplies a different type of power which is required for the production of the effect. Aquinas thinks that the primary cause is higher than the secondary causes since the primary cause's power has a more universal scope. For instance, beings with the powers to produce living material beings as such are of a higher nature than the animal father, which has a power for producing just one type of living being. Since the primary cause has a higher, more perfect power, Aquinas conceives of the secondary cause as depending upon the primary cause in exercising its causality, though both causes' causality is necessary for the production of the final effect.

Conclusion

This study has covered a lot of details in Aquinas's theories about efficient causation and causal powers. Thus, it might be useful to conclude by reiterating how his theories respond to some of the "big picture" philosophical questions about causation. One major question that arises when thinking about causation is: What is essential to the relationship between a cause and its effect? Put otherwise, what is it that ties certain phenomena together as cause and effect? What unifies disparate cases of causation as instances of causation? As noted in the introduction, many contemporary theories conceive of causation as a logical relationship between events. Attempts to specify this logical relationship are routinely defeated by counterexamples. Aquinas's theory offers an alternative way of conceiving of the relationship between cause and effect. Instead of construing causation as a logical relationship, he sees causation as an ontological phenomenon. As we have seen, causes influence the being of their effects and effects depend on their causes for their existence. The unique way in which efficient causes influence the being of their effects is by action, namely an exercise of power. Aquinas recognizes, on the one hand, that there are primary and paradigm exercises of power, namely in *per se* instances of efficient causation, and yet, on the other hand, not all exercises of power bring about their effects in a uniform way. While *per se* causes are simultaneous with their effects, advising and preparing causes act prior to their effects. While unimpeded *per se* causes necessitate their effects, other efficient causes do not necessitate their effects. Despite their difference, what all instances of efficient causation have in common is that the cause influences the being of its effect by exercising a power in action. By conceiving of causation as an ontological relationship of dependence, Aquinas is able to find a common feature between pairs of causes and effects that bear different temporal, modal and logical relationships to each other. This gives his view flexibility to account for varied instances of causation which might pose counterexamples to more rigid views that define causation in terms of a single logical relationship.

One of the reasons why understanding causation is so important is because of its predictive and manipulative value in the real world. Once we understand what sorts of realities are regularly tied together as cause and effect, we can predict effects on the basis of their causes and bring about effects by bringing about their causes. A central philosophical question about causation is: Why do certain lawlike regularities hold in the natural world? For example, what explains why water routinely dissolves salt? We saw in the Introduction that Humeanism conceives of the regular connections between certain causes and effects as merely a brute fact with no further explanation. Nomicism appeals to abstract laws to ground the regularities observed in natural causation. Yet, the abstract laws are themselves taken to be brute or rooted in an arbitrary choice of the divine will. Aquinas's theory offers a more satisfying explanation for why there are regularities in natural causation. On his theory, the reason why certain causes routinely produce certain effects is found in the real features of material substances. The particular active and passive powers of material substances ground the generalizations we make about cause and effect. This has the consequence that on Aquinas's view the project of natural science is not about discovering matters of fact about which regularities happen to hold. Nor is it about uncovering abstract laws. Rather, the goal of natural science, and even the ordinary person's endeavor to understand the things around her, is to come to a deeper understanding of the powers of observable material substances. As we have seen in this study, Aquinas recognizes that efficient causes do not operate in isolation from one another. Rather the instances of efficient causation which we observe in the material world are the result of many diverse substances operating through varied powers. Aquinas's theories offer a conceptual framework for understanding and distinguishing the various ways in which efficient causes can cooperate, or in some cases impede one another.

Of course, power theories of causation like Aquinas's raise many questions. Once the move is made to root causation in powers and actions, questions naturally arise, such as what are powers and actions ontologically, how they are individuated, and how the powers of diverse substances fit together. Throughout this study we have seen that Aquinas's texts propose conceptually rich answers to such questions. Though he wrote no separate treatise on causation or causal powers, a detailed and nuanced account of these central philosophical topics can be extracted from his works. My hope is that this study has highlighted the valuable ideas about causation and causal powers which medieval thinkers still have to offer us today.

Bibliography

PRIMARY SOURCES

Aristotle, *Metaphysics*, ed. W. D. Ross (Oxford: Clarendon Press, 1924).
The Basic Works of Aristotle, ed. Richard McKeon (New York: Random House, 1941).
Aristoteles Latinus XXV 3 Metaphysica, lib. I–XIV. Recensio et Translatio Guillelmi de Moerbeka, 2 vols., ed. Gudrun Vuillemin-Diem (Leiden: Brill, 1995).
Avicenna, *Liber de philosophia prima sive scientia divina*, ed. Gérard Verbeke (Leuven: Peeters, 1983).
Liber Primus Naturalium: Tractatus Secundus de Motu et de Consimilibus, ed. Simone Van Riet, Jules L. Janssens André Allard and Gérard Verbeke (Brussels: Académie Royale de Belgique, 2006).
Pattin, Adriaan (ed.), *"Le Liber de causis* : Édition établie à l'aide de 90 manuscrits avec introduction et notes par A. Pattin O.M.L.," *Tijdschrift voor Filosofie* 28 (1966): 90–203.
Pseudo-Dionysius, *De divinis nominibus*, in *Patrologiae cursus completus, Series Graeca*, ed. J. P. Migne, vol. 3 (Paris, 1857).
Spinoza, *Ethics*, trans. Edwin Curley (London and New York: Penguin Press, 2005).
Thomas Aquinas, *Opera omnia iussu impensaque Leonis XIII P. M. edita* (Rome: Ex Typographia Polyglotta S. C. de Propaganda Fide, 1888–).
In quatuor libros Sententiarum magistri Petri Lombardi episcopi Parisiensis, ed. Pierre Mandonnet and Marie Fabien Moos (Paris: P. Lethielleux, 1929–47).
In librum De causis expositio, ed. H. D. Saffrey (Fribourg [Suisse] and Louvain: Société Philosophique-Nauwelaerts, 1954).
Summa contra Gentiles, vols. 2–3, ed. P. Marc, C. Pera and P. Caramello (Taurini-Rome: Marietti, 1961).
In duodecim libros Metaphysicorum expositio, ed. M.-R. Cathala and R. M. Spiazzi (Taurini-Rome: Marietti, 1964).
Quaestiones disputatae de potentia, in *Quaestiones disputatae*, vol. 2, ed. P. M. Pession (Taurini-Rome: Marietti, 1965), 1–276.
Quaestiones disputatae de virtutibus, in *Quaestiones disputatae*, vol. 2, ed. E. Odetto (Taurini-Rome: Marietti, 1965), 707–828.

SECONDARY SOURCES

Adams, Marilynn McCord, *Some Later Medieval Theories of the Eucharist* (Oxford: Oxford University Press, 2012).

Albertson, J. S., "Instrumental Causality in St. Thomas," *New Scholasticism* 28 (1954): 409–35.

Anjum, Rani Lill and Mumford, Stephen, *What Tends to Be: The Philosophy of Dispositional Modality* (London and New York: Routledge, 2018).

Armstrong, D. M., *What Is a Law of Nature?* (Cambridge: Cambridge University Press, 1983).

Baldner, Stephen, "Aquinas on Celestial Matter," *The Thomist* 68:3 (2004): 431–67.
    "Albertus Magnus and the Categorization of Motion," *The Thomist* 70 (2006): 203–35.

Bobik, Joseph, Aquinas on Matter and Form and the Elements: A Translation and Interpretation of the *de Principiis Naturae* and the *de Mixtione Elementorum* of St. Thomas Aquinas (Notre Dame, IN: University of Notre Dame Press, 1998).

Boland, Vivian, "Aquinas and Simplicius on Dispositions," *New Blackfriars* 82 (2001): 467–78.

Brock, Stephen, *Action and Conduct: Thomas Aquinas and the Theory of Action* (Edinburgh: T&T Clark, 2000).
    "Causality and Necessity in Thomas Aquinas," *Quaestio* 2:1 (2002): 217–40.

Brower, Jeffrey E., *Aquinas's Ontology of the Material World: Change, Hylomorphism, and Material Objects* (Oxford: Oxford University Press, 2014).

Brower-Toland, Susan, "Causation and Mental Content: Against the Externalist Reading of Ockham," in Jenny Pelletier and Magali Roques (eds.), *The Language of Thought in Late Medieval Philosophy: Essays in Honour of Claude Panaccio* (Cham: Springer, 2017), 59–80.

Burrell, David, "Aquinas and Jewish and Islamic Authors," in Brian Davies and Eleonore Stump (eds.), *The Oxford Handbook of Aquinas* (Oxford: Oxford University Press, 2012), 65–72.

Calma, Dragos (ed.), *Reading Proclus and the Book of Causes Volume 1: Western Scholarly Networks and Debates* (Leiden: Brill, 2019).

Carl, Brian, "Action, Supposit, Subject: Interpreting *Actiones Sunt Suppositorum*," *Nova et Vetera* 17:2 (2019): 545–65.
    "Thomas Aquinas on the Proportionate Causes of Living Species," *Scientia et Fides* 8:2 (2020): 223–48.

Clarke, Norris, "Action as the Self-Revelation of Being: A Central Theme in the Thought of St. Thomas," in *Explorations in Metaphysics* (Notre Dame, IN: University of Notre Dame Press, 1994), 45–64.

Cory, David, "Thomas Aquinas on How the Soul Moves the Body," *Oxford Studies in Medieval Philosophy* 8 (2020): 146–87.

Cory, Therese Scarpelli, *Aquinas on Human Self-Knowledge* (Cambridge: Cambridge University Press, 2014).

"Rethinking Abstractionism: Aquinas's Intellectual Light and Some Arabic Sources," *Journal for the History of Philosophy* 53:4 (2015): 607–46.

Courtenay, William, "Covenant and Causality in Pierre D'Ailly," *Speculum* 46:1 (1971): 94–119.

"The King and the Leaden Coin: The Economic Background of 'Sine Qua Non' Causality," *Traditio* 28 (1972): 185–209.

Cross, Richard, "Accidents, Substantial Forms, and Causal Powers in the Late Thirteenth Century: Some Reflections on the Axiom 'actiones sunt suppositorum,'" in Christophe Erismann and Alexandrine Schniewind (eds.), *Compléments de substance: études sur les propriétés accidentelles offertes à Alain de Libera* (Paris: Vrin, 2008), 133–46.

de Libera, Alain, "Les actions appartiennent aux sujets: petite archéologie d'un principe leibnizien," in Stefano Caroti et al. (eds.), *Ad ingenii acuitionem: Studies in Honor of Alfonso Maierù* (Louvain-La-Neuve, BE: Fédération Internationale des Instituts d'Etudes Médiévales, 2007), 199–219.

Decaen, Christopher, "Elemental Virtual Presence in St. Thomas," *The Thomist* 64:2 (2000): 271–300.

"An Inductive Study of the Notion of Equivocal Causality in St. Thomas," *The Thomist* 79:2 (2015): 213–63.

Des Chene, Dennis, *Physiologia: Natural Philosophy in Late Aristotelian and Cartesian Thought* (Ithaca, NY: Cornell University Press, 1996).

Dodds, Michael J., *Unlocking Divine Action: Contemporary Science and Thomas Aquinas* (Washington, DC: Catholic University of America Press, 2012).

Doig, James, "Aquinas and Aristotle," in Brian Davies and Eleonore Stump (eds.), *The Oxford Handbook of Aquinas* (Oxford: Oxford University Press, 2012), 33–41.

Doolan, Gregory, *Aquinas on Divine Ideas as Exemplar Causes* (Washington, DC: Catholic University of America Press, 2008).

Fabro, Cornelio, *Participation et causalité selon St. Thomas D'aquin* (Louvain: Publications Universitaires de Louvain, 1961).

Fakhry, M., *Islamic Occasionalism and Its Critique by Averroës and Aquinas* (London: Routledge, 1958).

Finance, Joseph, *Être et agir dans la philosophie de Saint Thomas* (Paris: Beauchesne, 1945).

Fisher, Kendall, "Thomas Aquinas on Hylomorphism and the In-Act Principle," *British Journal for the History of Philosophy* 25:6 (2017): 1053–72.

Fitzpatrick, Antonia, *Thomas Aquinas on Bodily Identity* (Oxford: Oxford University Press, 2017).

Frost, Gloria, "Aquinas's Ontology of Transeunt Causal Activity," *Vivarium* 56 (2018): 47–82.

"Aquinas on the Intension and Remission of Accidental Forms," *Oxford Studies in Medieval Philosophy* 7 (2019): 116–46.

"What Is an Action? Peter Auriol vs. Thomas Aquinas on the Metaphysics of Causality," *Ergo* 6:43 (2020): 1259–85.

"Aquinas on Passive Powers," *Vivarium* 59:1–2 (2021): 33–51.

"Three Competing Views of God's Causation of Creaturely Actions: Aquinas, Scotus and Olivi," in Gregory Ganssle (ed.), *Divine Causation* (New York: Routledge, 2021), 66–81

Goddu, André, "William of Ockham's Arguments for Action at a Distance," *Franciscan Studies* 44 (1984): 227–44.

Haldane, John, "Identifying Privative Causes," *Analysis* 71:4 (2011): 611–19.

Hankey, Wayne, "Aquinas, Plato, and Neo-Platonism," in Brian Davies and Eleonore Stump (eds.), *The Oxford Handbook of Aquinas* (Oxford: Oxford University Press, 2012), 55–64.

Hausman, Daniel, *Causal Asymmetries, Cambridge Studies in Probability, Induction and Decision Theory* (Cambridge: Cambridge University Press, 1998), 36–54.

Heinaman, R., "Is Aristotle's Definition of Change Circular?" *Apeiron* 27:1 (1994): 25–37.

Hoffman, Paul, "Does Efficient Causation Presuppose Final Causation? Aquinas vs. Early Modern Mechanism," in Larry Jorgensen and Samuel Newlands (eds.), *Metaphysics and the Good: Themes from the Philosophy of Robert Merrihew Adams* (Oxford: Oxford University Press, 2009), 297–312.

Huisman, Tyler, "Aristotle on Accidental Causation," *Journal of the American Philosophical Association* 2 (2016): 561–75.

Jacobs, Jonathan (ed.), *Causal Powers* (Oxford: Oxford University Press, 2017).

Johansen, T. K., *The Powers of Aristotle's Soul* (Oxford: Oxford University Press, 2012).

Johnson, Joel, "Final Causality in the Thought of Thomas Aquinas," PhD diss., Purdue University, 2018, ProQuest Dissertations Publishing, 10840028.

Kane, W. Declan, "The Subject of Predicamental Action according to John of St. Thomas," *The Thomist* 22:3 (1959): 66–388.

Kedar, Yael, "Laying the Foundation for the Nomological Image of Nature: From Corporeity in Robert Grosseteste (c. 1168–1253) to Species in Roger Bacon (1220–1292)," in J. P. Cunningham (ed.), *Robert Grosseteste and the Pursuit of Religious and Scientific Learning in the Middle-Ages* (New York: Springer, 2016), 165–85.

Keele, Rondo, "Can God Make a Picasso? William Ockham and Walter Chatton on Divine Power and Real Relations," *Journal of the History of Philosophy* 45:3 (2007): 395–411.

Kenny, Anthony, *Aquinas on Mind* (London and New York: Routledge, 1993).

Kent, Bonnie, "Dispositions and Moral Fallibility: The UnAristotelian Aquinas," *History of Philosophy Quarterly* 29 (2012): 141–57.

"Losable Virtue: Aquinas on Character and Will," in Tobias Hoffmann, Jorn Muller and Matthias Perkams (eds.), *Aquinas and the Nicomachean Ethics* (Cambridge: Cambridge University Press, 2013), 91–109.

Kent, Matthew, "Prime Matter according to St. Thomas," PhD diss., Fordham University, 2006, ProQuest Dissertations Publishing, 3201130.

Kim, Yul, "Why Does the Wood Not Ignite Itself? Duns Scotus's Defense of the Will's Self-Motion," *American Catholic Philosophical Quarterly* 95:1 (2021): 49–68.

King, Peter, "Duns Scotus on the Reality of Self-Change," in Mary Louise Gill and James Lennox (eds.), *Self-Motion from Aristotle to Newton* (Princeton, NJ: Princeton University Press, 1994), 227–90.

Kovach, Francis J., "Aquinas's Theory of Action at a Distance: A Critical Analysis," in *Scholastic Challenges to Mediaeval and Modern Ideas* (Stillwater, OK: Western Publications, 1987), 147–78.

Kretzmann, Norman, "A General Problem of Creation," in Scott MacDonald (ed.), *Being and Goodness: The Concept of the Good in Metaphysics and Philosophical Theology* (Ithaca, NY: Cornell University Press, 1991), 208–28.

Künzle, P., *Das Verhältnis der Seele zu ihren Potenzen: Problemgeschichtliche Untersuchungen von Augustin bis und mit Thomas von Aquin* (Freiburg: Universitätsverlag, 1956).

Lagerlund, Henrik, "The Unity of Efficient and Final Causality: The Mind/Body Problem Reconsidered," *British Journal for the History of Philosophy* 19:4 (2011): 587–603.

Lewis, David, "Causation," *Journal of Philosophy* 70:17 (1973): 556–67.

Lisska, Anthony J., *Aquinas's Theory of Perception* (Oxford: Oxford University Press, 2016).

Little, Ambrose, "Are You What You Eat or Something More?," *American Catholic Philosophical Quarterly* 92:1 (2018): 1–20.

Lonergan, Bernard, Grace and Freedom: Operative Grace in the Thought of St. Thomas Aquinas, *in* The Collected Works of Bernard Lonergan, vol. 1, ed. Frederick Crowe and Robert Doran (Toronto: University of Toronto Press, 2013).

Lorkowski, C. M., "Hume, David: Causation," in *The Internet Encyclopedia of Philosophy*, www.iep.utm.edu/, accessed April 1, 2021.

Lovejoy, Arthur, *The Great Chain of Being: The Study of the History of an Idea* (Cambridge, MA: Harvard University Press, 2009).

Löwe, Can Laurens, "Mind over Matter: Aquinas's Transformation of Aristotle's Definition of Change," *Archives d'histoire doctrinale et littéraire du Moyen Âge* 82:1 (2015): 45–68.

"Peter Auriol on the Metaphysics of Efficient Causation," *Vivarium* 55:4 (2017): 239–72.

"Aristotle and John Buridan on the Individuation of Causal Powers," *Oxford Studies in Medieval Philosophy* 6 (2018): 189–222.

"John Duns Scotus versus Thomas Aquinas on Action–Passion Identity," *British Journal for the History of Philosophy* 26:6 (2018): 1027–44.

Thomas Aquinas on the Metaphysics of the Human Act (Cambridge: Cambridge University Press, 2021).

Lynch, Reginald, *The Cleansing of the Heart: The Sacraments as Instrumental Causes in the Thomistic Tradition* (Washington, DC: Catholic University Press, 2017).

MacDonald, Scott, "Aquinas's Parasitic Cosmological Argument," *Medieval Philosophy and Theology* 1 (1991): 119–55.

Majcherek, Kamil, "Walter Chatton's Rejection of Final Causality," *Oxford Studies in Medieval Philosophy* 7 (2019): 212–42.

Maier, Anneliese, "Causes, Forces and Resistance," in *On the Threshold of Exact Science*, trans. Steven Sargent (Philadelphia: University of Pennsylvania Press, 1982), 40–60.

"The Theory of the Elements and the Problem of Their Presence in Compounds," in *On the Threshold of Exact Science*, trans. Steven Sargent (Philadelphia: University of Pennsylvania Press, 1982), 124–42.

Makin, Stephen, "Aquinas, Natural Tendencies, and Natural Kinds," *New Scholasticism* 63.3 (1989): 253–74.

McDermott, Timothy, "The Subject of Predicamental Action," *The Thomist* 23 (1960): 189–210.

Meehan, Francis X., *Efficient Causality in Aristotle and St. Thomas* (Washington, DC: Catholic University of America Press, 1940).

Miller, Marianne T., "The Problem of Action in the Commentary of St. Thomas Aquinas on the *Physics* of Aristotle," *Modern Schoolman*, 23:3–4 (1946): 135–67; 200–26.

Morris, William Edward and Brown, Charlotte R., "David Hume," in Edward N. Zalta (ed.), *The Stanford Encyclopedia of Philosophy* (Spring 2021 Edition), ehttps://plato.stanford.edu/entries/hume/, accessed May 31, 2021.

Mumford, "The Power of Power," in Ruth Groff and John Greco (eds.), *Powers and Capacities in Philosophy* (New York: Routledge, 2013), 9–24.

Mumford, Stephen and Anjum, Rani Lill, "The Irreducibility of Dispositionalism," in Rafael Hüntelmann and Johannes Hattler (eds.), *New Scholasticism Meets Analytic Philosophy* (Heusenstamm: Editiones Scholasticae, 2014), 105–28.

Nadler, Steven, "No Necessary Connection: The Medieval Roots of the Occasionalist Roots of Hume," *The Monist* 79:3 (1996): 462–63.

"Malebranche on Causation," in Steven Nadler (ed.), *The Cambridge Companion to Malebranche* (Cambridge: Cambridge University Press, 2000), 112–38.

"Doctrines of Explanation in Late Scholasticism and Mechanical Philosophy," in Daniel Garber and Michael Ayers (eds.), *Cambridge History of Seventeenth Century Philosophy* (Cambridge: Cambridge University Press, 2008), 513–52.

Oderberg, David, *Real Essentialism* (New York: Routledge, 2007).

Ott, Walter R., *Causation and Laws of Nature in Early Modern Philosophy* (Oxford: Oxford University Press, 2009).

Paasch, J. T., *Divine Production in Late Medieval Trinitarian Theology: Henry of Ghent, Duns Scotus, and William Ockham* (Oxford: Oxford University Press, 2012).

Page, Ben, "Thomas Aquinas, 'the Greatest Advocate of Dispositional Modality'," *Studia Neoaristotelica* 14:2 (2017): 167–88.

Pasnau, Robert, "Intentionality and Final Causes," in Dominik Perler (ed.), *Ancient and Medieval Theories of Intentionality* (Leiden: Brill, 2001), 301–23.

Thomas Aquinas on Human Nature: A Philosophical Study of Summa Theologiae 1a, 75–89 (Cambridge: Cambridge University Press, 2002).

"Scholastic Qualities, Primary and Secondary," in Lawrence Nolan (ed.), *Primary and Secondary Qualities: The Historical and Ongoing Debate* (New York: Oxford University Press, 2011), 41–61.

Metaphysical Themes: 1274–1671 (Oxford: Oxford University Press, 2011).

"Teleology in the Later Middle Ages," in Jeffrey McDonough (ed.), *Teleology: A History* (Oxford: Oxford University Press, 2020), 90–115.

Pawl, Timothy, "The Five Ways," in Brian Davies and Eleonore Stump (eds.), *The Oxford Handbook of Aquinas* (Oxford: Oxford University Press, 2012), 115–31.

Péghaire, Julien, "L'axiome 'bonum est diffusivum sui' dans le néoplatonisme et le thomisme," *Revue de l'Université d'Ottawa* 1 (1932): 5–30.

Perler, Dominik and Rudolph, Ulrich, *Occasionalismus: Theorien der Kausalität im arabisch-islamischen und im europäischen Denken* (Göttingen: Vandenhoeck & Ruprecht, 2000).

Pierson, Daniel, "Thomas Aquinas on the Principle *omne agens agit sibi simile*," PhD diss., Catholic University of America, 2015, ProQuest Dissertations Publishing, 3705731.

Pilsner, Joseph, *The Specification of Human Actions in St. Thomas Aquinas* (Oxford: Oxford University Press, 2006).

Richardson, Kara, "Avicenna's Conception of the Efficient Cause," *British Journal for the History of Philosophy* 21 (2013): 220–39.

"Causation in Arabic and Islamic Thought," in Edward N. Zalta (ed.), *The Stanford Encyclopedia of Philosophy* (Winter 2015 Edition), https://plato.stanford.edu/archives/win2015/entries/arabic-islamic-causation/, accessed May 31, 2021.

Rosemann, Philip, *Omne agens agit sibi simile: A "Repetition" of Scholastic Metaphysics* (Leuven: Leuven University Press, 1996).

Rota, Michael, "Causation," in Brian Davies and Eleonore Stump (eds.), *The Oxford Handbook of Aquinas* (Oxford: Oxford University Press, 2012), 104–14.

Russell, John, "Action and Reaction before Newton," *British Journal for the History of Science* 9:1 (1976): 25–38.

Sangiacomo, Andrea, "*Sine qua non* Causation: The Legacy of Malebranche's Occasionalism in Kant's *New Elucidation*," *Oxford Studies in Early Modern Philosophy* 9 (2018): 215–48.

Schmaltz, Tad M., *Descartes on Causation* (New York: Oxford University Press, 2008).

Schmid, Stephan, "Teleology and the Dispositional theory of Causation in Thomas Aquinas," *Logical Analysis and the History of Philosophy* 14 (2011): 21–39.

Shanley, Brian, "Divine Causation and Human Freedom in Aquinas," *American Catholic Philosophical Quarterly* 72:1 (1998): 99–122.

Solère, Jean-Luc, "Scotus versus Aquinas on Instrumental Causality," *Oxford Studies in Medieval Philosophy* 7 (2019): 147–85.

Storck, Michael Hector, "Parts, Wholes, and Presence by Power: A Response to Gordon P. Barnes," *Review of Metaphysics* 62:1 (2008): 45–59.

Swanstrom, Julie, "Creation as Efficient Causation in Aquinas," *American Catholic Philosophical Quarterly* 93:1 (2019): 1–27.

Te velde, Rudi, *Aquinas on God* (London: Routledge, 2006).

Tomarchio, John, "Four Indices for the Thomistic Principle *Quod recipitur in aliquo est in eo per modum recipientis*," *Mediaeval Studies* 60:1 (1998): 315–67.

"Thomistic Axiomatics in an Age of Computers," *History of Philosophy Quarterly* 16:3 (1999): 249–75.

"Aquinas's Division of Being according to Modes of Existing," *Review of Metaphysics* 54:3 (2001): 585–613.

Torrell, Jean-Pierre, *Saint Thomas Aquinas: The Person and His Work* (Washington, DC: Catholic University Press of America, 1996).

Toth, Zita, "Medieval Problems of Secondary Causation and Divine Concurrence," PhD diss., Fordham University, 2017, ProQuest Dissertations Publishing, 10273316.

Trifolgi, Cecilia, "Thomas Wylton on Motion," *Archiv für Geschichte der Philosophie* 77:2 (1995): 135–54.

Tuttle, Jake, "Suárez's Non-Reductive Theory of Efficient Causation," *Oxford Studies in Medieval Philosophy* 4 (2016): 125–58.

Vucu, Simona, "Henry of Ghent and John Duns Scotus on Self-agency and Self-motion: An Inquiry into the Medieval Metaphysics of Causal Powers," PhD diss., University of Toronto, 2018, ProQuest Dissertations Publishing, 10641101.

Watts, Jordan, "Natural Final Causality at the University of Paris from 1250 – 1360," PhD diss., The Catholic University of America, 2015, ProQuest Dissertations Publishing, 3705758.

Weisheipl, James, "The Principle *Omne quod movetur ab alio movetur* in Medieval Physics," *Isis* 56 (1965): 36–45.

Wippel, John, "Thomas Aquinas's Derivation of the Aristotelian Categories (Predicaments)," *Journal of the History of Philosophy* 25:1 (1987): 13–34.

The Metaphysical Thought of Thomas Aquinas (Washington, DC: The Catholic University of America Press, 2000).

"Aquinas on God's Freedom to Create or Not," in *Metaphysical Themes in Thomas Aquinas II* (Washington, DC: The Catholic University of America Press, 2007), 218–39.

"Thomas Aquinas and the Axiom 'What Is Received Is Received According to the Mode of the Receiver'," in *Metaphysical Themes in Thomas Aquinas II* (Washington, DC: The Catholic University of America Press, 2007), 113–22.

Wood, Adam, "The Faculties of the Soul and Some Medieval Mind–Body Problems," *The Thomist* 75 (2011): 585–636.

Wood, Rega, "The Influence of Arabic Aristotelianism on Scholastic Natural Philosophy," in Robert Pasnau and Christina Van Dyke (eds.), *The Cambridge History of Medieval Philosophy* (Cambridge: Cambridge University Press, 2009), 247–66.

Index

For EU product safety concerns, contact us at Calle de José Abascal, 56–1°,
28003 Madrid, Spain or eugpsr@cambridge.org.

www.ingramcontent.com/pod-product-compliance
Ingram Content Group UK Ltd.
Pitfield, Milton Keynes, MK11 3LW, UK
UKHW020354140625
459647UK00020B/2458